BLACK AMERICA SERIES

# SYRACUSE AFRICAN AMERICANS

BLACK AMERICA SERIES

# SYRACUSE AFRICAN AMERICANS

Barbara Sheklin Davis

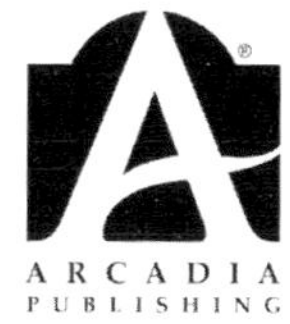

ISBN 978-0-7385-3880-8

Published by Arcadia Publishing
Charleston, South Carolina

Printed in the United States of America

Library of Congress Catalog Card Number: 2005926956

For all general information contact Arcadia Publishing at:
Telephone 843-853-2070
Fax 843-853-0044
E-mail sales@arcadiapublishing.com
For customer service and orders:
Toll-Free 1-888-313-2665

Visit us on the Internet at www.arcadiapublishing.com

# Contents

# FOREWORD

Syracuse is a city of vision and a light on a hill. It is the people of any city that build its character and defines its destiny. We dedicate this pictorial history to the African American men, women, and families who believed in the destiny of prosperity that America promised to all. This pictorial displays the intelligent ingenuity of African Americans and honors the courage of those who stood against the perils of slavery. We pay our deepest respect to the black slaves who made salt in the late 18th century and to the two ministers who freed the famous runaway slave William Henry, known by his slave name, Jerry, from jail, rescuing him from the potential bond of slavery. Today a monument known as the Jerry Rescue has been erected in Clinton Square Park in downtown Syracuse in honor of this heroic event.

It is this foundation that was laid by the colored people before the present-day African American that gave us the privilege of much success. Syracuse is also the home of great performers such as Libba Cotten, the first and only Grammy Award winner who resided in Syracuse; Ernie Davis, the only Heisman Trophy winner from Syracuse University; and Jim Brown, the only college athlete to be enshrined into the College Hall of Fame in both football and lacrosse. Sports and music have not been the only avenues of success. Education, politics, medicine, and dentistry are all areas where the black community has made significant progress here.

Vision could never be realized in the African American community without faith in God and love for family. It was this great faith in God that propelled the black family through slavery, the Jim Crow Laws, the Ku Klux Klan, and segregation. It was faith in God that motivated great black men and women to achieve despite any obstacles that were placed in their way. It was this faith that gave us Harriet Tubman, who wrote history with every step she took as she walked through Syracuse leading slaves to freedom, and Dr. Martin Luther King Jr., who stood his ground in a nonviolent manner against the racists that wanted to diminish any person of color. In addition, there is the Dunbar Center that was established in the late 1930s to improve the social, cultural, and educational needs of Negro people. To this day, the mission of the Dunbar Center is still the same. It thrives as a beacon of light and a ray of hope for all of the modern-day African Americans who dare to dream.

As you view the pictorial, please keep in mind these pictures are a true representation of our culture. Black people have intact families, enjoy life, and create thriving communities. It has been stated that a picture is worth a thousand words. Studying these photographs reestablishes and reconnects me to who I am in my very core. Even though I was born in New York City, African American culture is deeply intertwined. This is a culture of which I am proud to be a part.

—Ronald Otis Jennings

# *One*

# The Earliest Years

The history of Syracuse's African American community begins, like that of the city itself, with salt. More than a decade before Ephraim Webster and Asa Danforth began to manufacture it, black men were making salt. Silas Bowker, later to be a senator from Cayuga County, visited the Onondaga salines in 1774, and in 1823, an account of what he saw was recorded in the journal of the New York State Senate: "The manufacture of salt was wholly in the hands of two negro men, deserters from their master in Esopus, who used brass kettles for this purpose, and whose only customers were the neighboring Indians." There were black slaves in Syracuse in the early days. Some came with their owners from elsewhere in New York State or from the South; others were purchased by settlers to help with the heavy labor. When Asa Danforth built his mills, he purchased a slave from a tavern keeper in Herkimer Flats to do the grinding. All early census records show both slave and free black populations; the county African American population in 1810 was 153, of whom 41 were slaves.

**Notice.**

THE subscriber offers his services to the people of this city who desire to have their vaults cleaned. His residence is 56 Ash street, near the Court House.

ISAAC WALES.

Syracuse, Feb. 4, 1852—dlw

In 1824, Isaac Wales became the first African American to settle in the young village of Syracuse. He had come in 1810 as the property of John Fleming. According to contemporary accounts, "Wales in youth had but few accomplishments, yet learned to read and write." He was able to get work on the Erie Canal, then being dug, and, as his habits "were industrious and frugal," he saved enough money to buy his freedom for $80. Wales married, purchased property and a home at 56 Ash Street, and advertised his services in the *Daily Standard*.

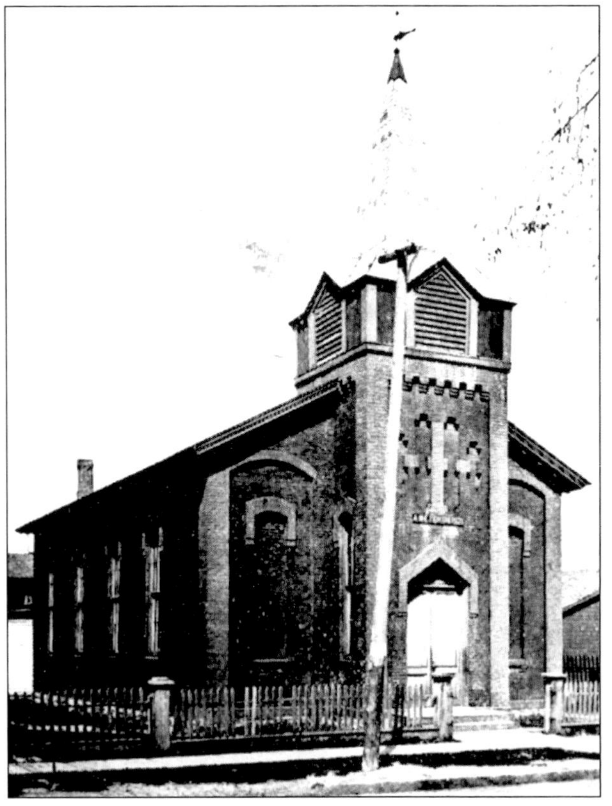

The 1830s saw increasing attention paid to abolitionist activities. In 1831, opponents of slavery met in Syracuse to form an abolitionist society. Notices of antislavery meetings in Syracuse and surrounding areas began to appear in local papers. In 1837, Syracuse's first African American church, the African Methodist Episcopal Zion Church, was founded.

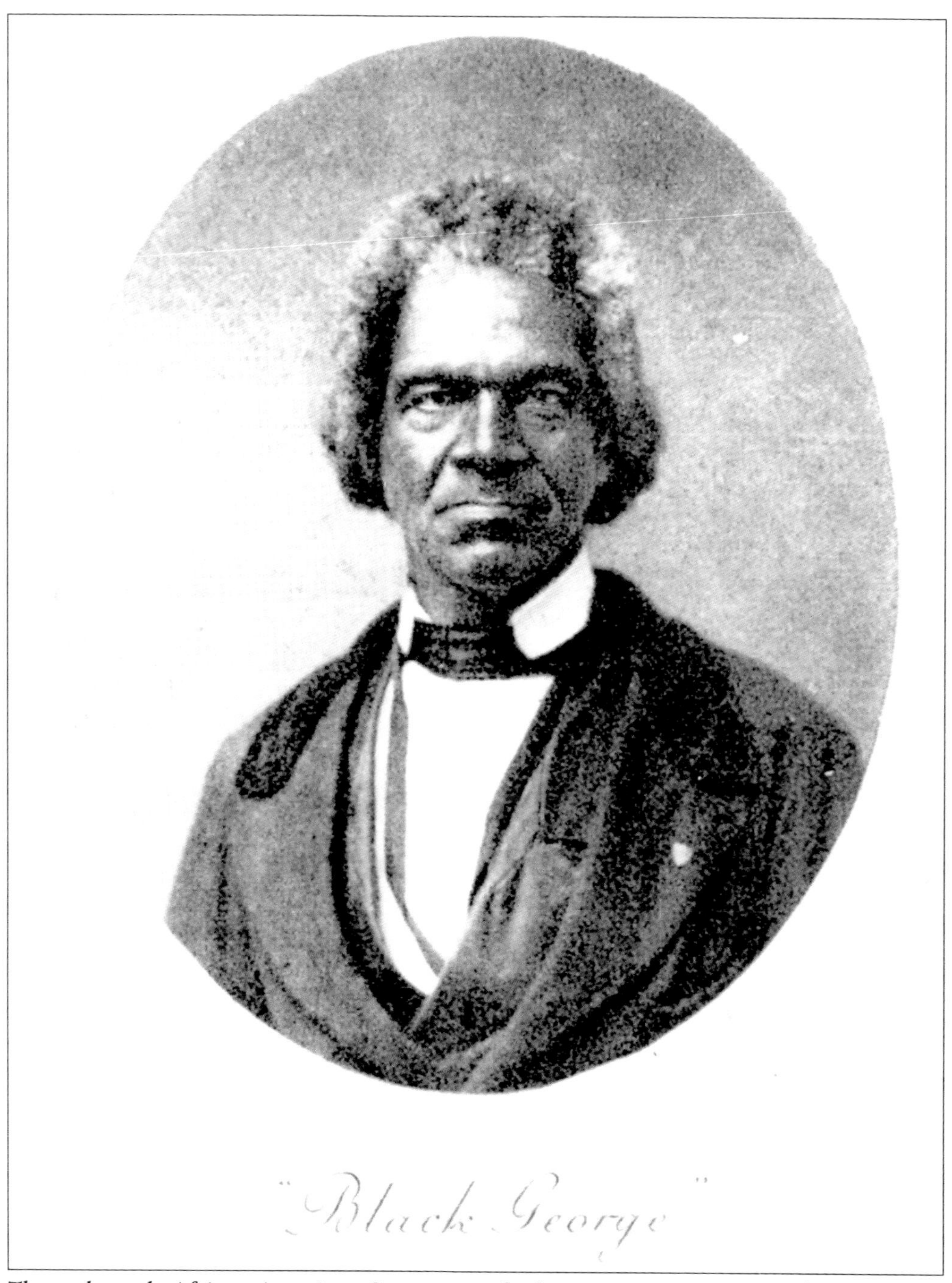


The only early African American Syracusan of whom a portrait exists today is George Johnson. Johnson was an indoor servant in the home of the Wheaton family, and his likeness appeared in the diary of Ellen Birdseye Wheaton with the caption "Black George." Johnson worked for the Wheaton family for 14 years, from 1846 until 1860, and then was employed by the Longstreet family until his death.

**$200 Reward**

**Left the service of the subscriber on the evening of the 7th inst. a Bright Quadroon Servant-girl, about twenty four years of age, named HARRIET. Said girl was about 5 feet high, of a full and well proportioned form, straight light brown hair, dark eyes, approaching to black, of fresh complexion, and so fair that she would generally be taken for white; a prominent mouth with depressed nostrils and receding forehead, readily betrayed to the critical observer the leading traits of the African race. Her demeanor is very quiet, and her deportment modest.**

**At the time of leaving she had on a black dress of figured poplin. She took with her one green Merino dress; one pink Gingham (checked) do.; one French Muslin figured do.; one Buff, and one light purple Calico do. She wore small rings (with stones) in her ears, and had three chased Gold Rings on her fingers, two of which were set with green and the other with transparent chrystal. She also took with her a plaid blanket Shawl, but left her bonnet, so that her head-dress cannot be described.**

In leaving the service of the subscriber, she leaves her aged mother and a younger sister, who are devotedly attached to her, and to whom she has ever appeared much attached. It may be proper also to state, that her conduct as a servant, and her moral deportment so far as the same have come to the knowledge of the subscriber, have hitherto been irreproachable. It is believed that she has been spirited away from the service of the undersigned, by the officious and persevering efforts of certain malicious and designing persons, operating through the agency of the colored people of Syracuse, at which place he had been induced to spend a few days. The subscriber would further add, that he has refused several importunate offers of $2,500 for said girl, for the sole reason that he would never consent to part her from the other members of her family, and it is chiefly with

In 1839, an event occurred that served to focus Syracuse's attention on the issue of slavery. Harriet Powell was a beautiful girl of modest manner and lavish attire who was owned by the J. Davenports of Mississippi. The African American employees of Syracuse House plotted to free her with the assistance of local abolitionists. A hue and cry was raised, but searching proved fruitless. Although Davenport issued a handbill offering a hefty $200 reward for the return of his possession, Harriet Powell was successfully transported to freedom in Canada.

**THE IMPARTIAL CITIZEN.**

NEW SERIES— The Wisdom which is from above is without Partiality. VOL. 1—NO. 31

S. R. WARD & CO. SYRACUSE, WEDNESDAY, SEPTEMBER 12, 1849. PUBLISHERS

The *Impartial Citizen* was the first African American newspaper published in Syracuse. It was strictly abolitionist and began publication in 1848.

Jermain Wesley Loguen came to Syracuse in 1841 to head the African Methodist Episcopal Zion Church. Pastor, orator, and abolitionist, Loguen's efforts on behalf of fugitive slaves earned Syracuse the name of "Canada of the United States."

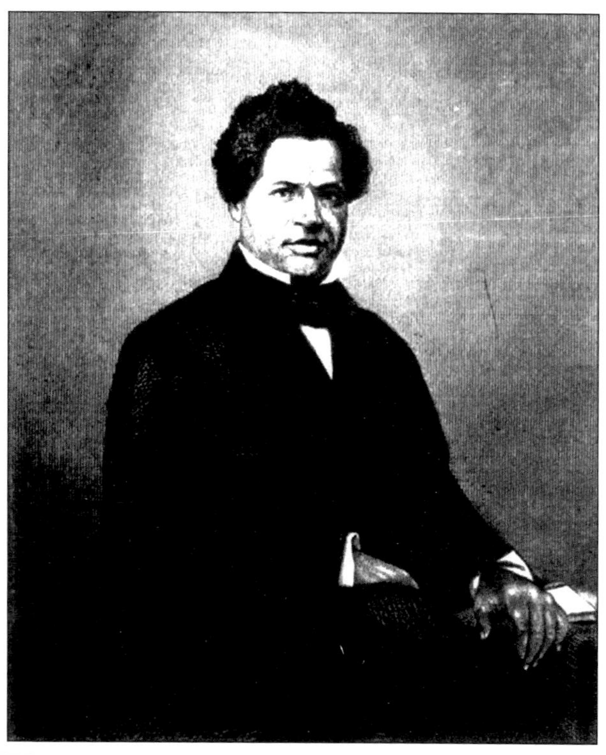

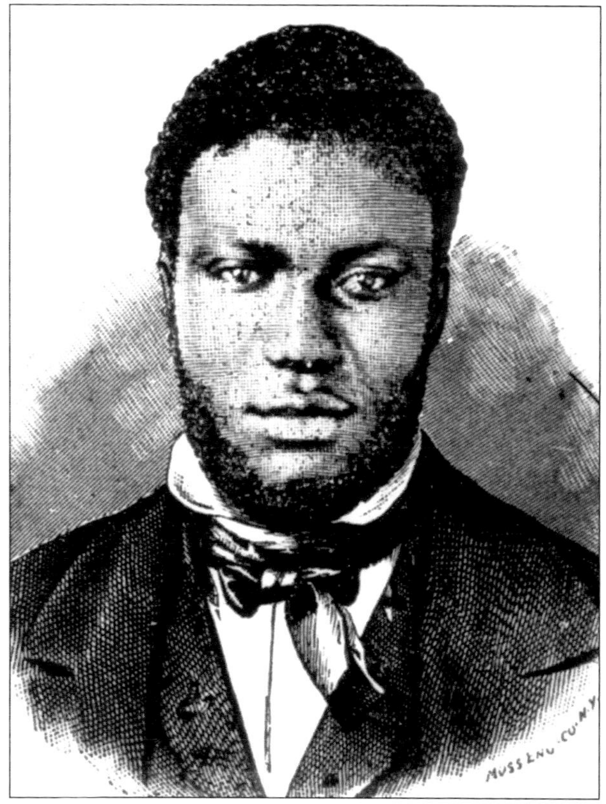

Samuel Ringgold Ward became pastor of the Congregational church in Cortland in 1846 and, in 1848, began to publish the *Impartial Citizen* in Syracuse. A spellbinding orator, Ward was known as "the black Daniel Webster."

# PUBLIC SENTIMENT!

## TO THE ELECTORS OF

# CAMILLUS!

**Those of you who are opposed to the FUGITIVE SLAVE LAW—to the extension of *Slavery over Free Soil*—to the admission of any more SLAVE STATES, and are disposed to waive former political preferences and party predilections, and unite your strength that your influence may be felt in the cause of *Freedom* and *Humanity*, are cordially invited to meet with us at Rowe's Hotel, on the**

## 27th day of January inst.,

**at 2 o'clock P. M., to nominate officers to be elected at the next town meeting.**

***Camillus, January* 3d, 1852.**

D. A. Munro,
Charles Land,
Daniel Abrams,
C. S. Elderkin,
D. Gleason,
Geo. Plumb,
John Case,
E. Shead,
E. Marks,
M. Lyon,
H. C. Hughes,
James M. Munro,
W. Truesdell,
N. N. Pickard,
James Bennett,
Harry Weed,
Martin W. Lyon,
M. Armstrong,
E. R. Harmon,
D. L. Pickard,
Wm. Jones,
E. B. Soles,
T. Briggs,
Isaiah Wilcox,
B. S. Harrington,
Charles L. Beach,
Charles L. Land,
Thom. Hand,
S. B. Lee,
A. Harmon,
A. Richmond,
W. H. Barrett,
William Stack,
John G. Kimberley,
C. B. Way,
Byron Freeman,
Loren Richmond,
Sylvester Richmond,
James I. Slote,
Calvin Wheeler,
Aaron Miller,
James Lybolt,
Henry Osman,
George W. Cook,
W. R. Wheeler,
[illegible] Sims,
[illegible] B. Sherwood,
[illegible] T. Darling,
[illegible] W. Clark,
[illegible] Gleason,
[illegible] Lybolt,
[illegible] Cole,
[illegible] Holden,
[illegible] Carpenter,
[illegible] Hutcheson,
[illegible] C. Sweeting,
[illegible] Green,
[illegible]

Ambrose Kelsey,
George Eagerty,
James Patten,
H. A. Mungear,
Seth Dunbar,
J. H. Earll,
George W. Cornwell,
George W. Borden,
W. R. Cooper,
C. B. Wheeler,
H. Rawe,
W. H. Lee,
David H. Kingsley,
I. B. Worden,
Isaac Clute,
C. B. Fish,
B. Bucklin,
D. H. Abrams,
Jeremiah W. Hall,
Moses Harrington,
Hugh McCole,
J. W. Skinner,
Wm. Gilley,
Alex. McColl,
David Shearer,
Samuel Sutherland,
S. D. Barnard,
Gabriel Tompkins,
J. S. Tompkins,
Ananias Ashby,
Egbert E. Ashby,
George Dixon,
George M. Dixon,
Stephen Ketchum,
Nathan Ashby,
J. B. Condon,
Benj. Brown,
Albert N. Glynn,
A. J. Dallas,
Abram Martin,
Aaron Clark,
R. Field,
Wm. S. Johnson,
Henry Wolven,
R. L. Dill,
A. S. Worden,
Wm. Felter,
J. H. Sims,
Alvin Myers,
Patrick Barigon,
Lewis Whitmore,
Perry Delano,
Thos. Sweetman,
I. M. Peck,
Lyman Smith,
D. B. Paddock,
L. C. Skinner.

Alfred Thomson,
Jerry Eagerty,
Nathaniel Paddock,
G. W. Barrows,
Samuel Dill,
Jonathan Thompson,
Leonard Peck,
Guy Nearing,
Simon Veeder,
Lawrence Lamberson,
Jesse Sims,
D. Z. Suits,
B. Sidnam,
Matthew Sherwood,
Wm. C. Thompson,
Wm. Thompson,
L. Farnham,
John B. Miller,
C. Staley,
Wm. Miller,
D. Scofield,
Horace Woodruff,
A. Staley,
John Spores,
G. Shonnus,
Wm. Miller, Jr.
David Clark,
Nelson Burrell,
S. H. Campbell,
Daniel Bennett,
N. G. Wood,
Loren Tyler,
Jeremiah Paddock,
Ira Paddock,
C. Lyon,
Gilbert Sweet,
J. B. Lyon,
D. B. Burch,
Wm. Chapman,
L. Mack,
N. Bryan,
M. B. Manwaring,
S. S. Manwaring,
Geo. Harper,
Simon Marshall,
Reuben Straws,
Jonathan Marshall,
Orrin Brewer,
Thomas Sherwood, Jr.
J. W. Starks,
J. B. Bennett,
L. B. Bennett,
George Carter,
L. Richmond,
C. M. Coon,
John J. Cook,
Jonathan Paddock.

John Burch,
John Cook,
Felix Benton,
H. A. Richmond,
I. T. Richmond,
John Harper,
C. D. Manwaring,
L. Richmond, Jr.
Ethan Campbell,
Alden Brown,
Alanson Cook,
Michael Harper,
Henry McDowell,
Edwin McDowell,
Isaac Paddock,
Daniel Sharp,
Chauncey Vanalstine,
P. F. Vanalstine,
A. J. Vannistine,
D. E. Rockwell,
Oliver Beers,
I. G. Parker,
Alfred Bartlett,
Henry Clift,
P. Malony,
P. J. Wood,
C. Shehan,
Wm. Whedon,
Jas. M. Baker,
H. G. White,
L. Linsday,
James Sidnam,
James Isham,
Peter Johnson,
Joseph Johnson,
James Kinney,
Horatio Plumb,
S. C. Johnson,
James T. Hay,
C. C. Phinney,
Sylvester Whedon,
M. H. Hubbard,
Ezra Whedon,
L. Whedon,
Dennison Whedon,
Hiram Whedon,
M. A. Sweeting,
S. P. Sweeting,
Mason Sweeting,
John Wright,
W. L. Sheldon,
Asa Bingham,
C. D. Bingham,
W. Burt,
Phillip Holden,
Horace Ward,
John Trumbull,

George Jerome,
F. Colehan,
Jonas Secor,
Abm. Johnson,
Pardy Ladd,
Harry Isham,
Henry Gifford,
John Clapper,
Daniel Hervey,
John Saunders,
Solomon Hess,
Henry W. Casler,
Wm. C. Thorp,
O. V. Kasson,
J. W. Kasson,
A. Kasson,
John Scott,
Nathan Williams,
James Wood,
Wm. North,
Isaac W. Saunders,
John H. Wood,
John E. Saunders,
Asa Dye,
Asa M. Dye,
A. P. Brooks,
Horace Ritter,
Alonzo McNett,
James Cook,
Alva Wood,
James Fredenburgh,
Oliver E. Ham,
Harry Fancher,
E. A. Bennett,
Platt Richards,
John Richards,
Arial Spaulding,
John Moss,
Asa Kenyon,
A. B. Sprague,
Nathan Paddock,
R. Q. Coure,
Peter Ten Eyck,
Ezra Woodruff,
Edmond Cox,
Moses H. Lamberson,
Giles Lamberson,
John Vosburgh,
Wm. Smith,
R S Veeder,
John Doyle,
Wm. B. Fish,
A. Q. Thompson,
A. Thompson,
Ebenezer Thompson,
Arthur White,
Russel Dyer,

James Whitney,
James Cox,
Isaac Sherwood,
John Craver,
Luther Sims,
Caleb F. Steves,
Jeremiah Steves,
George Coburn,
Luther Jones,
James Jones,
Thomas Meachem,
Byron Lent,
Wm. S. Cox,
John W. Steves,
Oliver Coburn,
Levi M. Steves,
J. F. Steves,
James Sidnam, jr.,
Joel Winchell,
Hiram Jones,
W. W. Lockwood,
Samuel Thorp,
Chauncey Green,
John Cornish,
Le Roy Barns,
John Osman,
Silas Cornell,
Wm. W. Barker,
Alanson Brown,
R. Veeder,
A. Guilford,
E. Quackenbush,
A. T. Mattison,
Patrick Bucklin,
Henry Winchel,
Stephen Winchel,
Anson Byard,
M. C. [illegible]
Philander Gleason,
Harvey Winchel,
[illegible]
Wm. D. Chase,
[illegible]

By 1842, public sentiment had changed sufficiently to allow both the county and state antislavery conventions to be held in Syracuse. Notices appeared in the newspaper advertising events designed to raise money for abolitionist activities. In the five years between 1845 and 1850, there were 12 major antislavery meetings in Syracuse. A meeting called in Camillus in 1852 to protest the Fugitive Slave Law was one of about 25 smaller gatherings that were held for this purpose.

# *Two*

# From Slavery to Freedom

The two-year-old city of Syracuse's definitive confrontation with the issue of slavery came as a result of the Compromise of 1850, which included the Fugitive Slave Law, providing for the return of all runaway slaves to their masters even without identification or a jury trial. At a mass meeting in Syracuse, resolutions were passed declaring the law "a most flagrant outrage upon the individual rights of man." A vigilance committee was formed to ensure that "no person is defrauded of his liberty without due process of law," and plans were made to ensure the safety of fugitives from slave catchers and kidnappers. Thus the stage was set for one of the most dramatic events in Syracuse history: the rescue of William Henry, known by his slave name of Jerry. The Jerry Rescue put Syracuse on the national stage as a center of abolitionist activity. Not all sympathized with the city's position, however. The *Albany Argus* declared Syracuse to be a "burning disgrace to the State at large," and some in Syracuse itself expressed abhorrence of "the Jerry Rescue outrage." Still, Syracuse maintained its defiance of slavery and engaged openly and effectively in antislavery activities, especially the Underground Railroad. Rev. Jermain Loguen was among its most active "stationmasters," and Syracuse papers of the time provided regular reports of over 300 slaves who fled through Syracuse to safety.

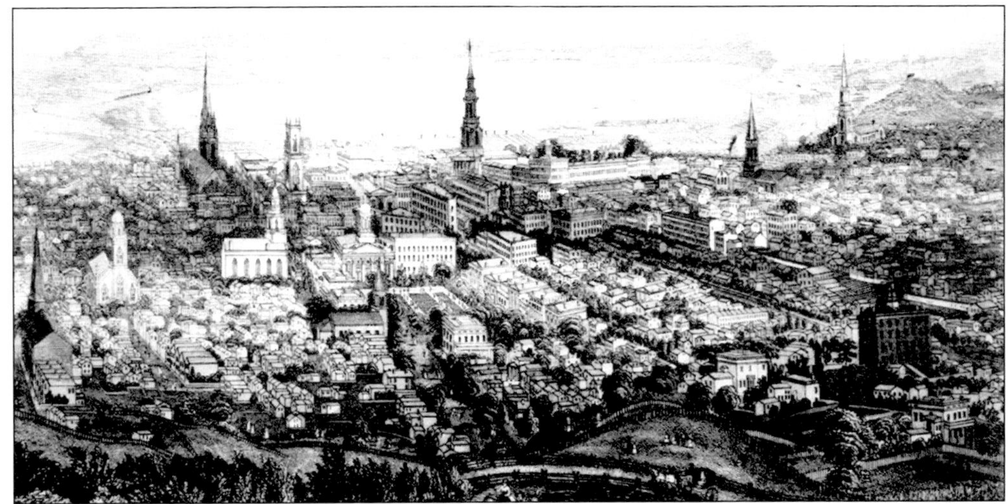

Support for African American suffrage was strong in Syracuse, and the passage of the 15th Amendment in 1870 was greeted with jubilation. This is a view of Syracuse in the early 1850s at the time of the Jerry Rescue.

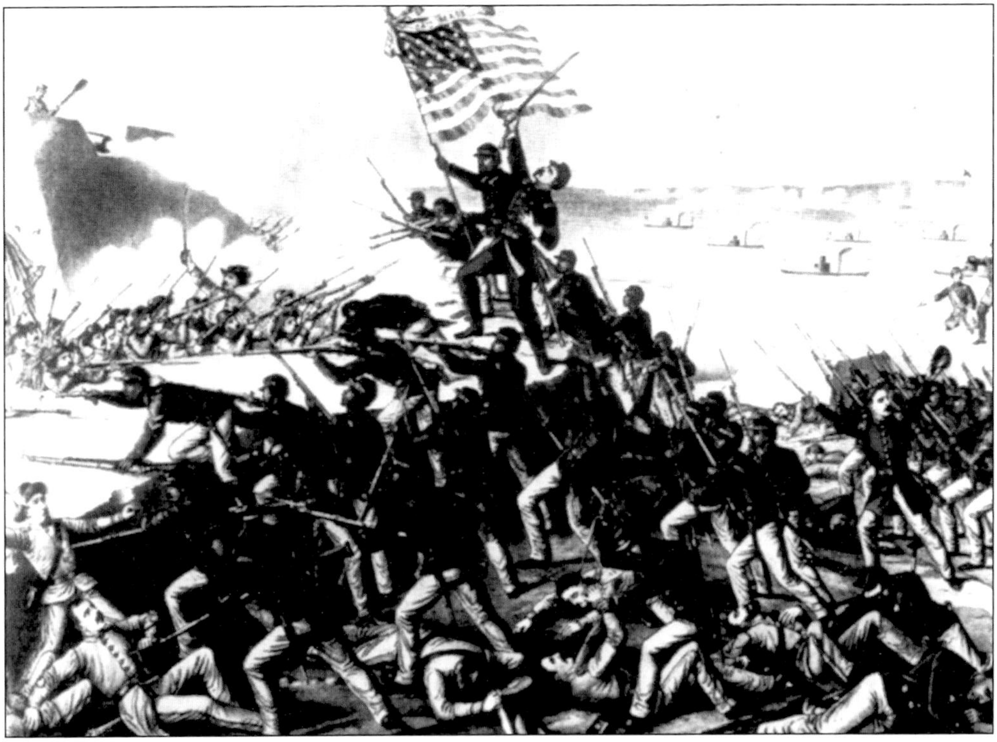

When the War between the States commenced, the black men and women of Syracuse responded as best they could. Although ready to stand by the Stars and Stripes, 33 African American men were rejected from military service from 1861 to 1863. But by the fall of 1863, a black company from Syracuse, recruited by Reverend Loguen, volunteered and enlisted in the Massachusetts and Rhode Island black regiments. Seven years later, a company of African American soldiers was organized in Syracuse to serve with the 51st Regiment of New York.

Portraits from the period show a proud people, with faith in the promise of freedom and opportunity for which a civil war was fought and won. This portrait of Reverend Brown shows his strength and determination.

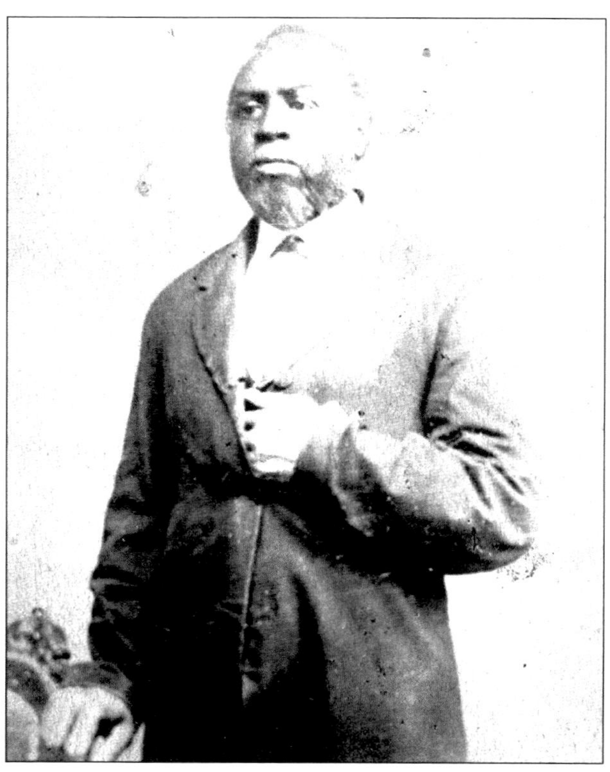

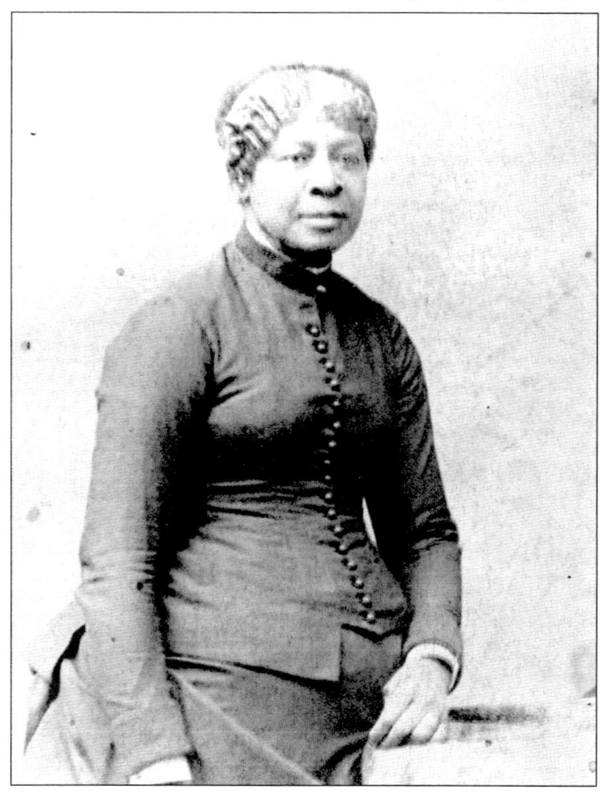

Louisa Brown, Reverend Brown's wife, is shown in costume and pose typical of the era.

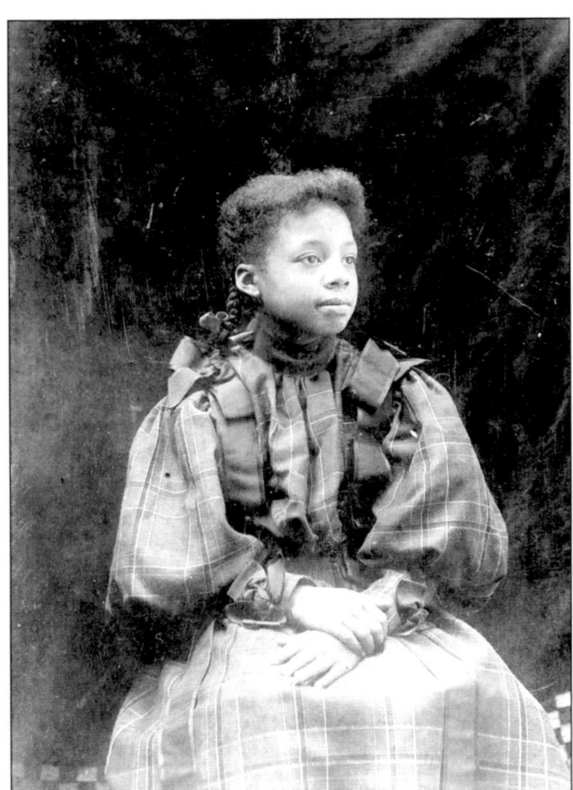

This unknown girl is dressed in her best attire for her portrait.

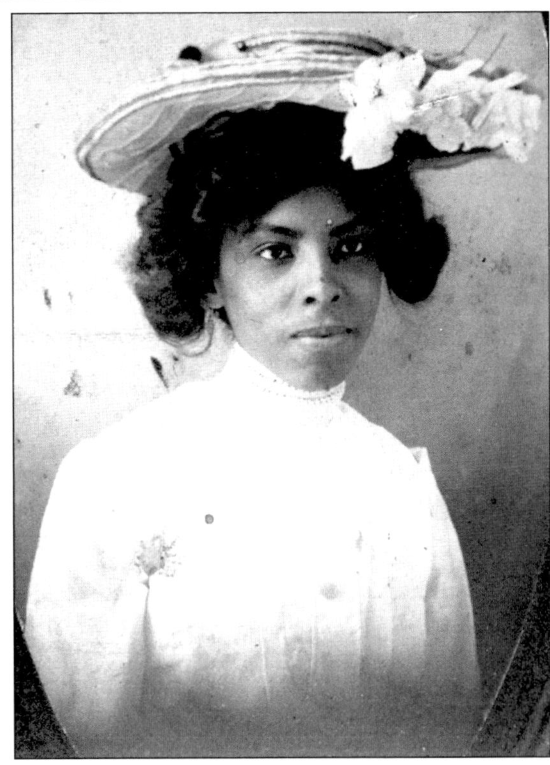

Catherine Johnson looks particularly lovely in her bonnet.

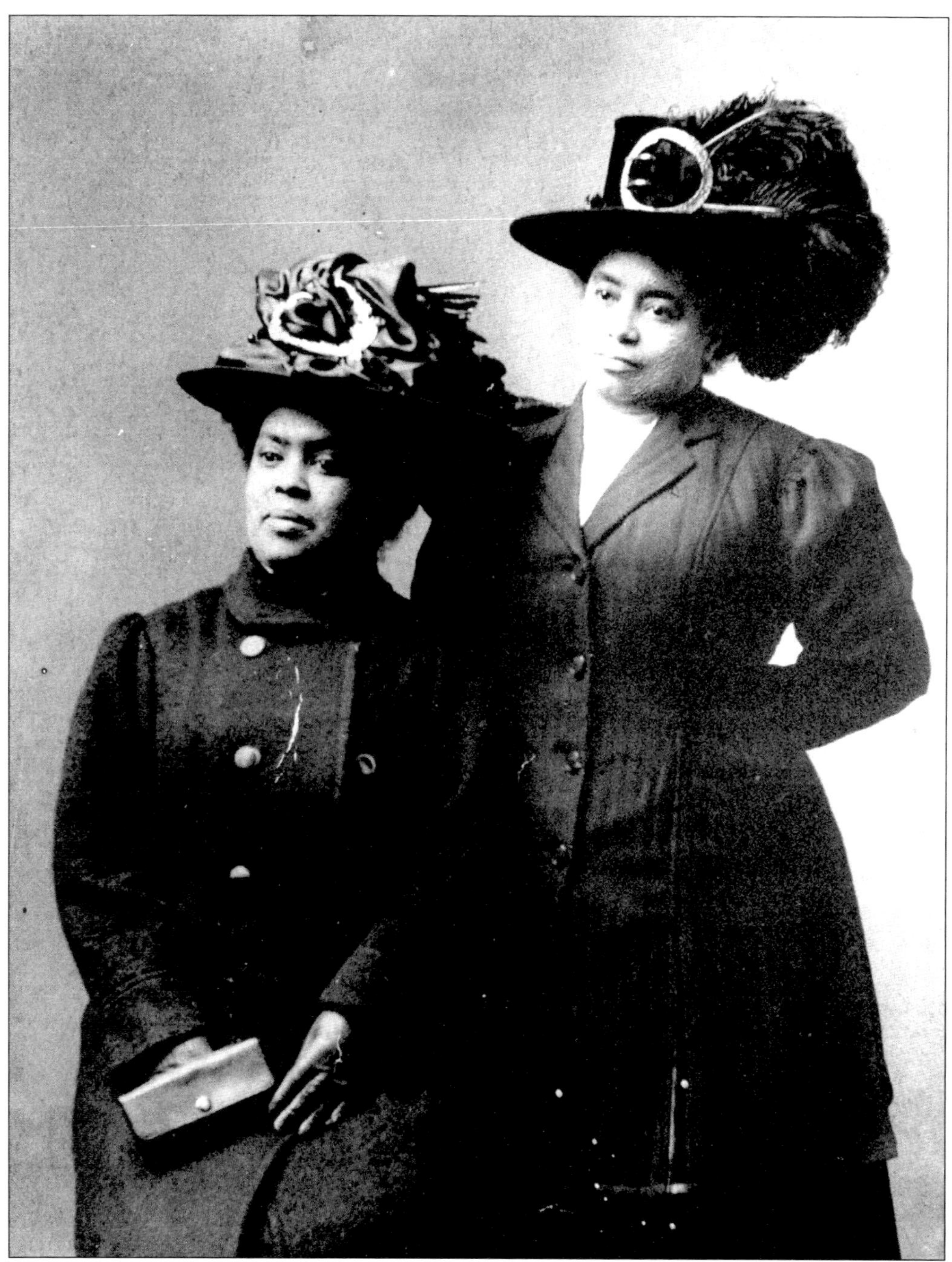

This is a portrait of Frances Towns and her sister Blanche.

Another unnamed young woman from the period is seen here.

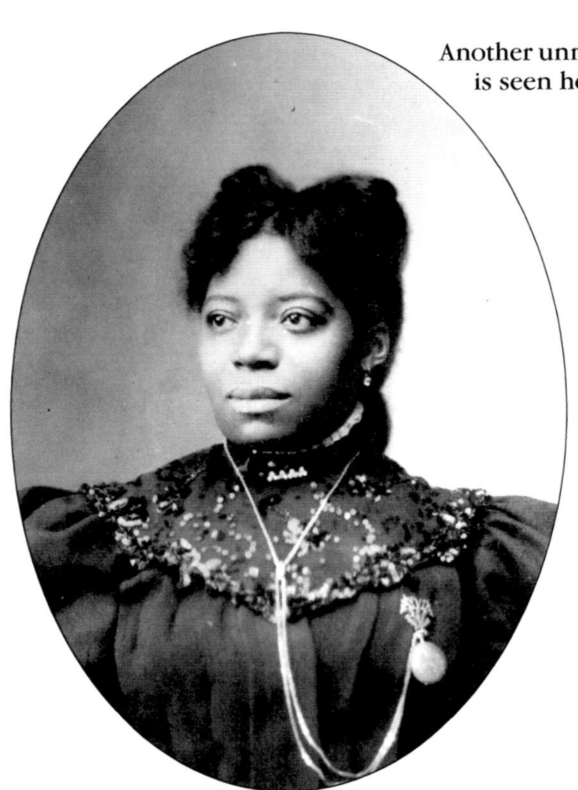

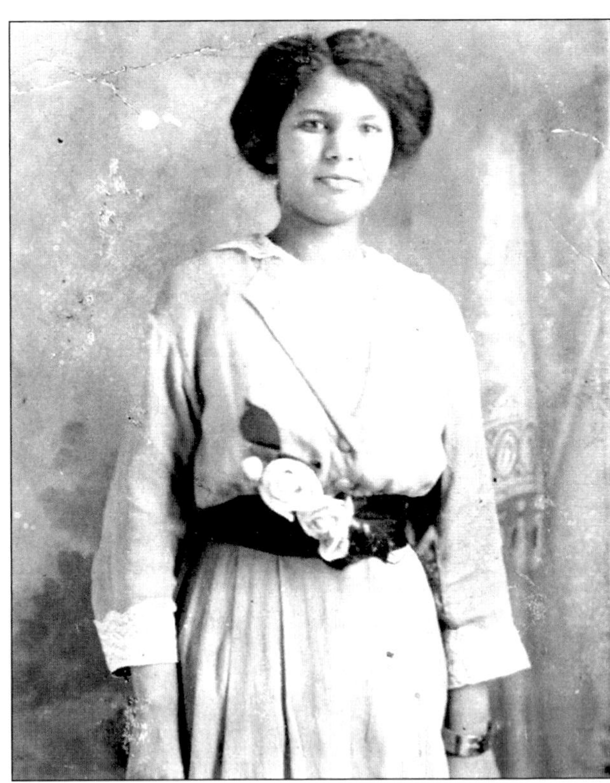

Mrs. Crocker poses for her portrait in a gallery.

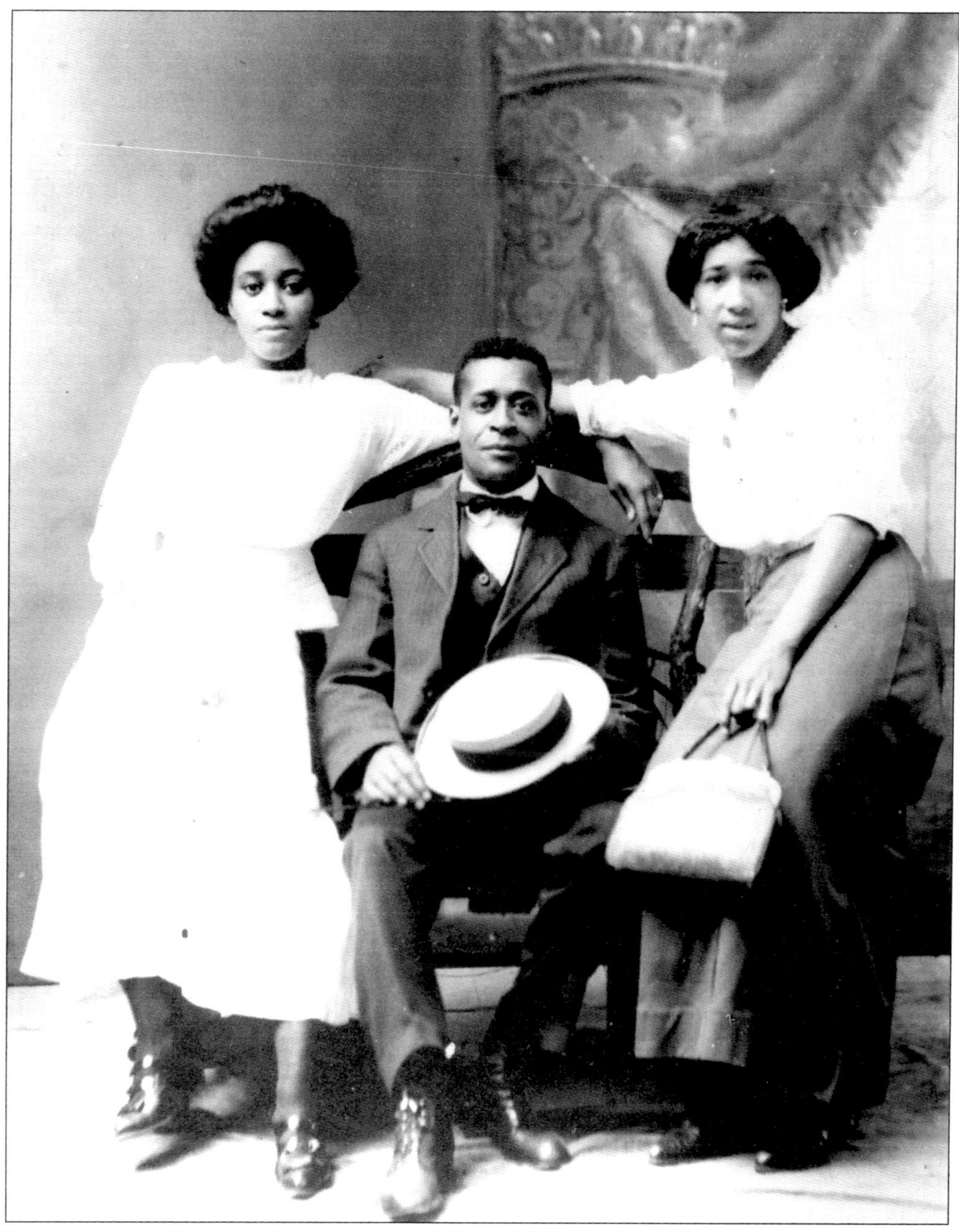

This lovely studio portrait shows, from left to right, Geneva Robinson, Frank Robinson, and Dorothy Gordon.

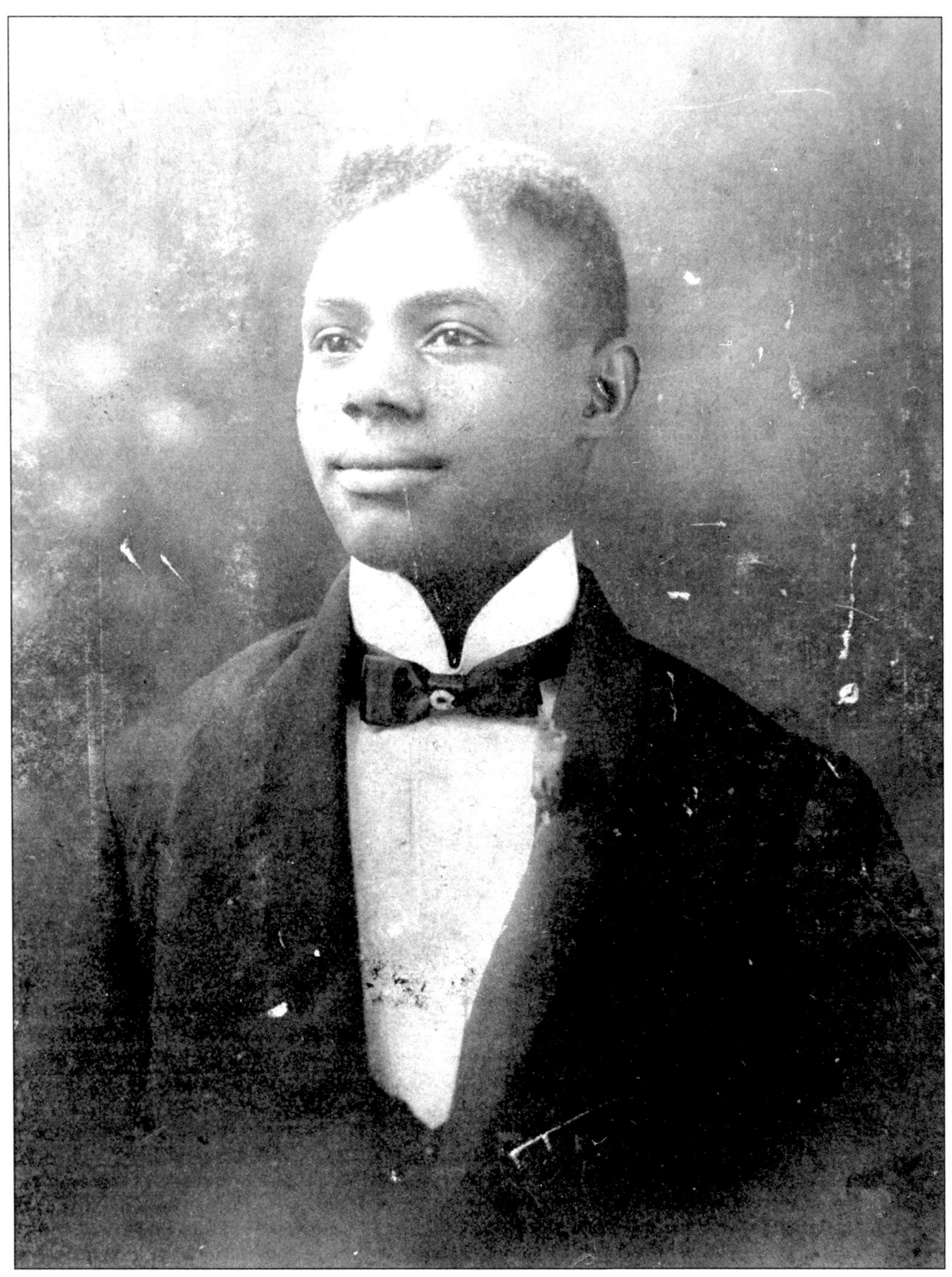

An unidentified man smiles proudly as his portrait is made.

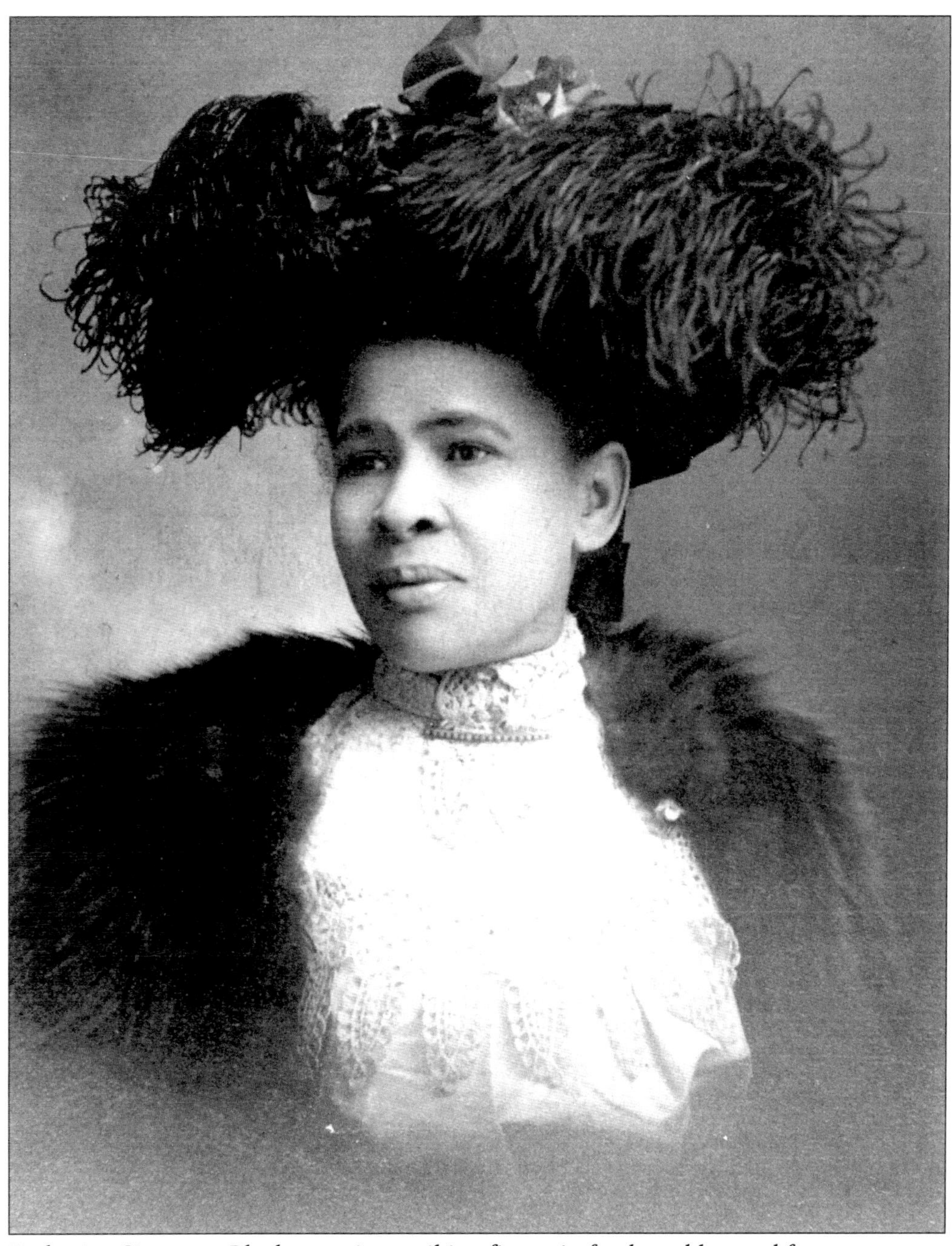

Katherine Simmons Blackstone is a striking figure in feathered hat and fur.

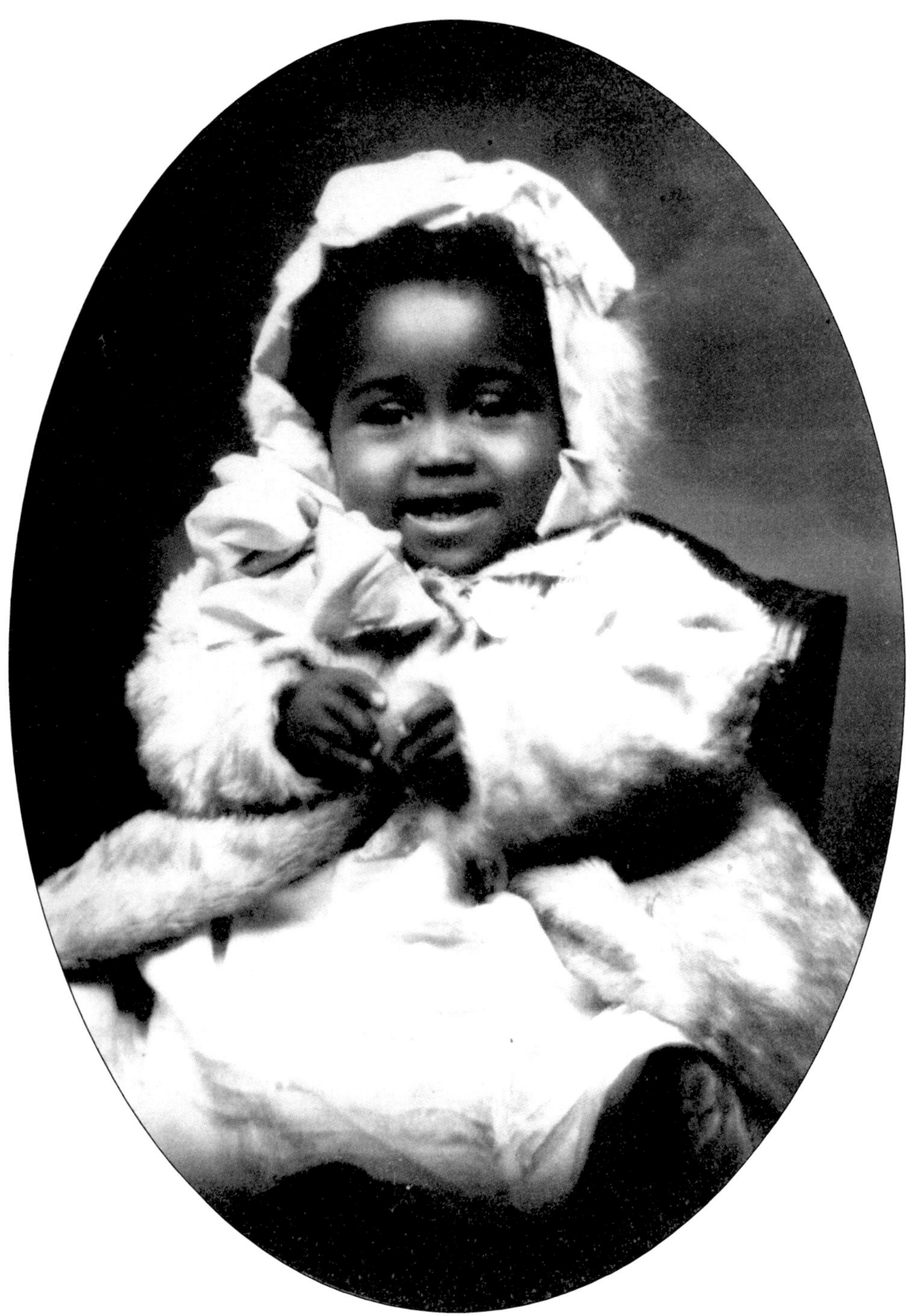

An unknown but delightful little girl poses for an early portrait.

The African American churches of the community numbered three: the African Methodist Episcopal Zion Church, Bethany Baptist Church (established in 1887 as Union Baptist), and St. Philip's Episcopal Church, organized about 10 years later.

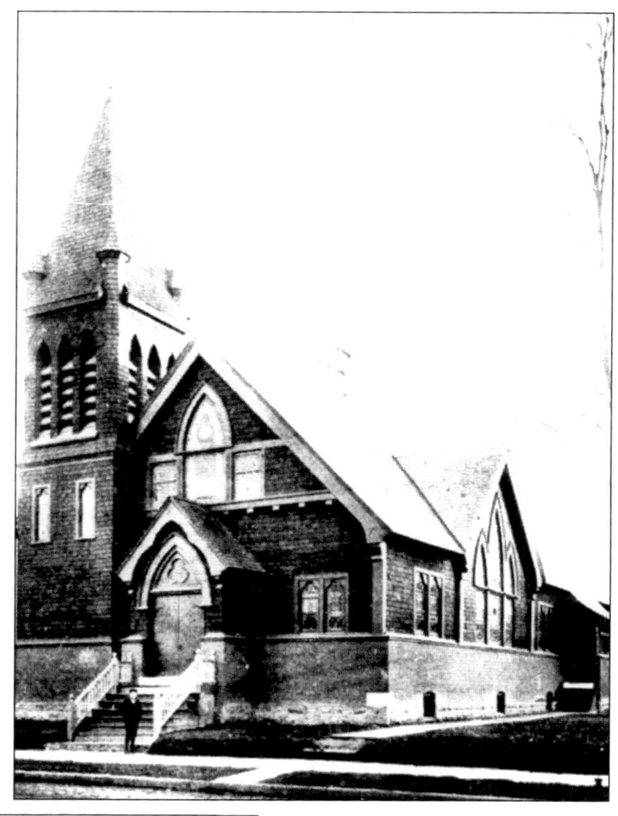

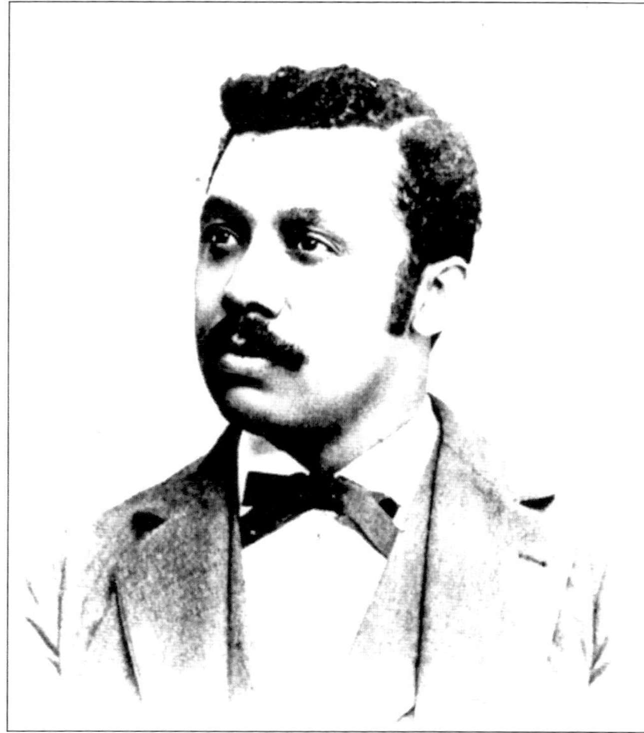

The school system in Syracuse was free and open to all. Education was highly valued by the African American community. Rev. George Stevens, pastor of Bethany Baptist Church, instructed the community, "Let us educate our children. You say you are not allowed positions as clerks or bookkeepers, well, let [us] aspire to something higher. When the white people of our community see our children coming from schools and colleges, then they will see that we are determined to be men."

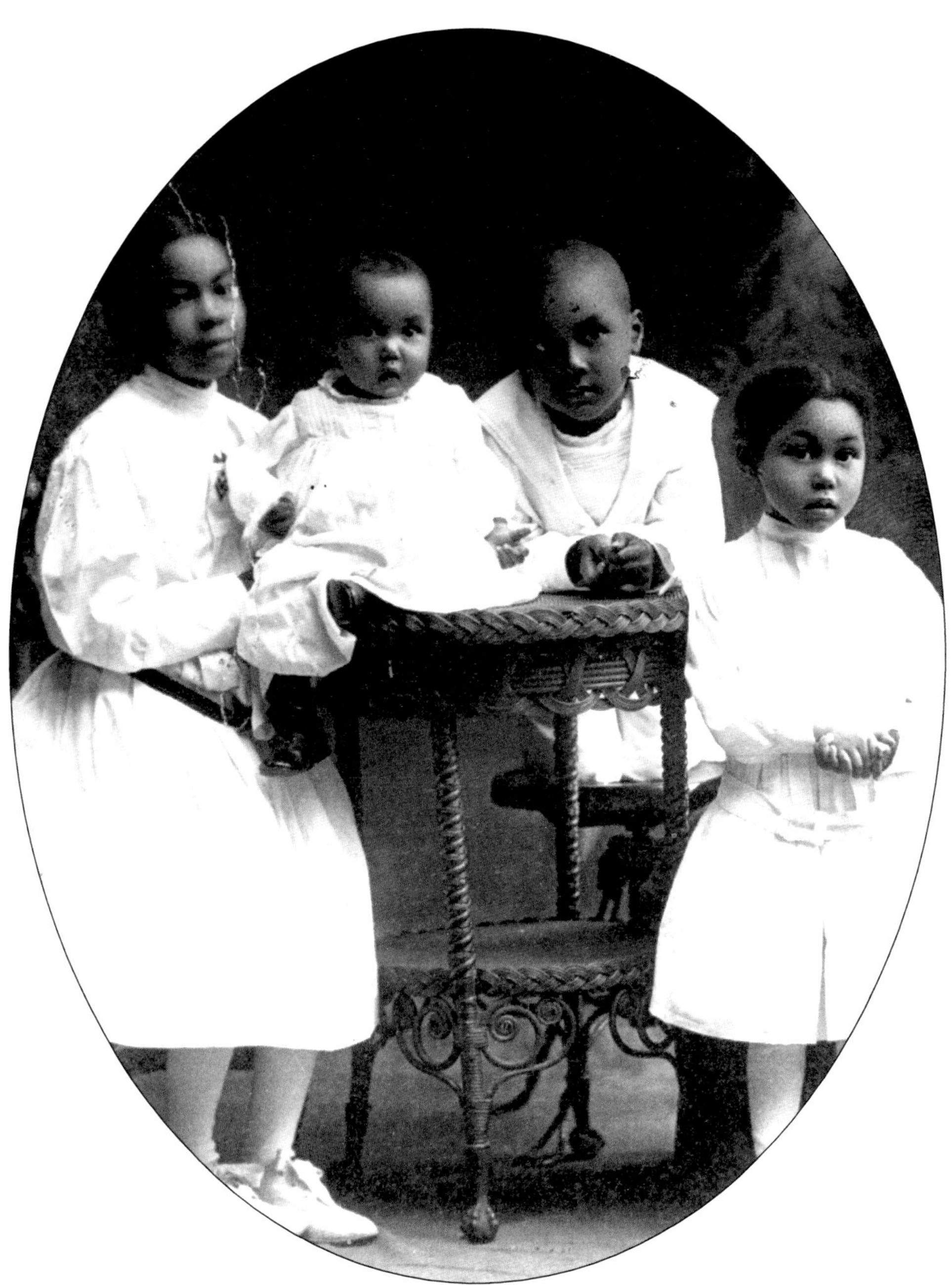

Corrine, Viola, Alexander, and Elmira Jordan (named from left to right) make a beautiful family picture. African American parents sent their children to school more regularly than did white parents. Almost 89 percent of African American children attended primary school regularly compared to 87.9 percent of all white children and 83.3 percent of white children of immigrant parents. Attendance at school, however, must have seemed pointless to many young African Americans who had only domestic service open to them as a career. Accordingly, attendance dropped drastically at the high school level. In 1890, Rev. George Stevens decried the fact that "in this city is a grand university. Not one of our race is there. It is a shame! I go to High School and there I find one, only one!"

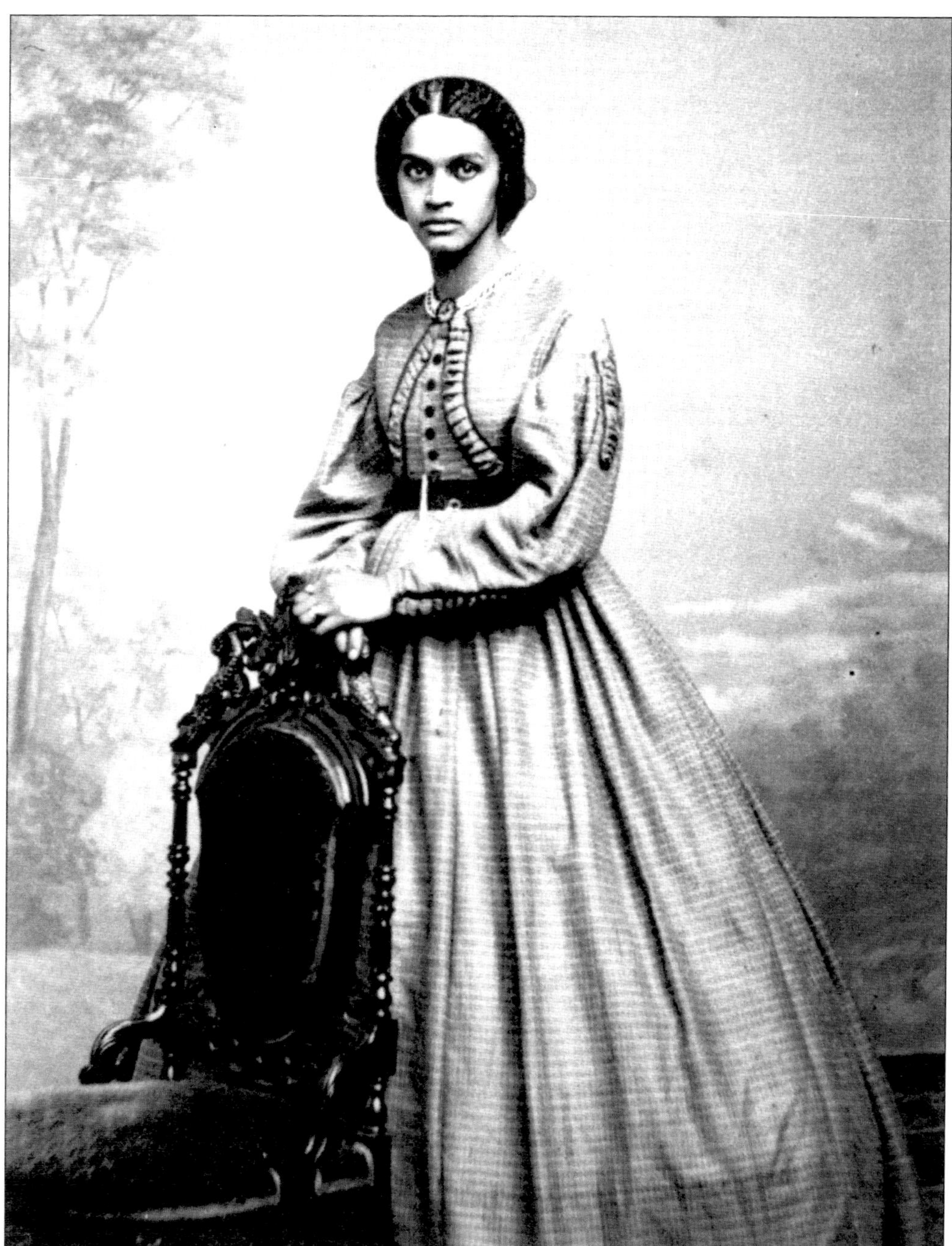

Politically, the African American community in Syracuse had little power, although it was active and vocal. Since the Civil War, Syracuse blacks had allied primarily with the Republicans, the party of Lincoln, although their voting strength was small and was divided among several districts. African American delegates were sent to New York State Republican conventions. In 1878, Gerrit Loguen, son of Jermain Loguen, was elected an inspector of elections, the first African American man to hold that post in New York State. His sister, Helen Amelia Loguen, married the son of Frederick Douglass, thus uniting two powerful African American families.

Another proud and lovely, although unidentified, woman is pictured here.

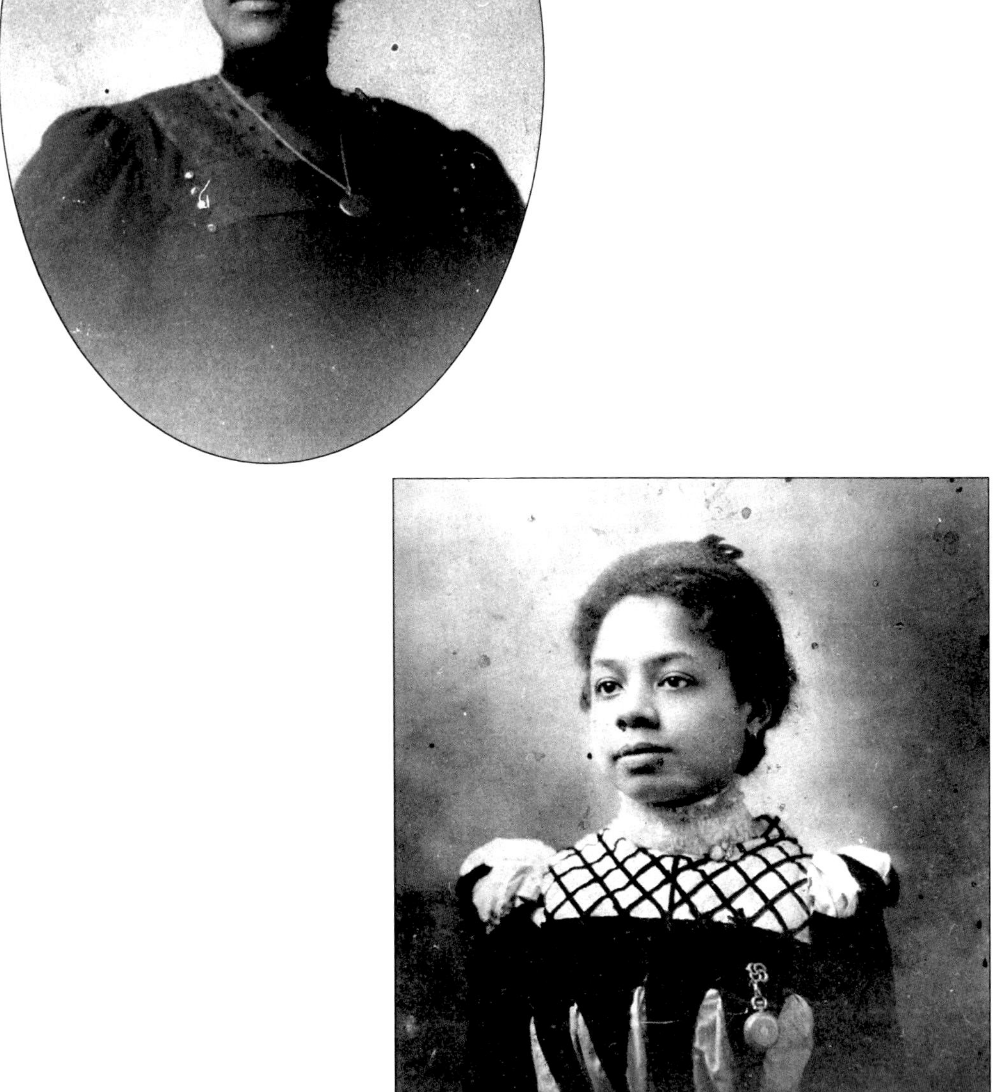

Costumes of the period were painstakingly made and lovingly worn for portraits.

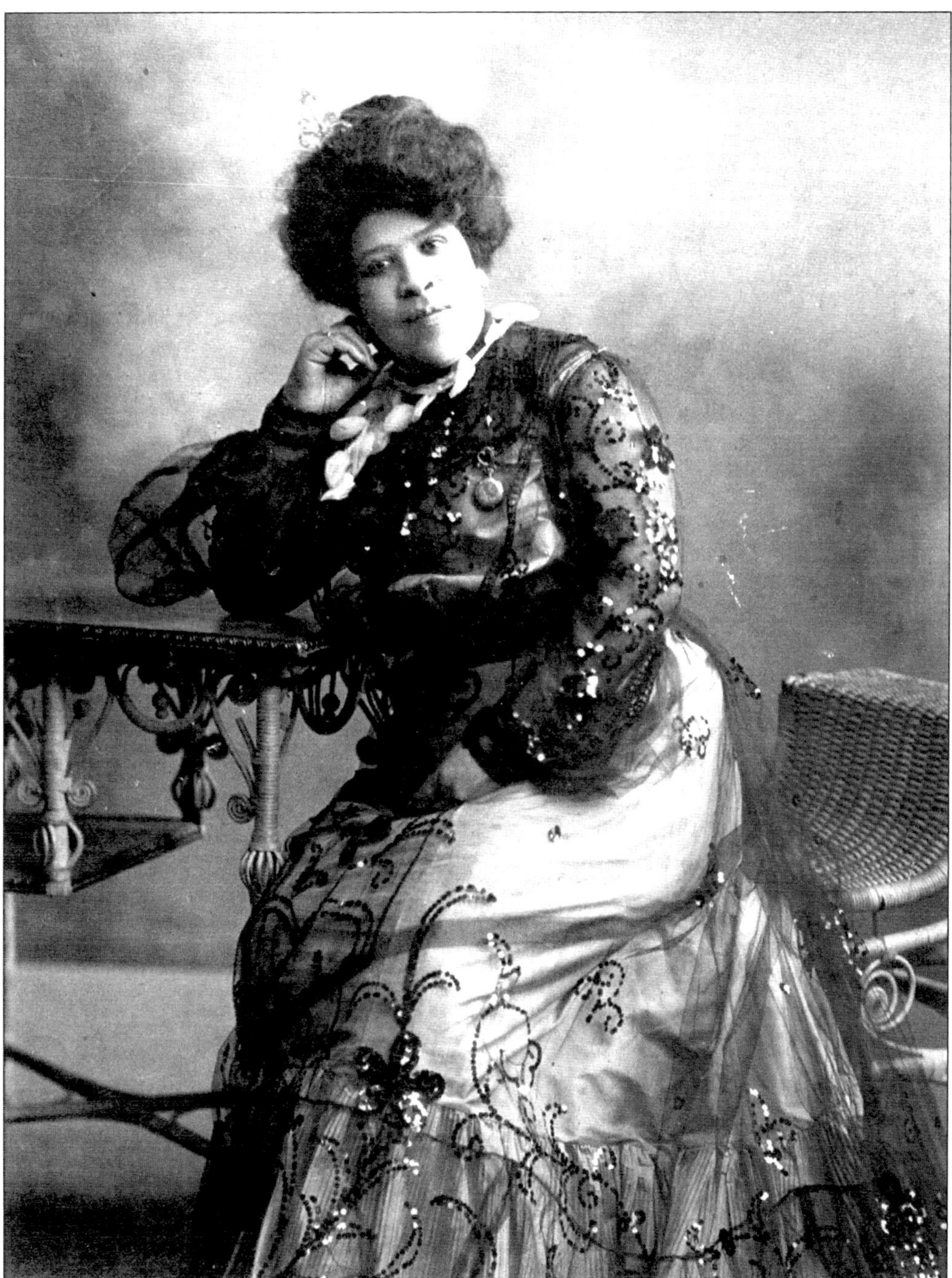

Harriet Terrill Simmons cut a beautiful figure in her elaborate costume.

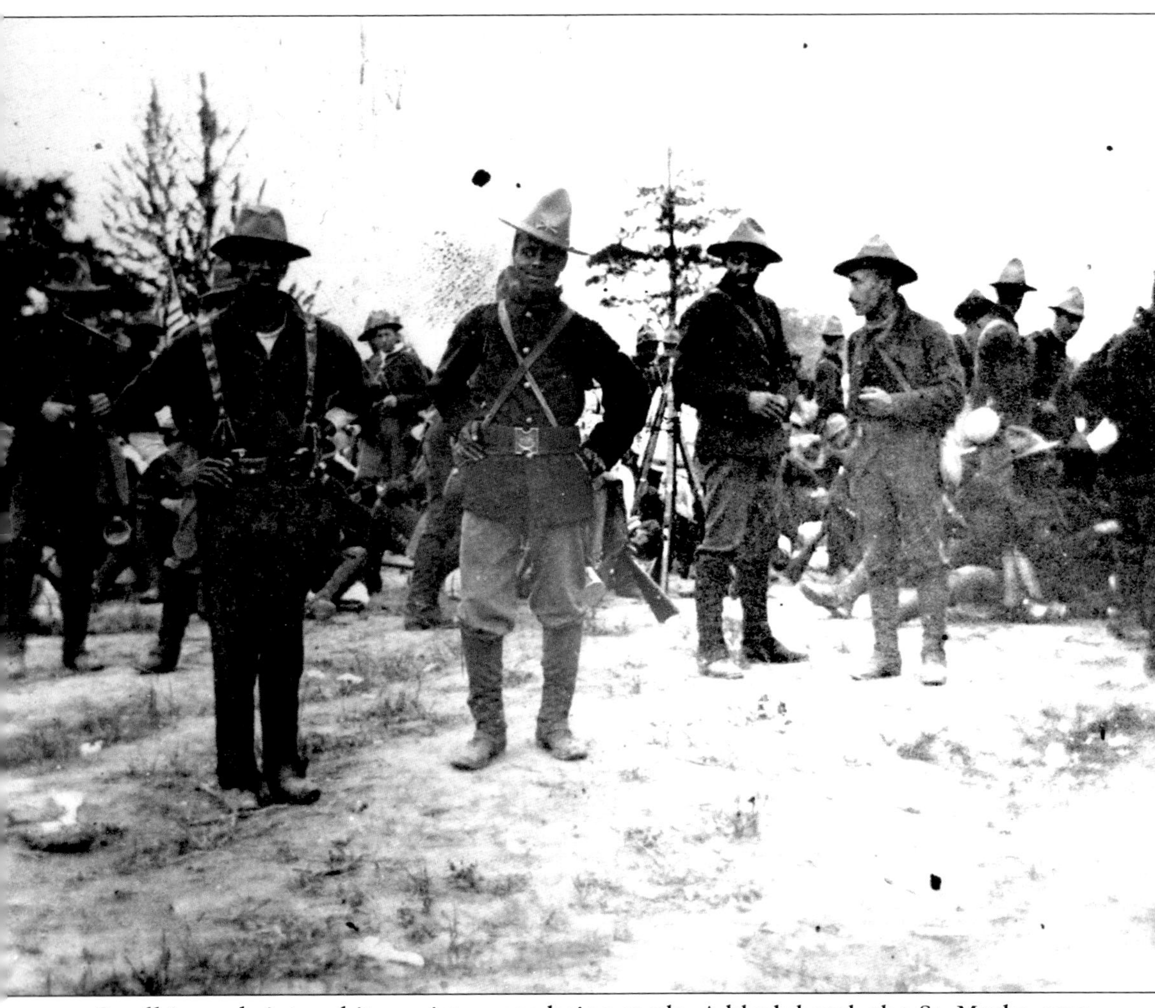

Small inroads into white society were being made. A black hotel, the St. Marks, was established in 1899, and a black baseball club was formed, as were several benefit and temperance groups. African American soldiers from Syracuse served with the army in the Spanish-American War, encountering a situation where they were valued for their skills rather than devalued for their color.

# *Three*

# SEEKING ENTRY

The African American population of Syracuse grew from 300 to 400 during the 1860s. These census figures were to double in the next 20 years, as black families returned from Canada or came up from the South to work as domestic servants or day laborers. The black community of this period comprised little more than one percent of the city's population and was concentrated in the area south of the Erie Canal, in the 6th, 7th, and 8th Wards. Black community life in this period centered around employment and religious activities. There existed what has been described as a "semi-fluid pattern of race relations," with a relatively free intermingling of whites and blacks. A few African American families owned homes in white neighborhoods, and relationships were friendly.

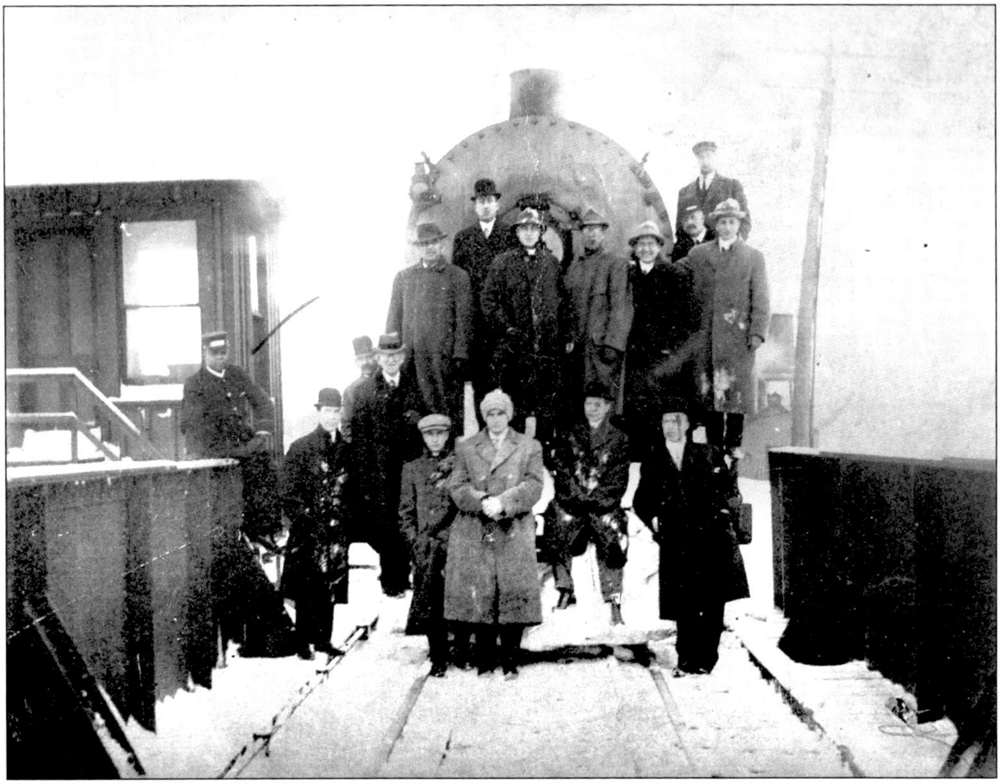

Most African American employment at the end of the 19th century was in casual labor, domestic service, or trades such as whitewashing, barbering, and hairdressing.

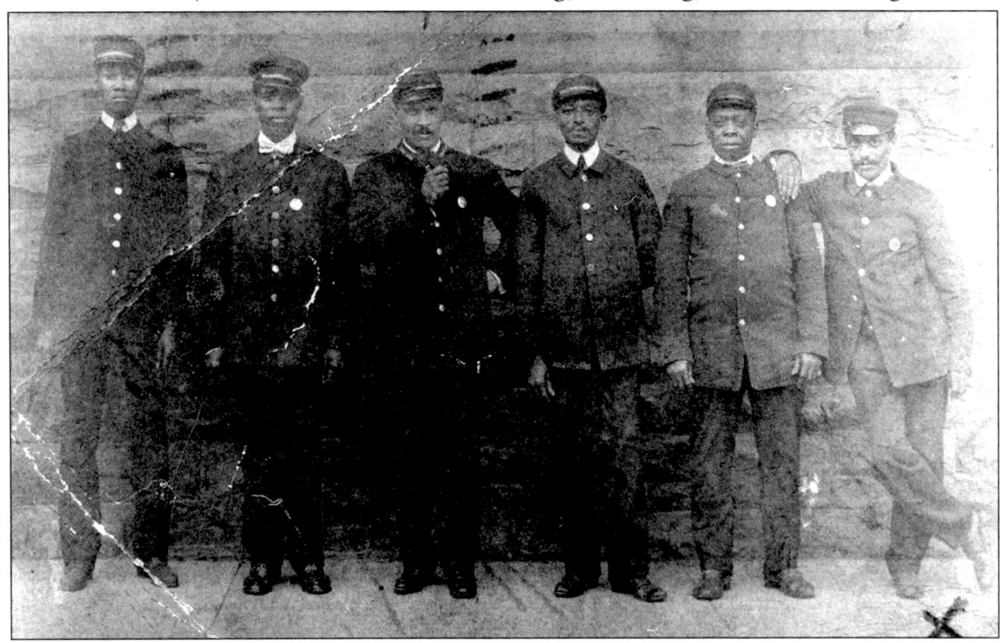

Syracuse's many hotels and the New York Central Railroad employed black men as waiters.

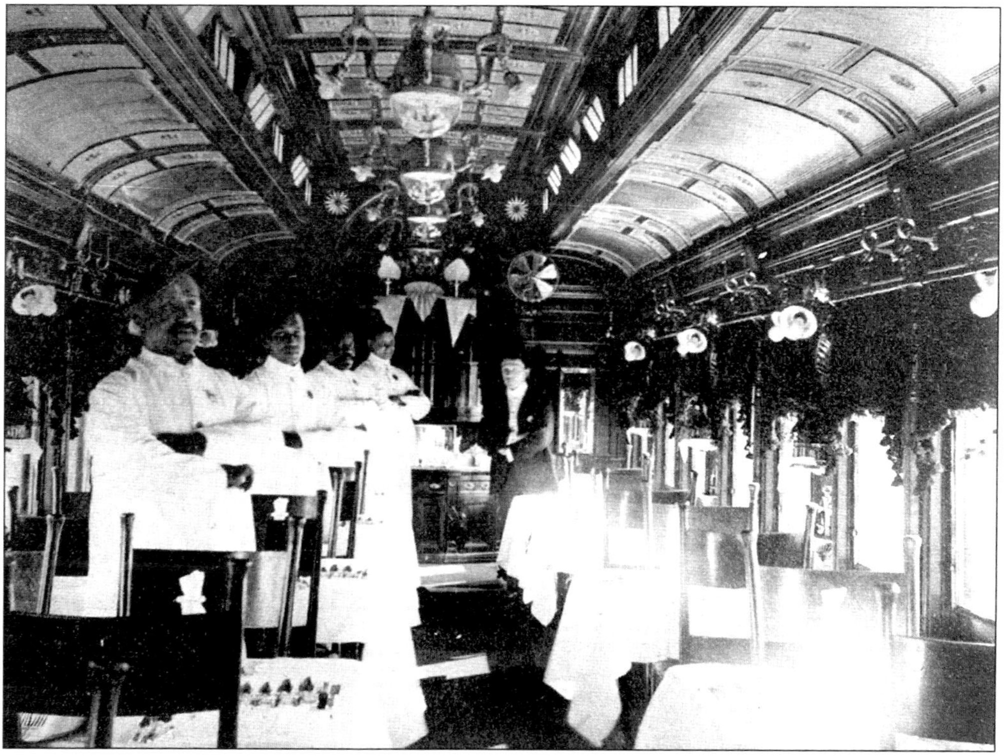

This type of employment gave rise to unique social organizations such as the Club, composed of waiters at the Globe Hotel, and the Hotel Burns Waiters Club.

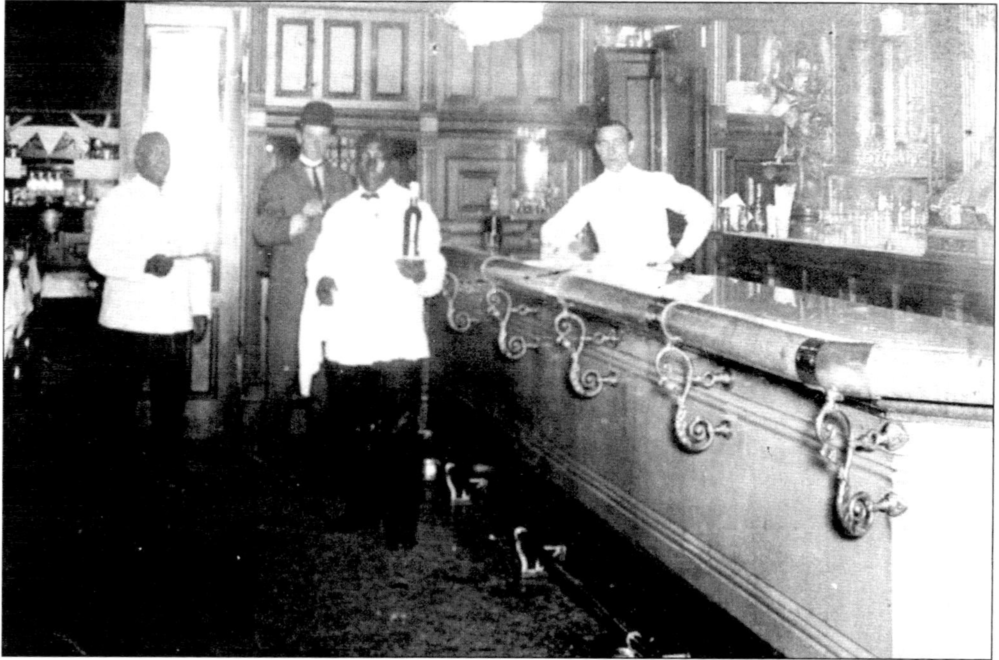

Beekman Hazel was headwaiter at the Yates Hotel bar, where many black men found work at the end of the 19th century.

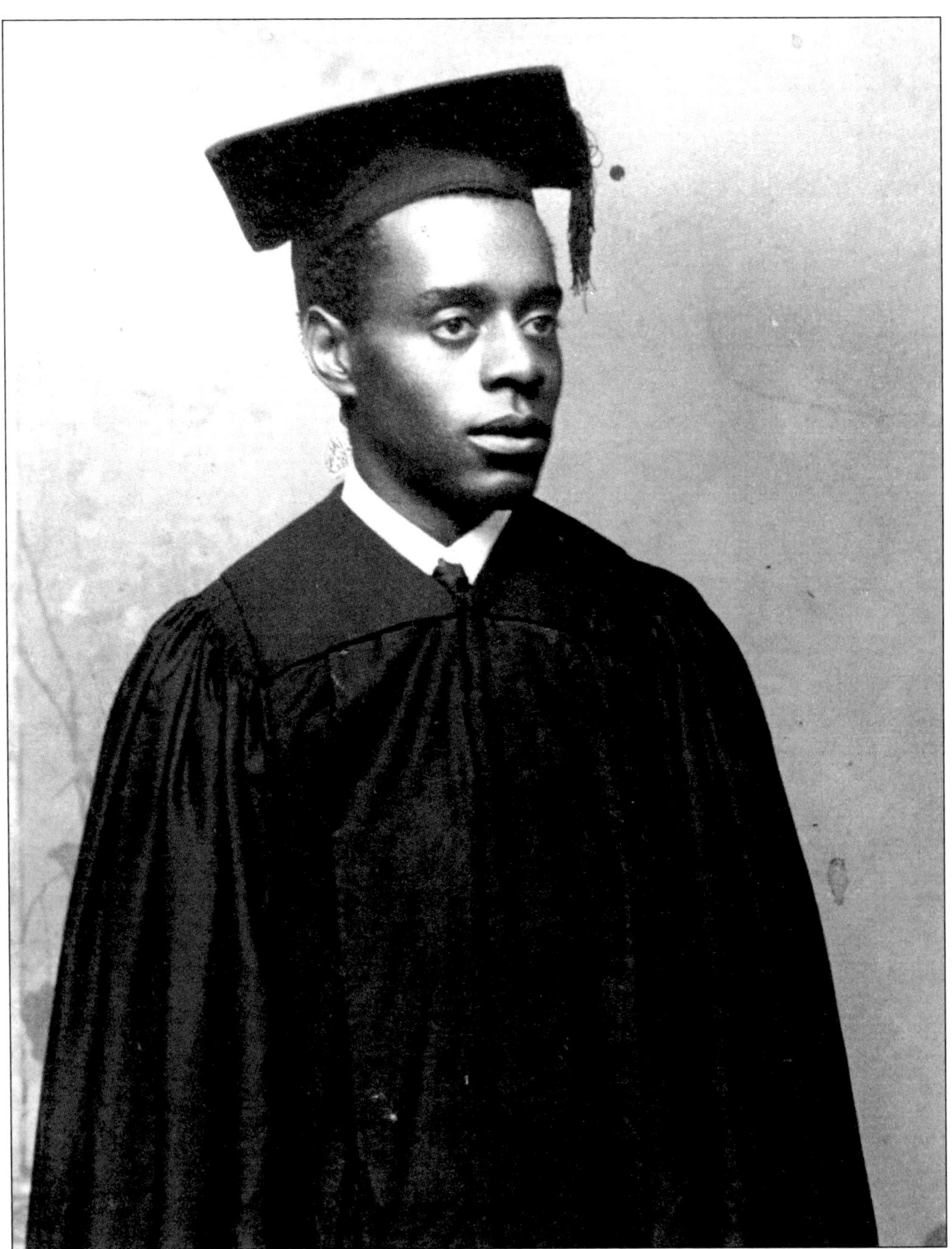

Discrimination in employment, though not official, was nonetheless widespread. Even African American professionals could not find work in Syracuse. William H. Johnson, the first black man to graduate from the Syracuse University College of Law, spoke of this in his 1903 address to his fellow graduates: "It seems strange that there are not more of the colored students taking up the legal profession and especially when what few have done so rank among the best and ablest lawyers in the country. Strange, yes, very strange, that the majority of the colored lawyers start for the west and south. Why is it? Tell me, fellow members, is it because there is race prejudice in this state?"

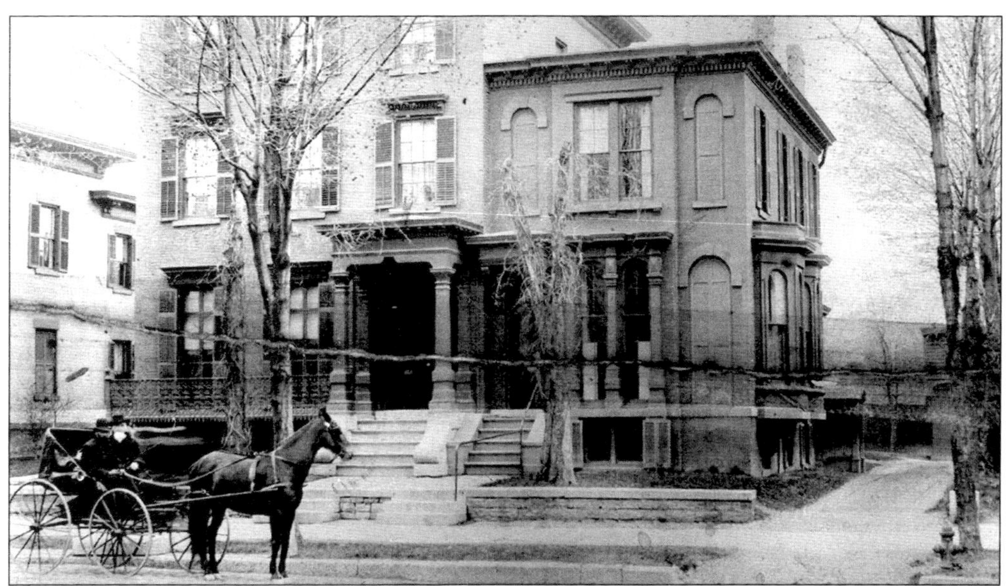

The African American community had its own social structure. George S. Schuyler describes the "definite classes in the tiny colored community" in his autobiography, *Black and Conservative*. "At the bottom were those associated with the underworld, an extensive midtown area. . . . Above this underworld class were the laborers and domestics who were poor but respectable, who had homes and families but little schooling. Finally, there were the men who worked for wealthy families, who were chefs, butlers, coachmen, and such; who had nice homes, well-reared families, and sought to maintain high cultural standards." Francis Johnson, coachman to Dr. Didama, appears in front of the latter's home.

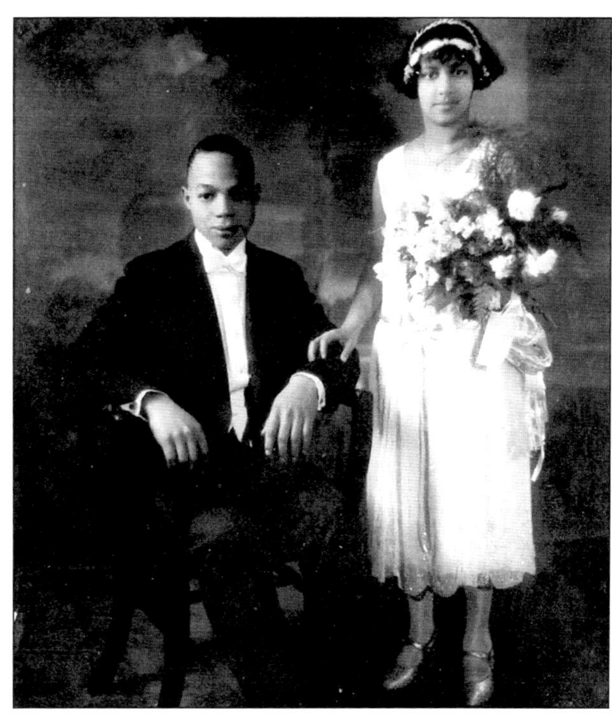

Social activities were sponsored by fraternal organizations, such as the Lodge of Colored Free Masons, formed in 1877, the Colored Odd Fellows, and the Colored Knights of Pythias, or by social organizations, such as the Colored Young Men's Social Club. Balls, receptions, picnics, and socials were frequent. Cakewalks were especially popular at the beginning of the century, and large numbers of participants and onlookers, both black and white, would attend, to be duly reported upon in the press.

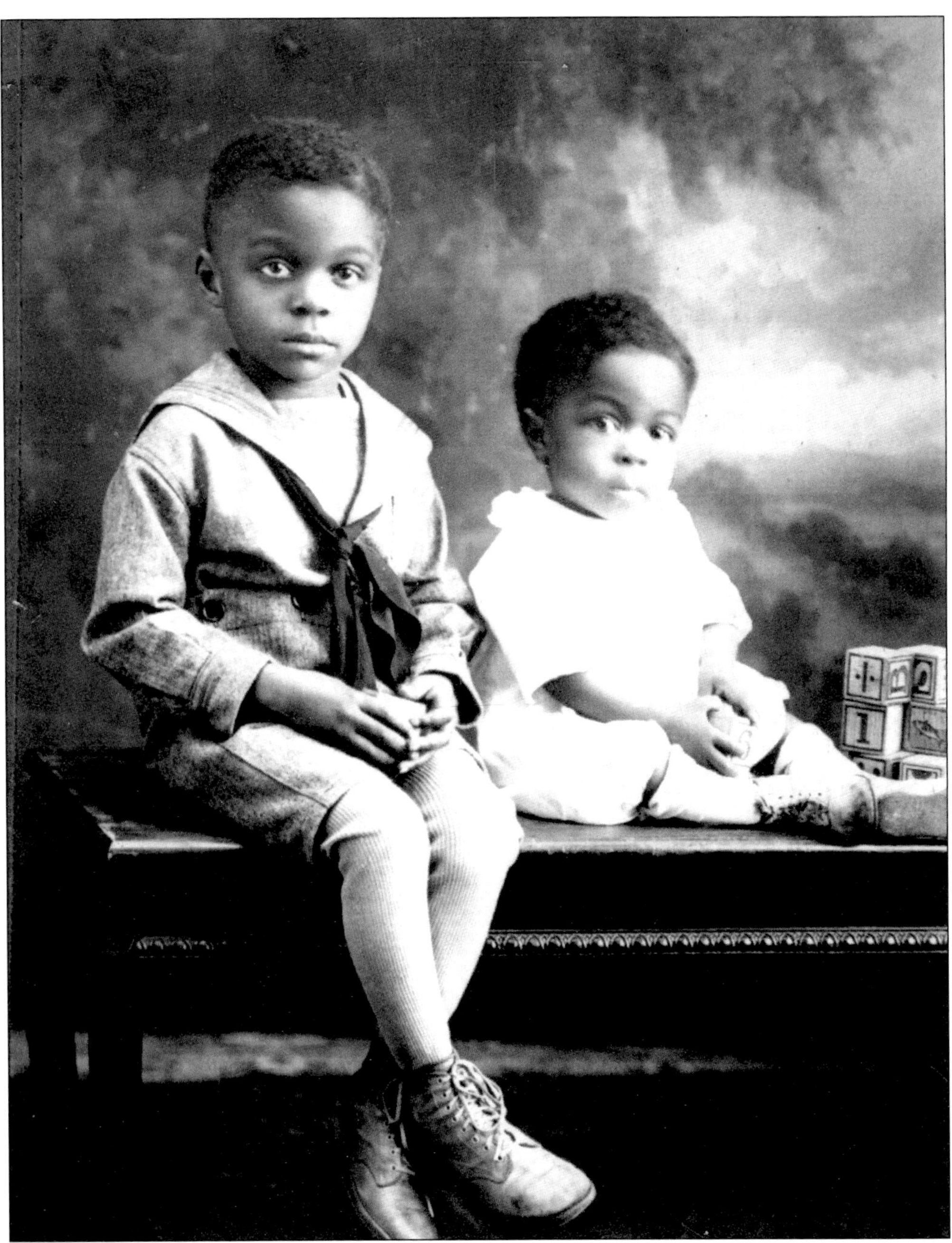

George Schuyler describes the effect discrimination in employment had on African American children like the Harrises (pictured above): "In Syracuse there was nothing to which a youngster could point with pride. Most Negroes were either laborers, janitors, messengers, butlers, maids, cooks, waiters, or bellhops, and they were in competition with whites. Thus, their employment was marginal and their income was low."

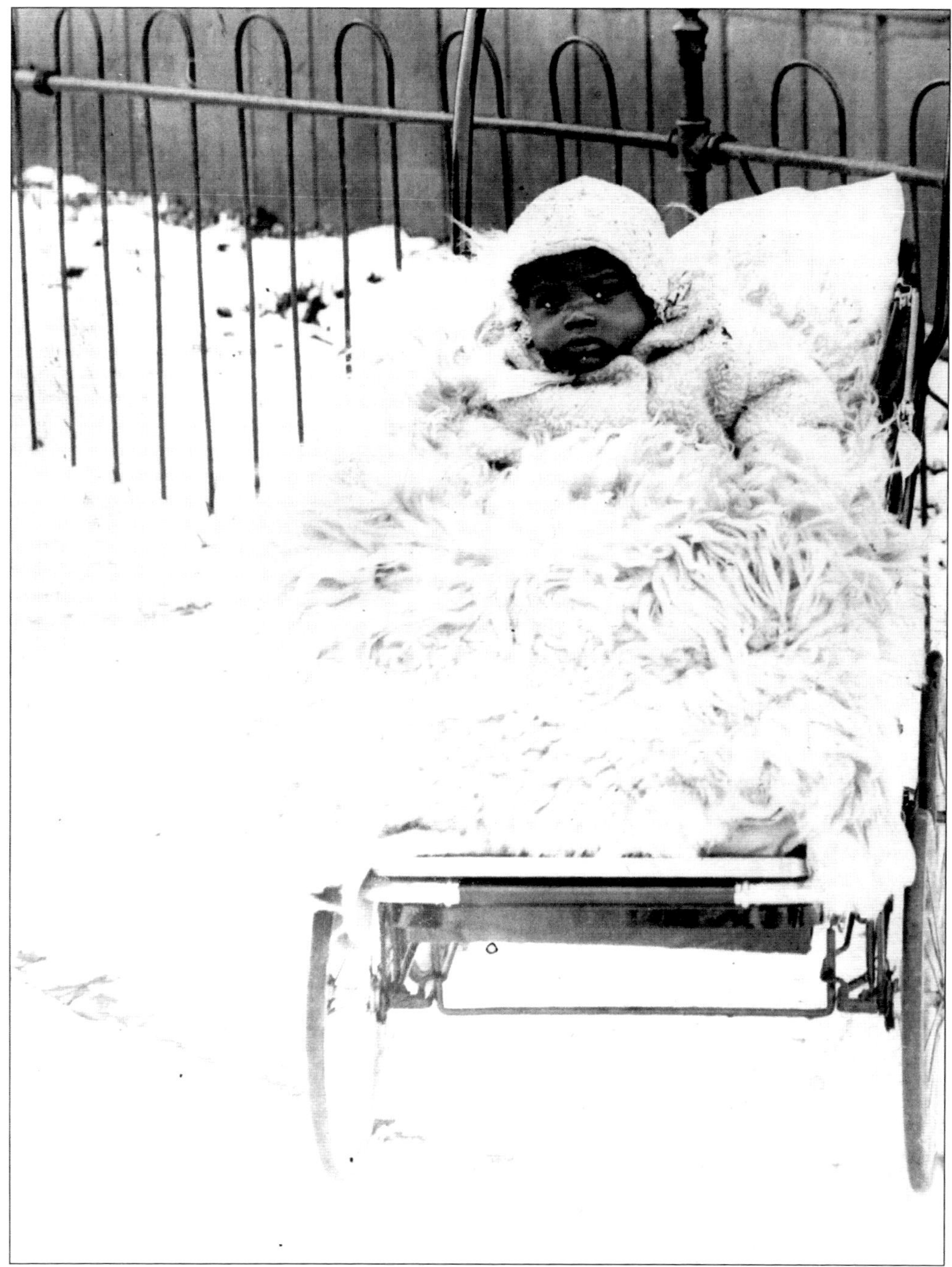

George Schuyler continues: "There were no Negro clerks, city employees, policemen or firemen, not even street-cleaners. Nor were Negroes employed in any of the factories, department stores, banks, warehouses, or other enterprises."

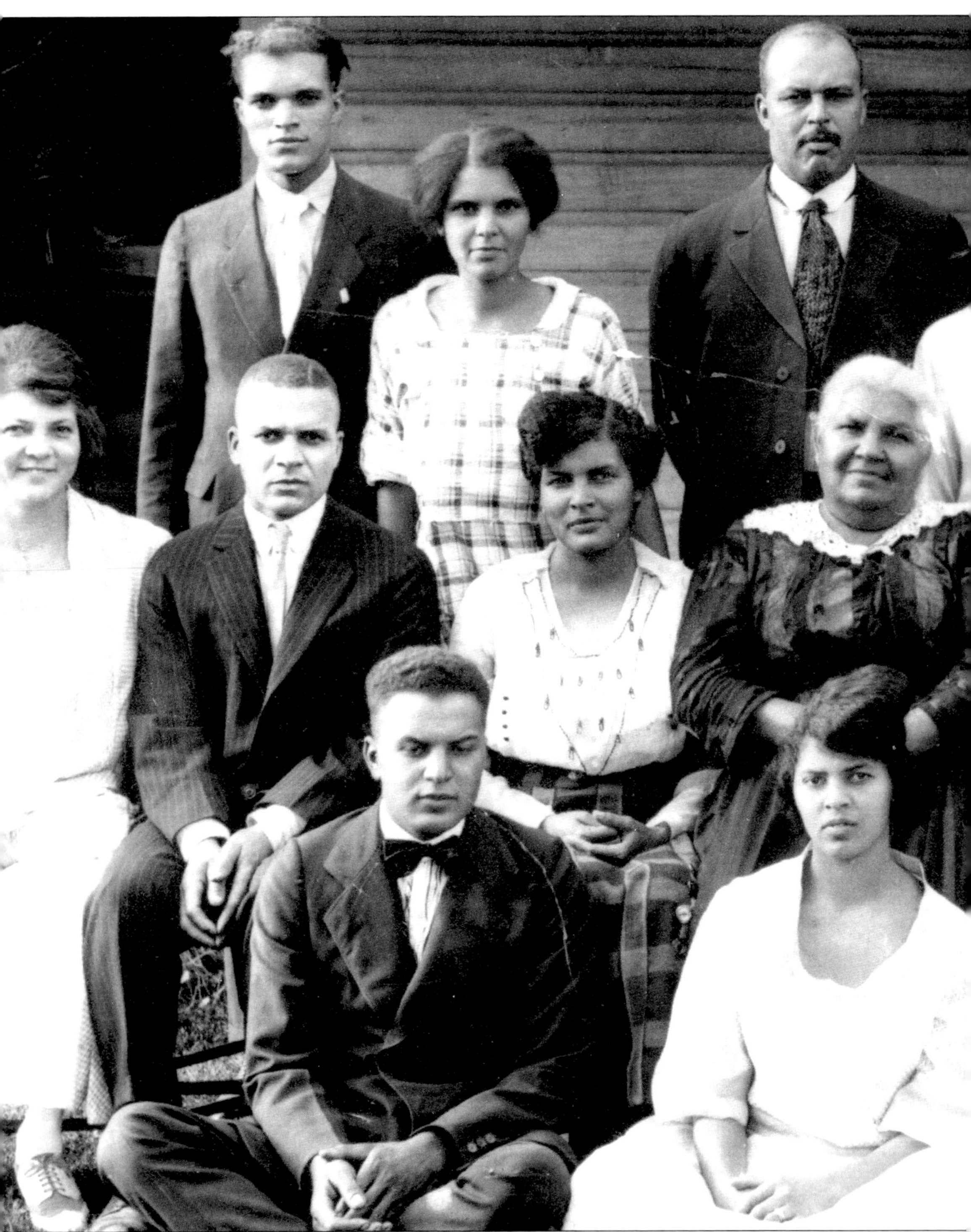

"Discrimination was *de facto* rather than *de jure*, but it affected Negroes just as much nonetheless." There was, as one observer has noted, "a pattern of almost total exclusion [of blacks] from the social and industrial life of the community."

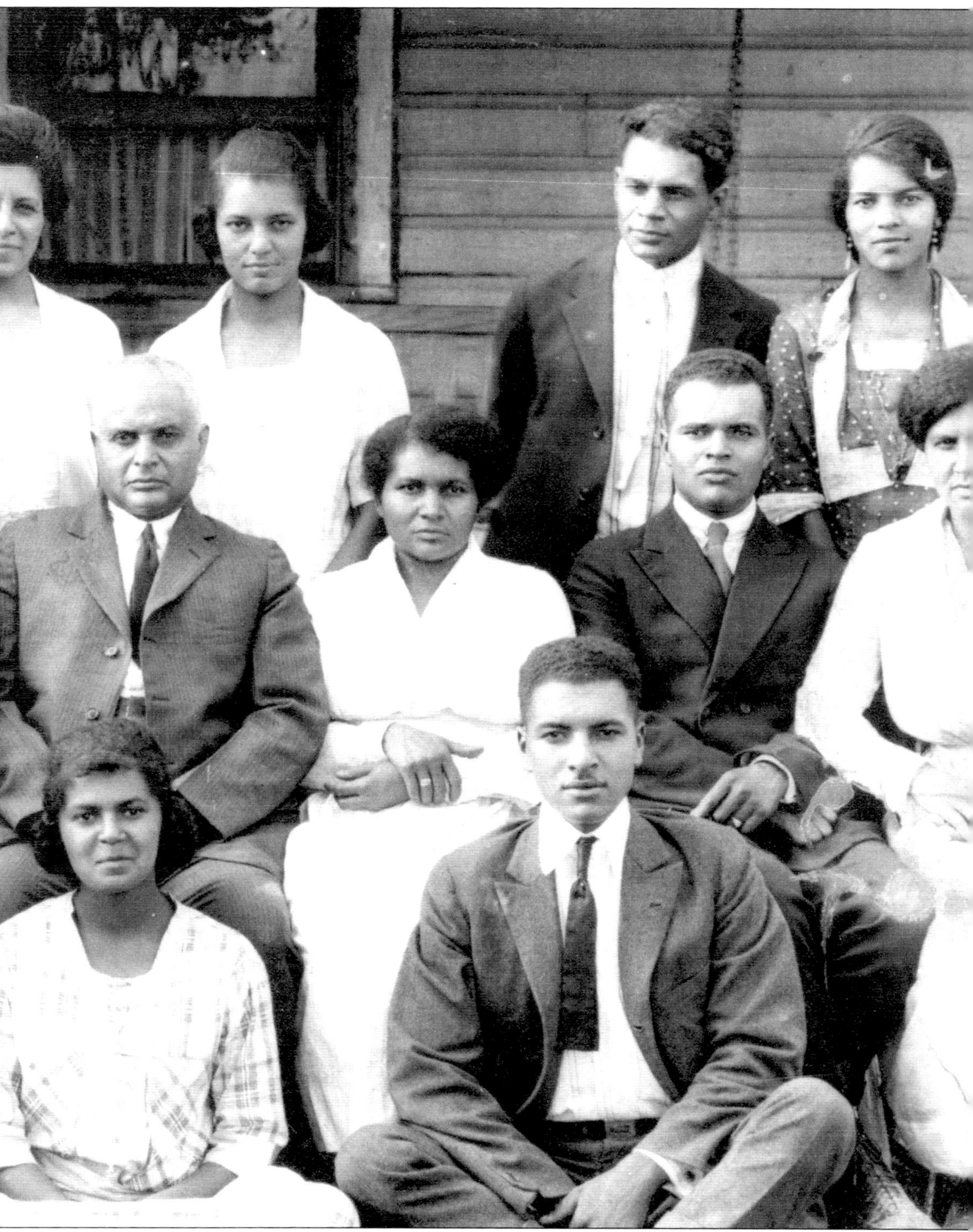

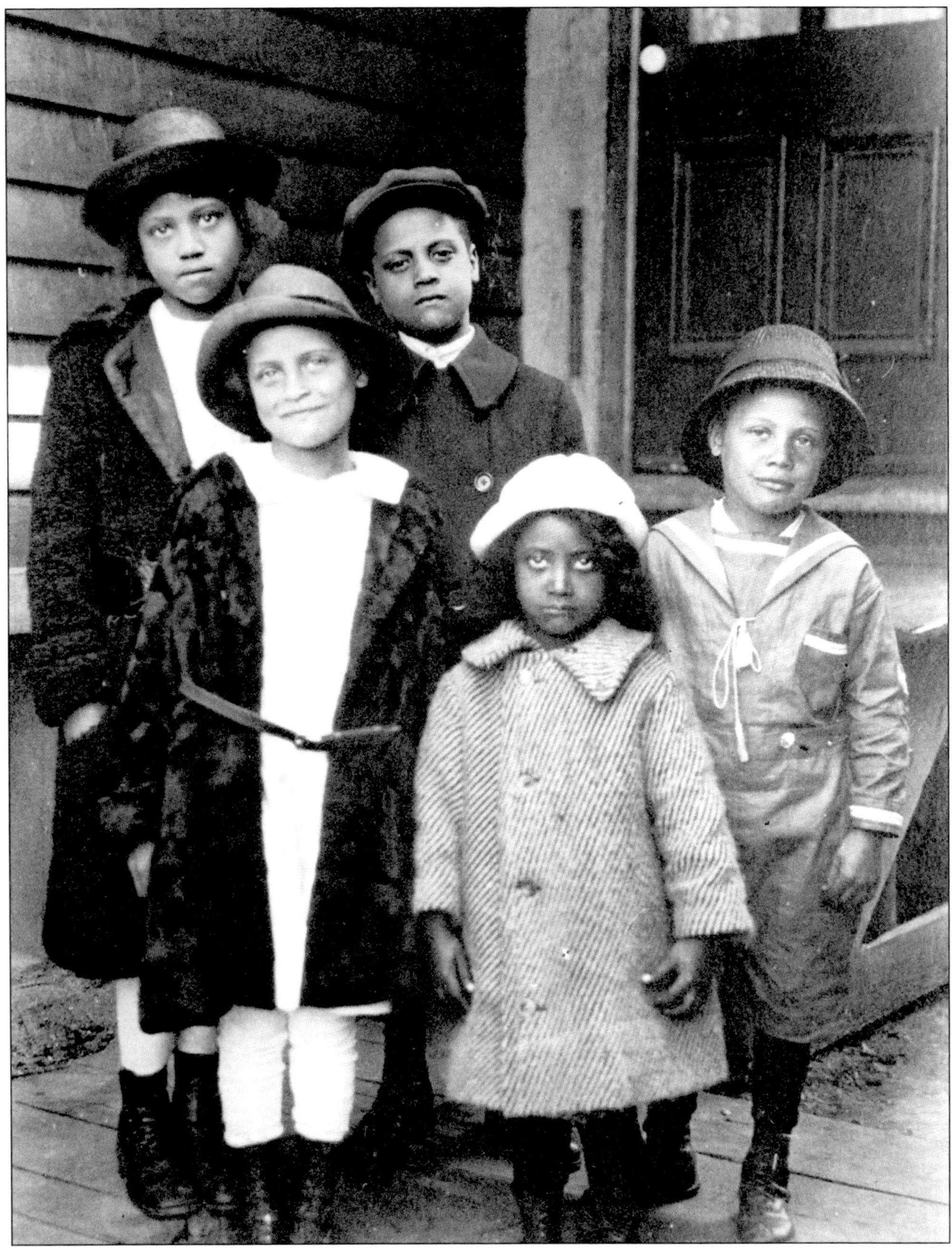

By the beginning of the 20th century, the Powell children, shown in this photograph, were part of a community which, while increasingly slowly in size, was declining as a percentage of the total community.

# *Four*

# SCENES OF A COMMUNITY

The advent of the 20th century brought about some notable changes in the life of Syracuse's African American community. Political activity declined significantly, as did social activities. The population grew, albeit slowly. As a proportion of the total city population, however, the black community declined from 1 percent to 0.7 percent. Census figures show 1,034 black residents in 1900, 1,124 in 1910, and 1,260 in 1920. Men who had come with their families in the mid-1890s to build the Woodlawn Reservoir were joined by others who came to work at the munitions plant. World War I changed the employment picture somewhat for African Americans, and a few jobs in industry were opened to them for the first time. But as employment opportunities broadened, racial discrimination became more overt. William M. Chiles, relocation director for the Urban Renewal Program, described the years from the Civil War to the Second World War as "the period of great accommodation where everyone knew his place and kept it. Gradualism was in the saddle and peace, not justice, was the order of the day."

Yet white attitudes were expressive of "indifference rather than hostility," as was the case in many other cities. George Schuyler noted that "there was surprisingly little talk in our home or in the town generally about the race problem. Prejudice on grounds of so-called race existed and one did not have to go far to find discrimination. There were people who did not want Negro neighbors, and there were fine restaurants and bars, I heard, where the patronage of colored people, no matter how well dressed and well behaved was not encouraged. Reportedly, colored theatergoers could with difficulty get seats in the orchestra section of the six theatres, but were welcomed mostly in the back balcony and gallery. Of course, few Negroes in our town could afford orchestra seats. If a colored person wanted to rent a home, he might encounter difficulties in certain areas of town, and not due just to lack of money."

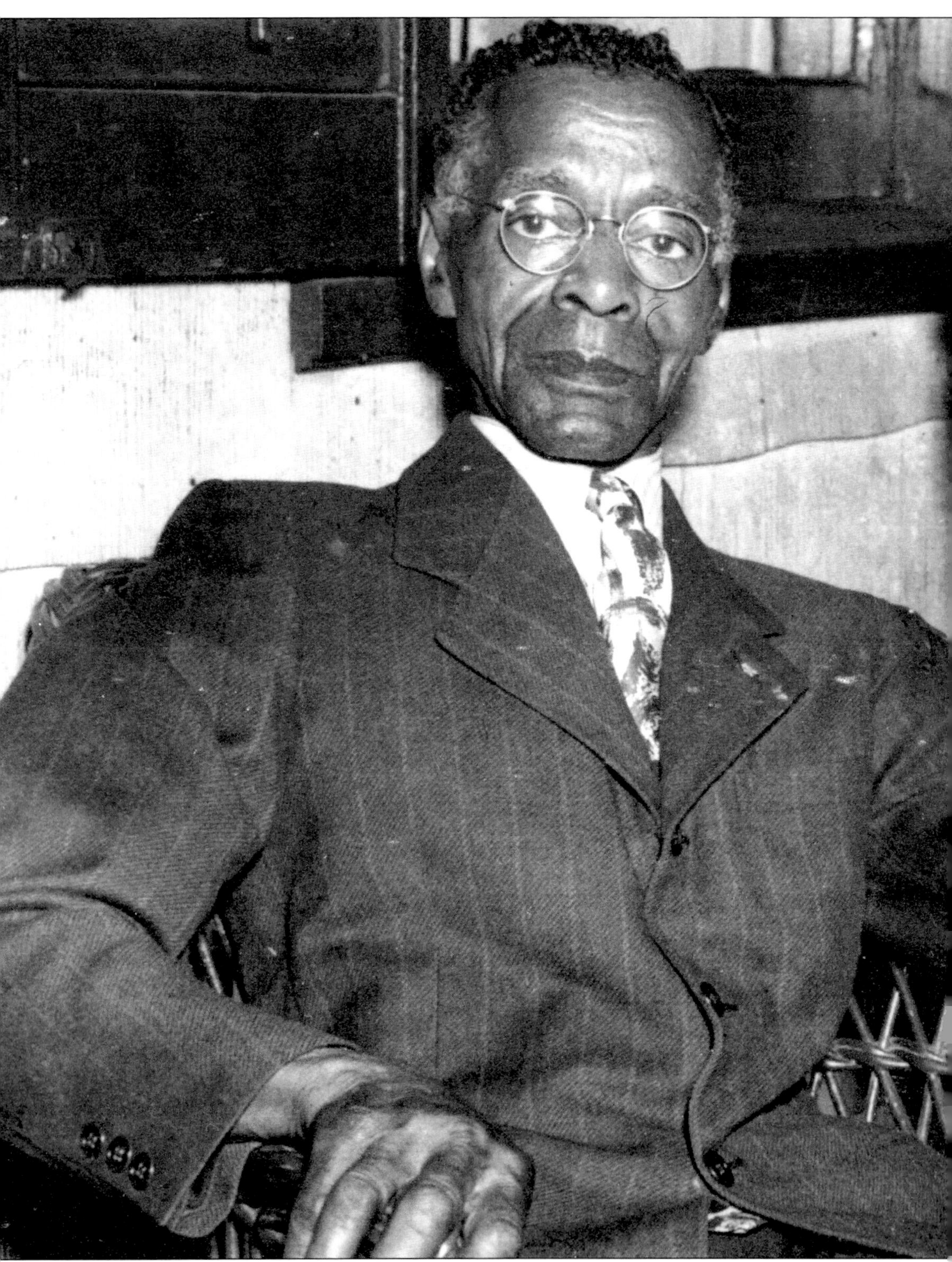

Mr. and Mrs. William Johnson are shown seated on the porch of their home.

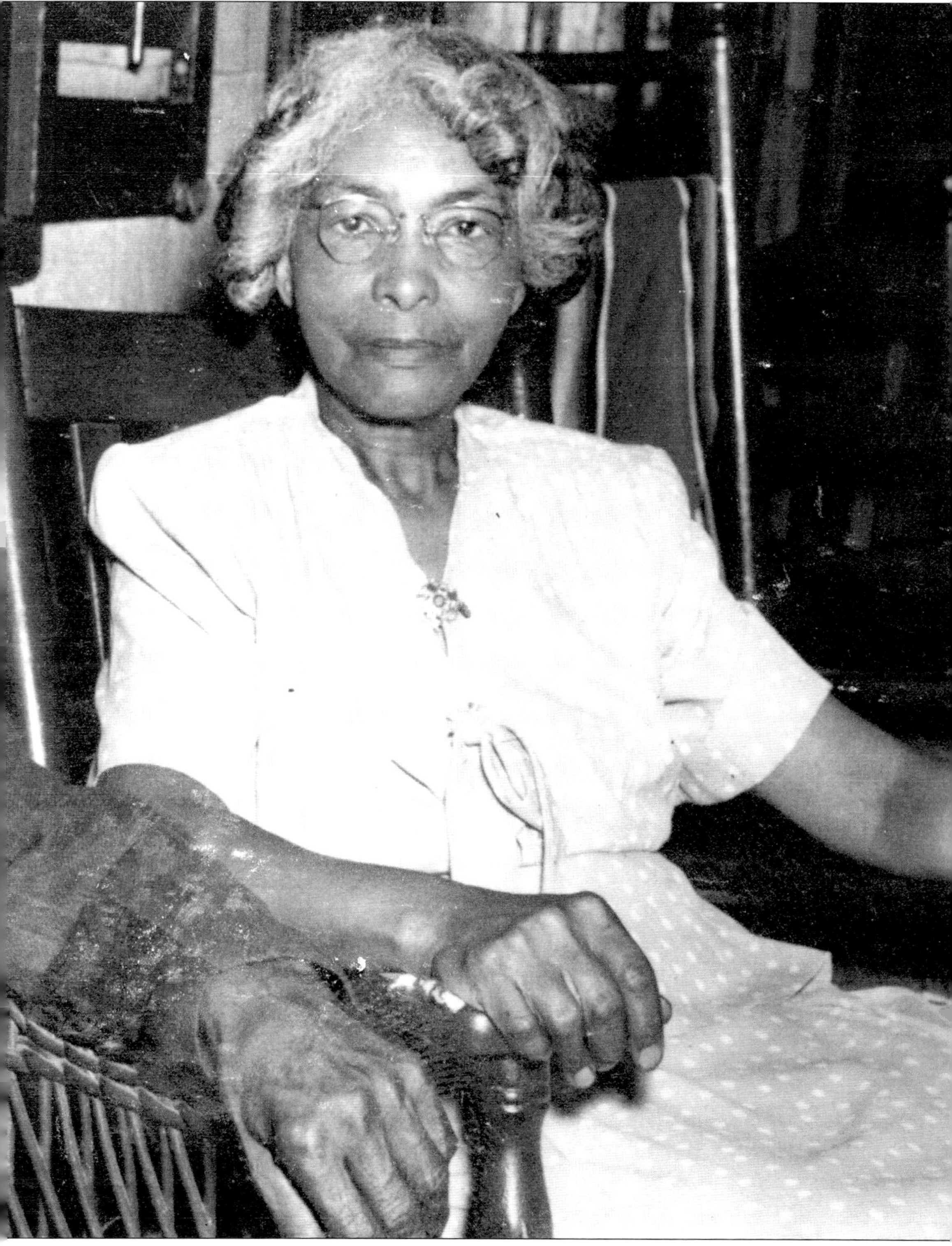

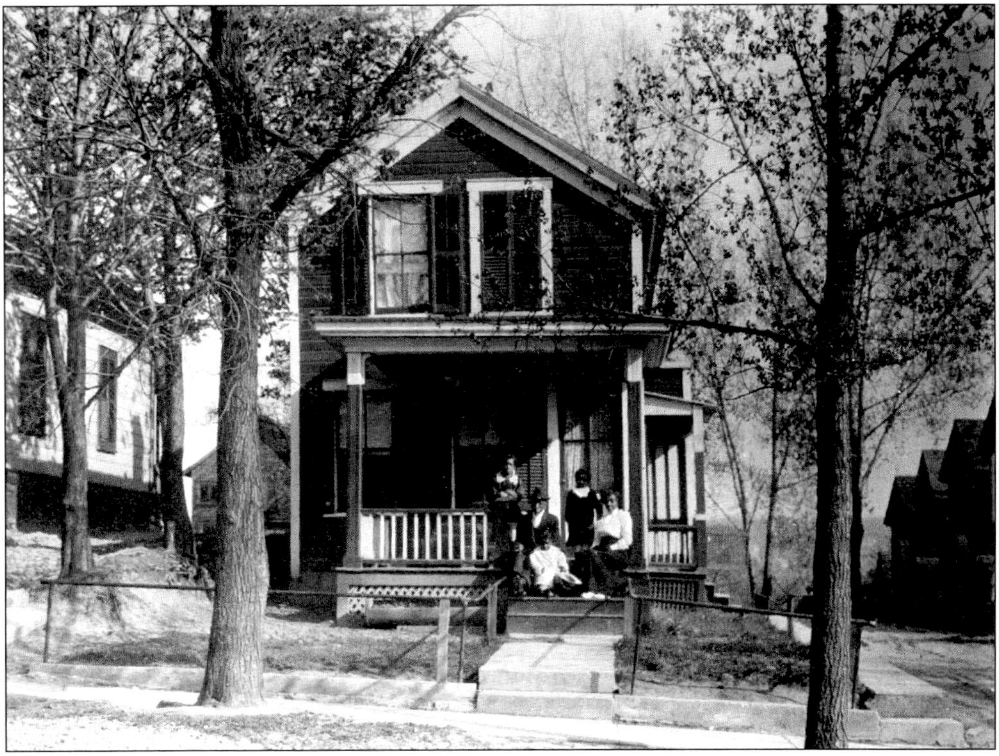

The house shown is located at 326 Green Street in Syracuse.

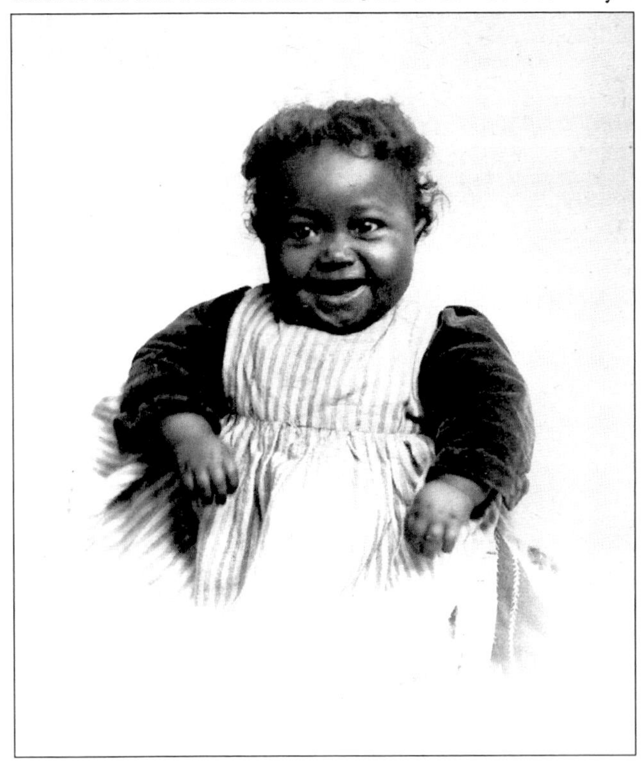

This delightful youngster is baby Marie Hazel.

This photograph is of Edith, Herbert, and Dorothy Johnson.

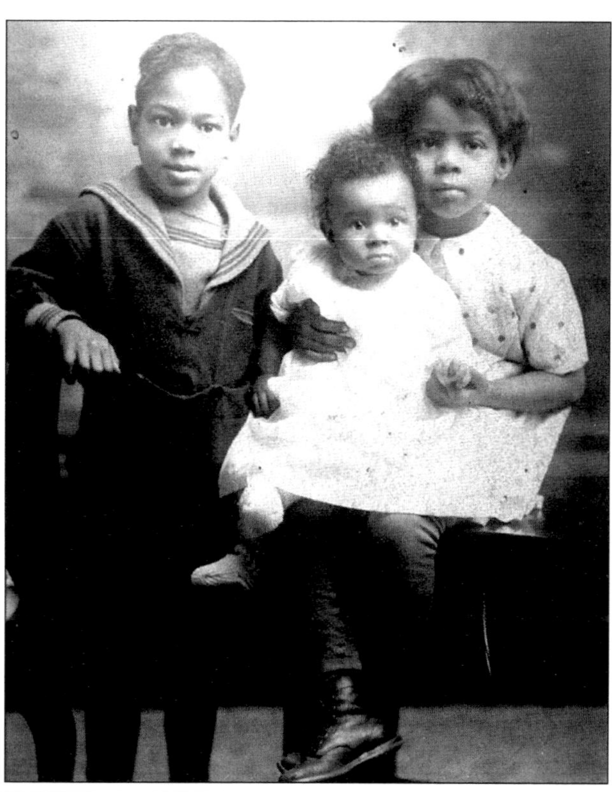

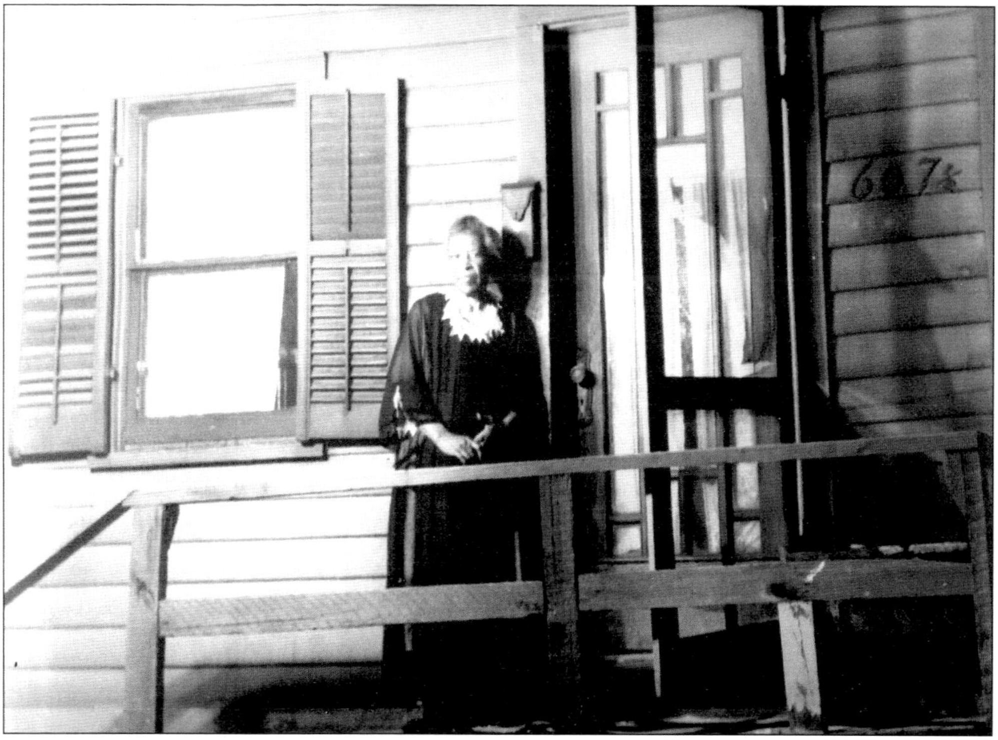

This photograph shows Mrs. Joseph Terrill on the porch of her home.

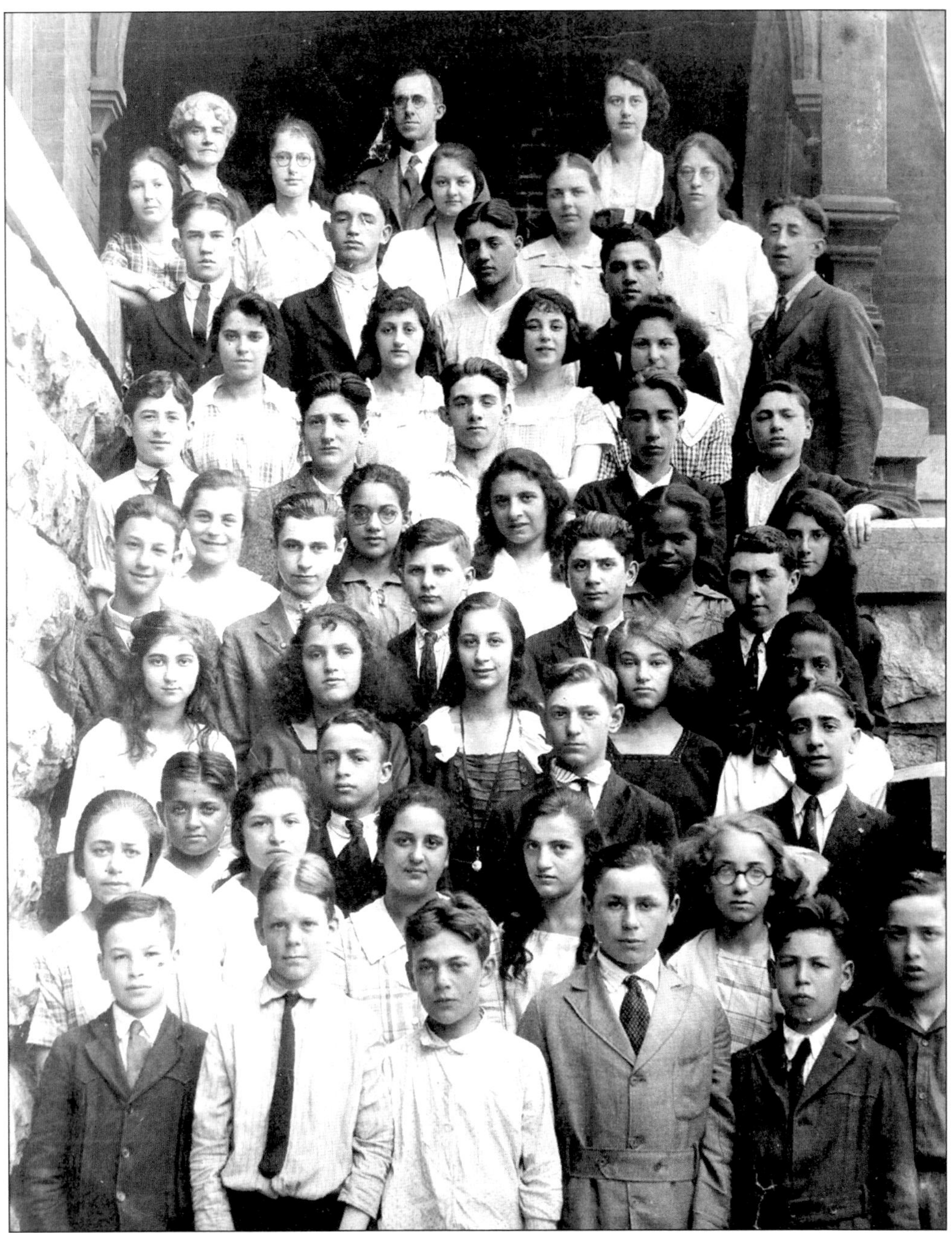

The African American community was not the only one that was segregated. Jews, Italians, and Germans also lived in separate areas and maintained their own ways of life. Syracuse in the first part of the 20th century was a quiet city with little organized activity.

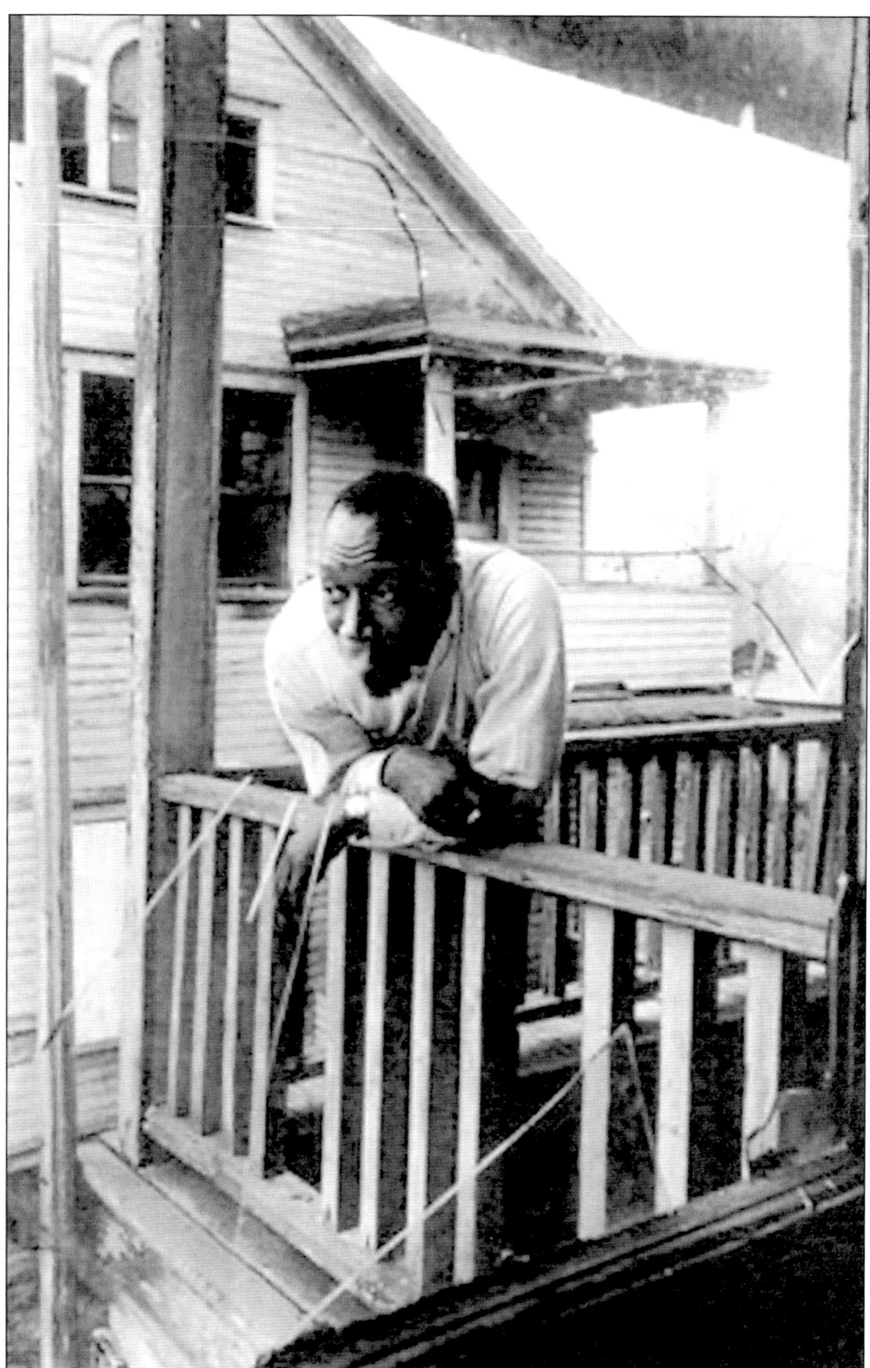

"The Ward" was a special neighborhood. The writer John Williams, seen here, who grew up in Syracuse, described the area known as "Jew Town" or "the Ward" in which he grew up: "Jew Town was a misnomer. Jews were not the only ones who lived there." Williams, who gained great fame as the author of *The Man Who Cried I Am* and many other novels, has fond memories of the close and neighborly Syracuse community in which he was raised.

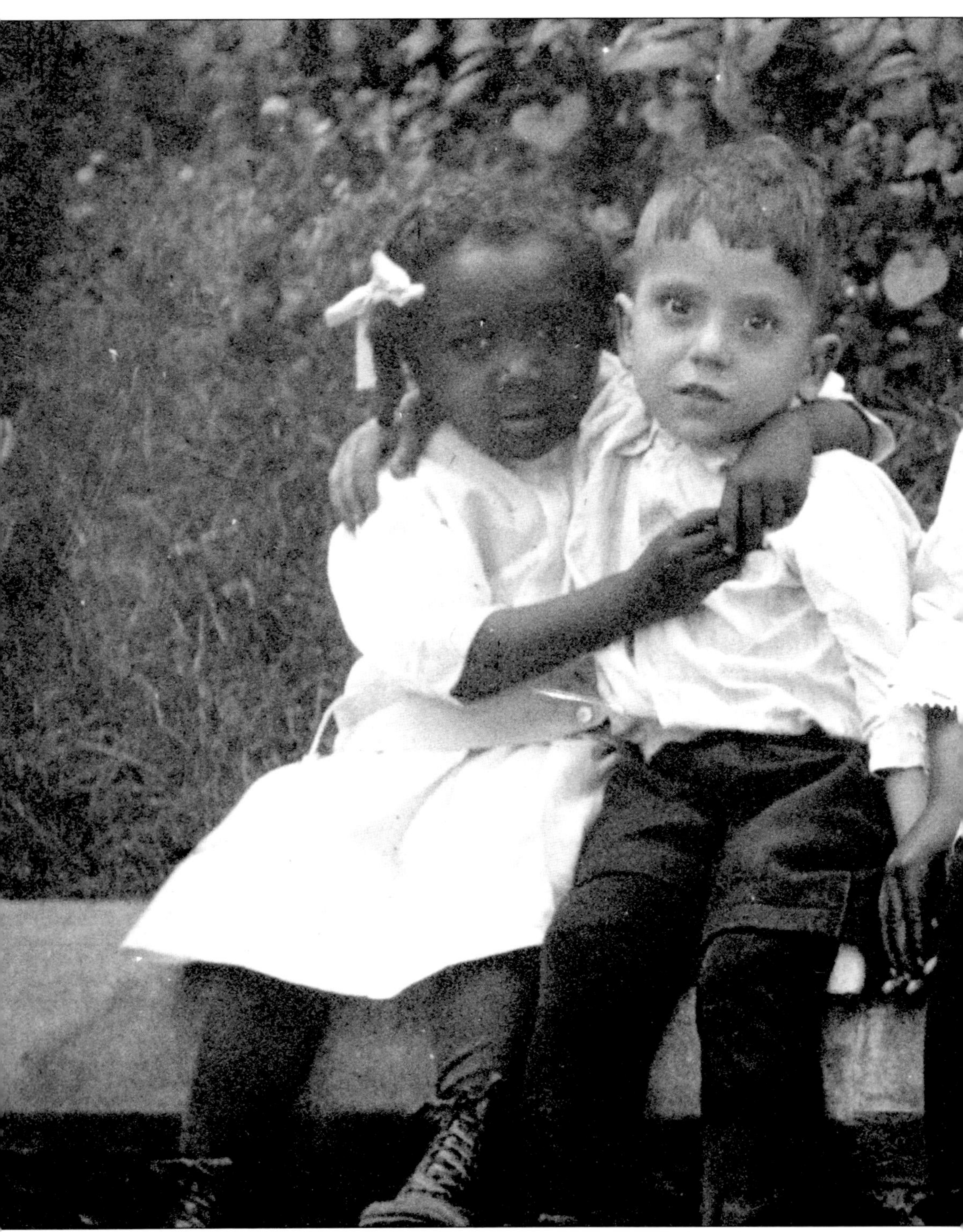

Williams wrote, "the Ward was an entity unto itself, integrated not because that was where the relatives were, or where the money ran out, or more money could be made, but because it was set in a lovely valley surrounded by green hills upon which sat the red

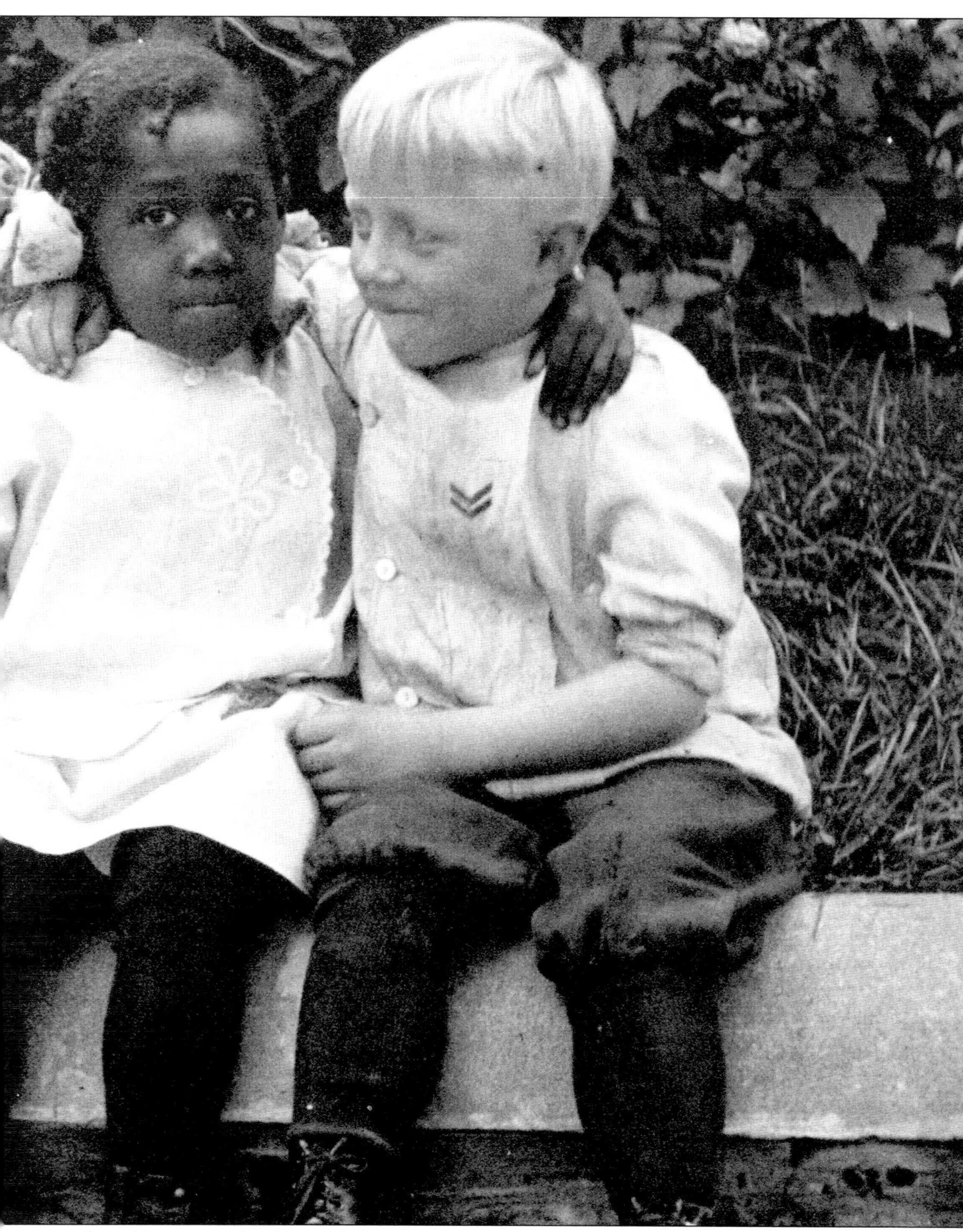

brick and limestone building of Syracuse University. Looking up at them reminded us of what could be achieved. Securing an education was the primary drive of all our parents." The photograph is of Vivian and Marie Cloyd, Raphael Nano, and Frank Keeler.

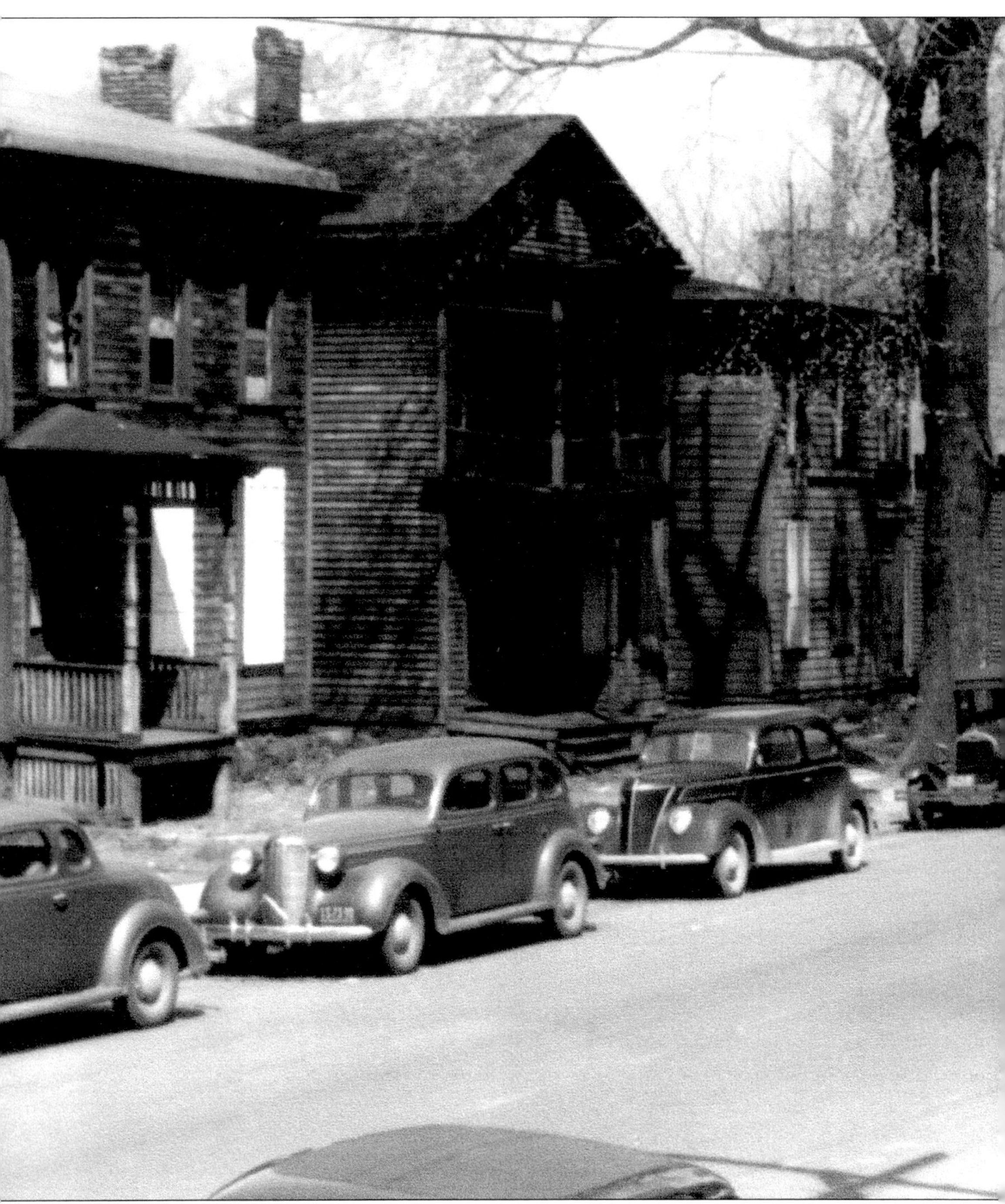

Into this setting, in the year 1918, came a young, black ex-convict named Jimmy LaGrin. He brought with him an idea that would greatly alter the social and economic life of Syracuse's black community for the next three decades. Determined that other black youth should not be led to lives of crime as he had been, he began to organize a recreational group dedicated to the young people in the city. Beginning first within the black community, LaGrin later sought the aid of white Syracuse through the Commonweal

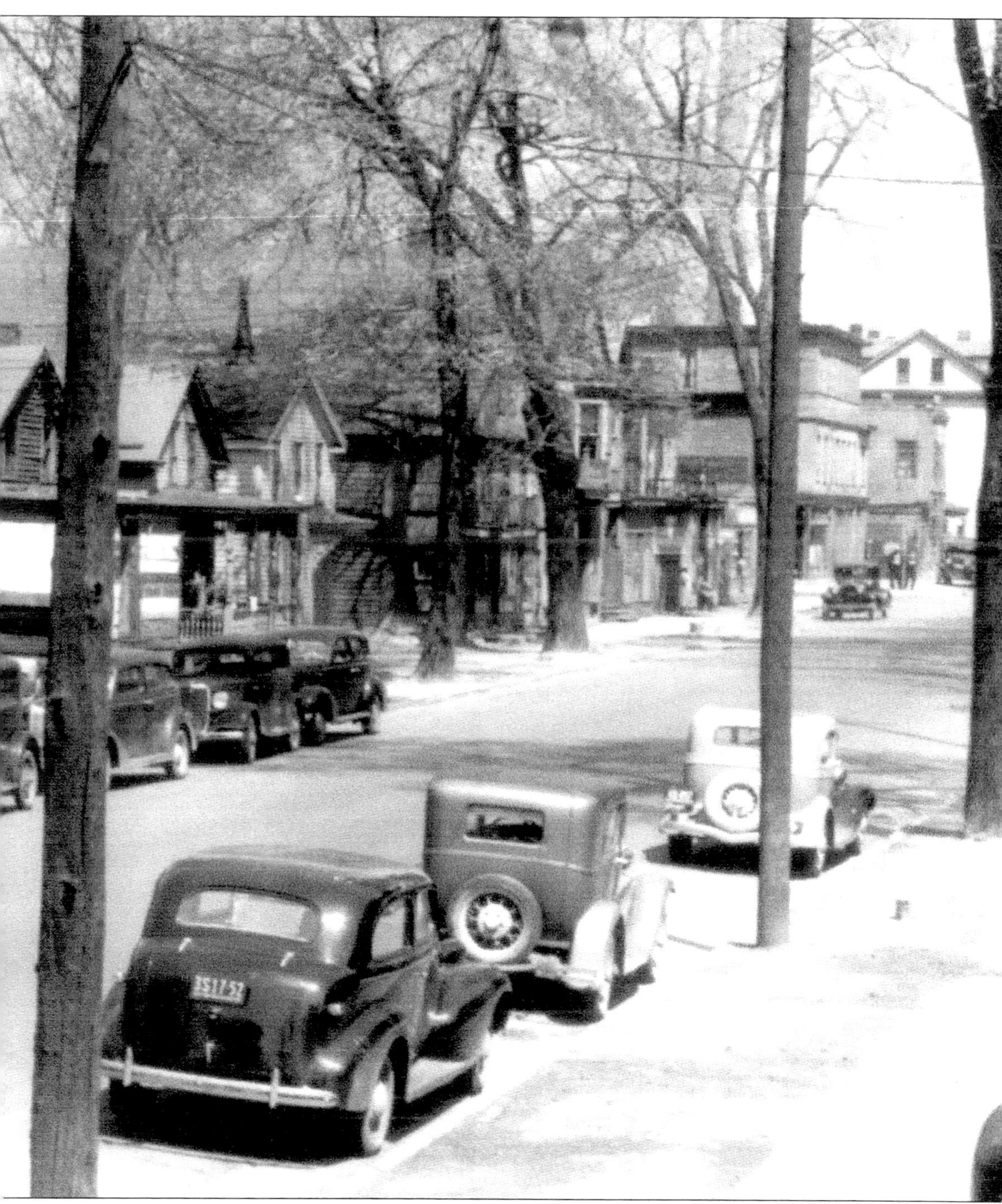

Club, an influential businesswomen's group interested in social service. When the African Methodist Episcopal Zion Church ended its sponsorship of LaGrin's programs in 1925, the Commonweal Club voted to provide financial backing to develop an African American community center, called the Dunbar Center after the African American poet, Paul Laurence Dunbar.

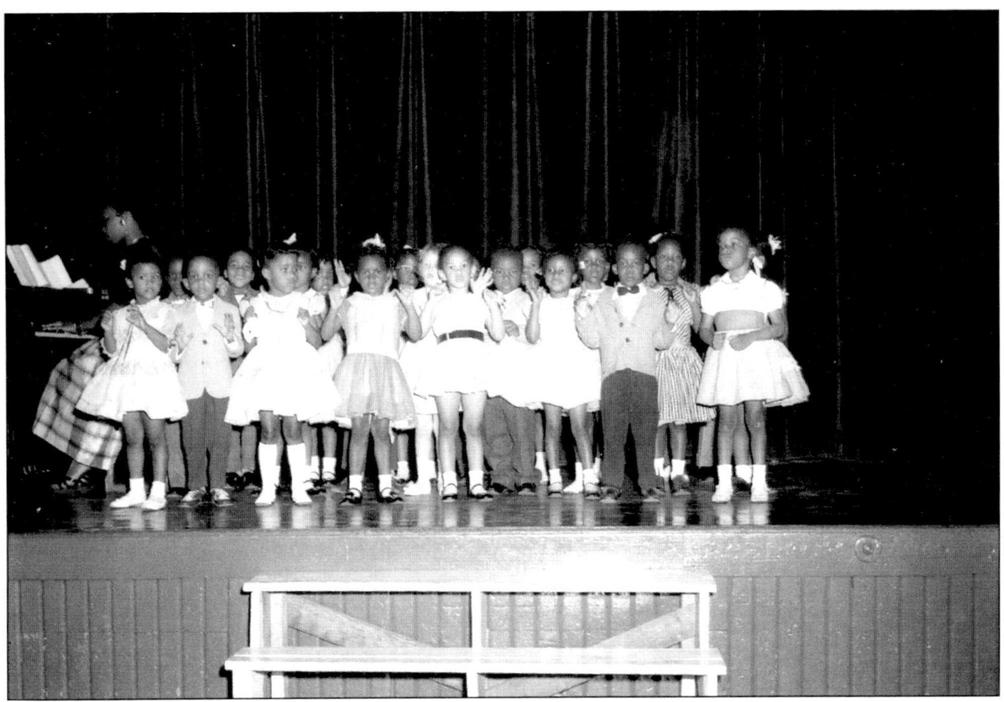

Syracuse University students were hired to direct established activities, which ranged from dances, lectures, and teas to play programs for children and a baseball team.

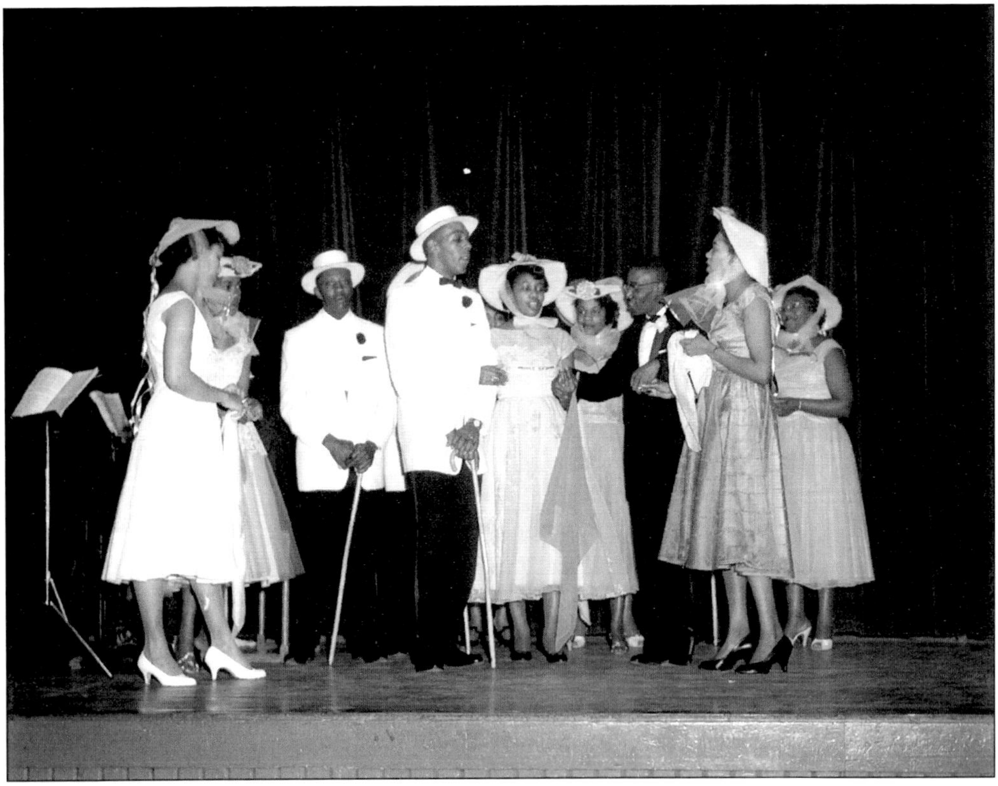

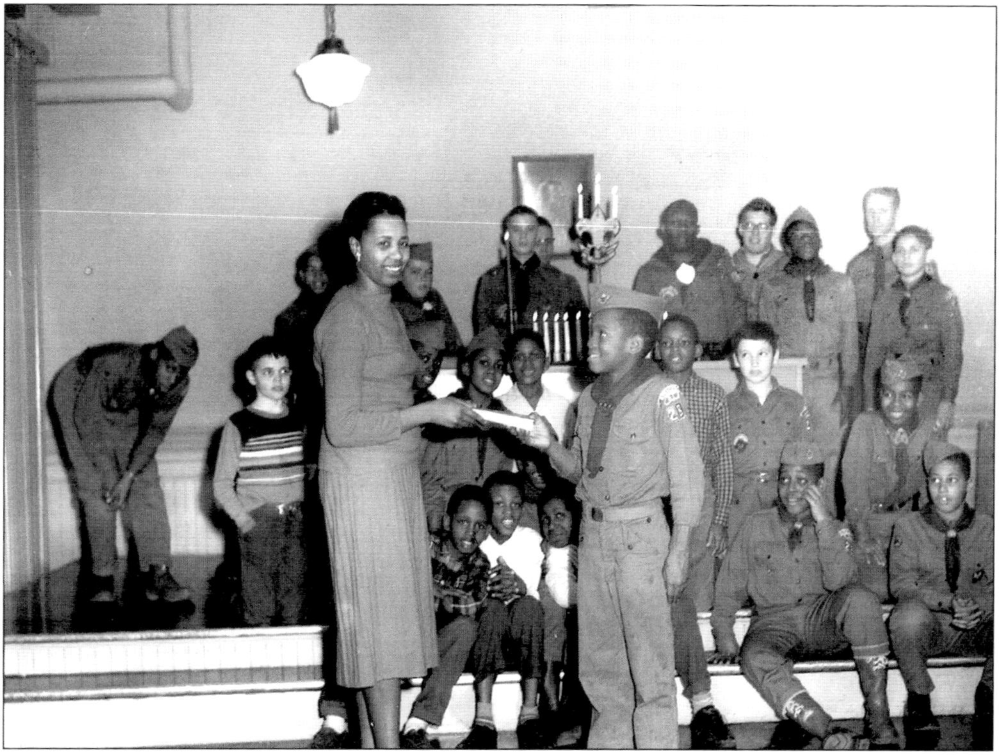

The Dunbar Center expanded and moved to larger, though not permanent, quarters on McBride Street. Laura Rowles was hired as the first full-time director, to be succeeded by Helen Blake.

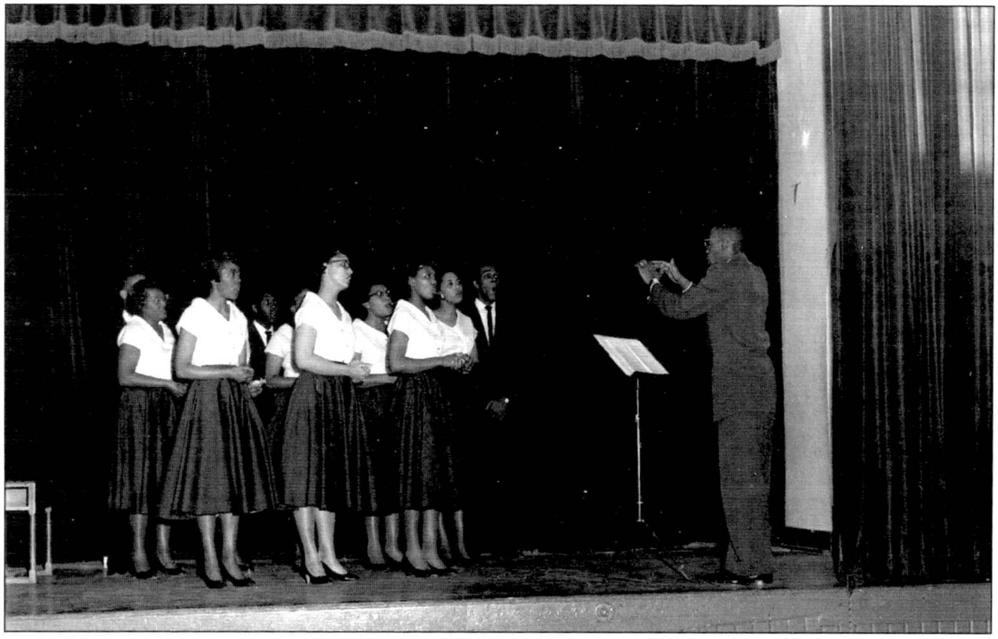

New activities included a chorus, scout troop, drama club, and basketball team. In 1929, the Dunbar Center became a community chest agency, and its future was secure.

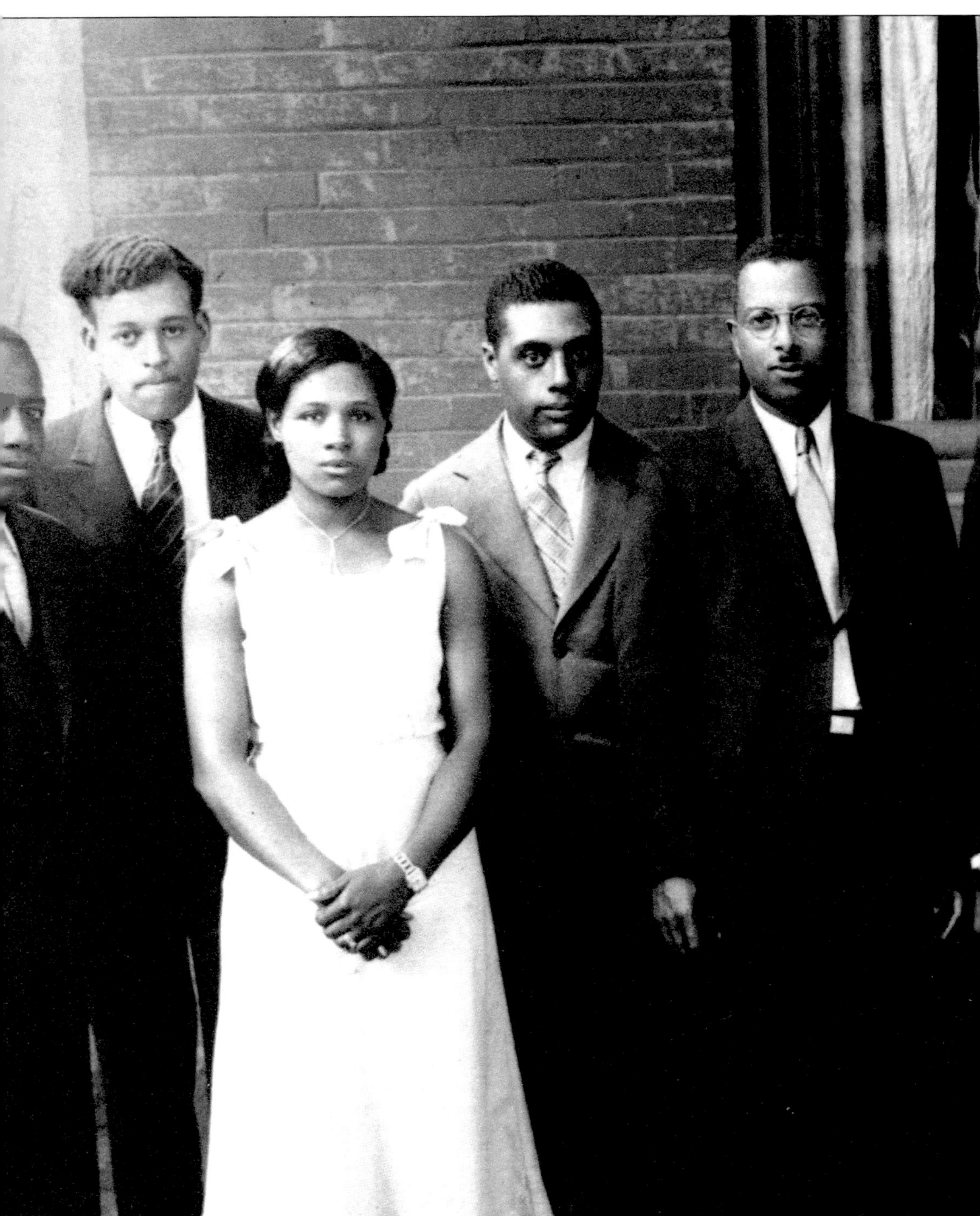

In 1930, Golden B. Darby was appointed the first executive secretary of the Dunbar Center, seen here fifth from left with the Dunbar Center staff. A forceful and active civic leader of the African American community, Darby led the center until 1937. The center and its programs were a great source of pride for the African American community.

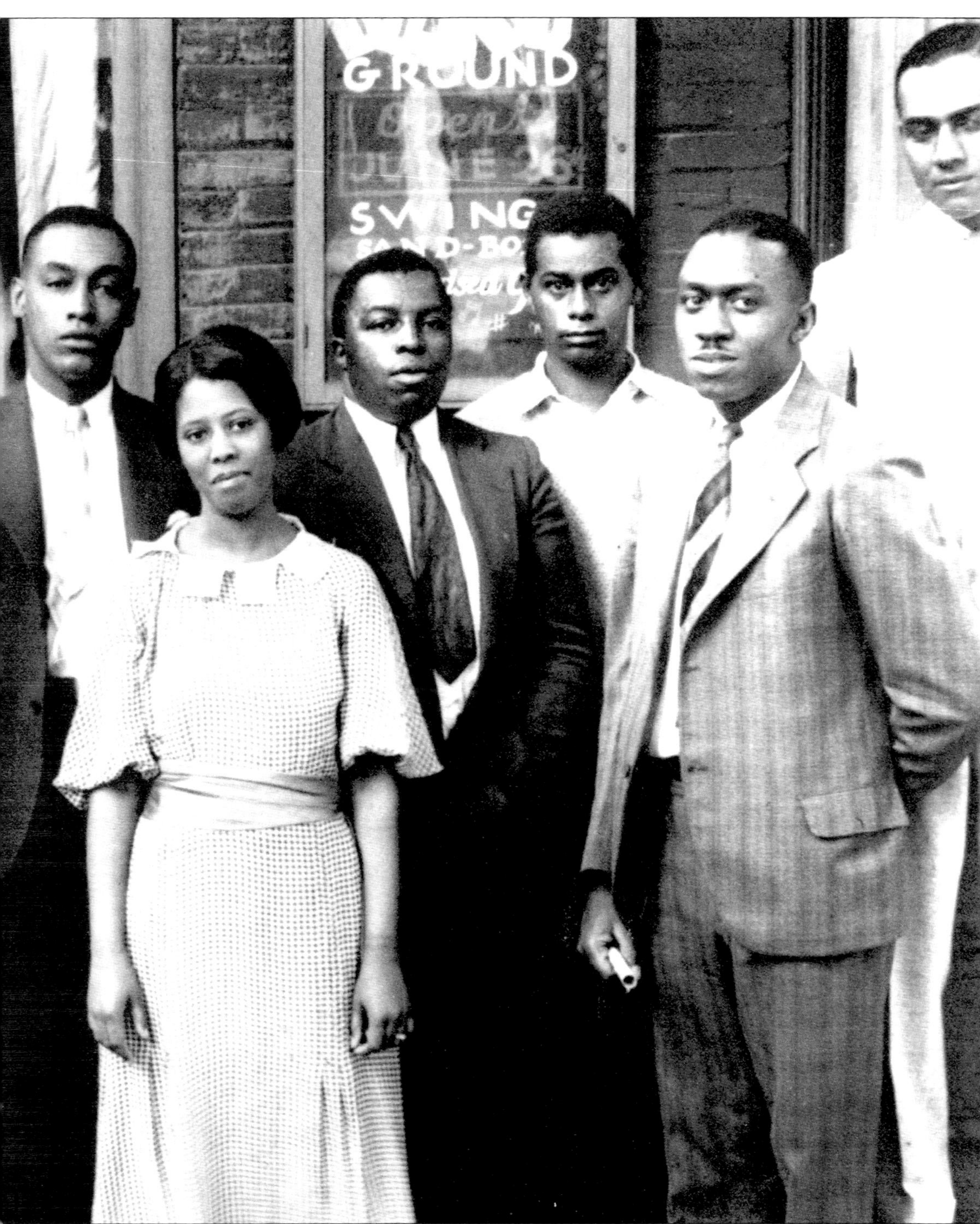


Dunbar originated within the community and was operated by and for the community. Though the board was biracial, the center's director and social workers were black, and they served both as models for and leaders of the people they served.

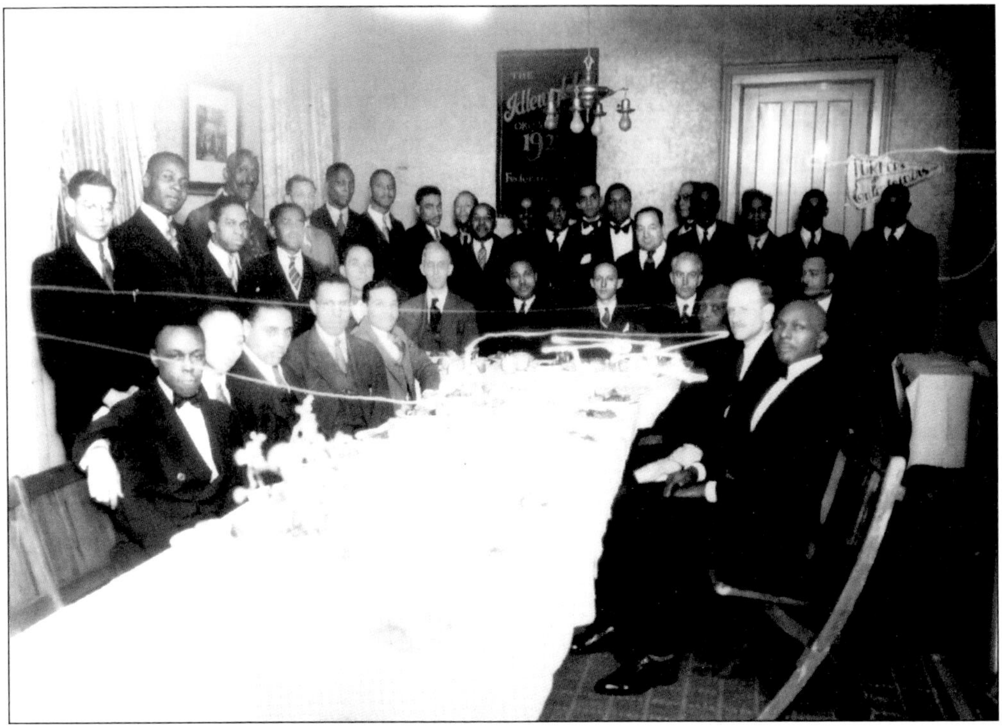

The board of the Dunbar Center, seen here, defined its mission: "to establish and maintain . . . recreational, social and cultural centers for the use of the Negro people of the city of Syracuse; to investigate conditions affecting the social well-being of the Negro people; to assist the Negro to improve his condition through the development of educational and vocational opportunity, health standards and good citizenship; to promote racial understanding and cooperation in the interest of community unity and solidarity."

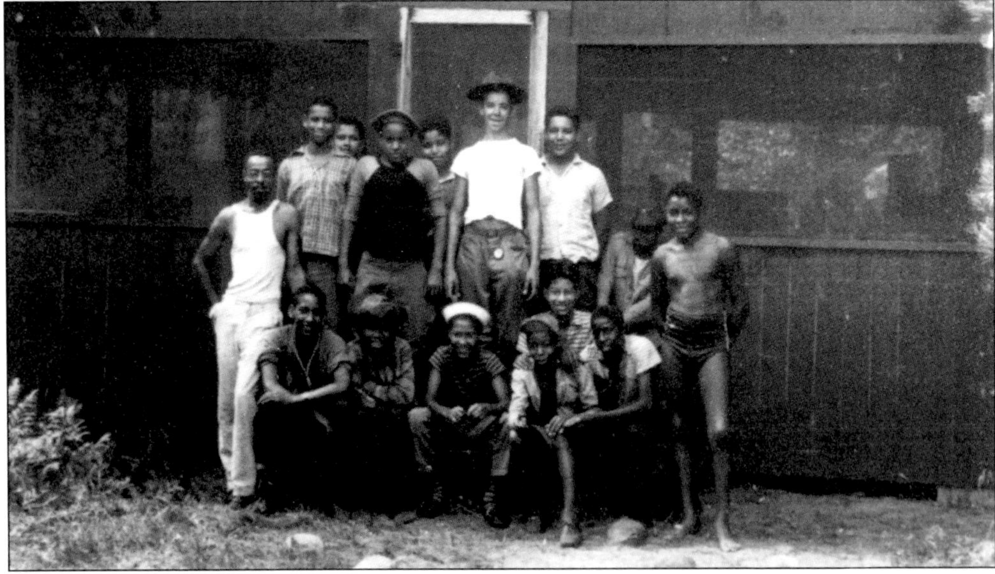

In the late 1930s and the 1940s, the Dunbar Center was the primary force behind programs of employment, housing, and recreation in the African American community.

Theodore Brown succeeded Golden Darby in 1937. Under Brown's leadership, the Dunbar Center acquired a permanent home on South Townsend Street. Dunbar initiated careful surveys of the employment and housing of Syracuse's black population. It served as a training center and employment agency and offered job placements in domestic service, construction work, and business.

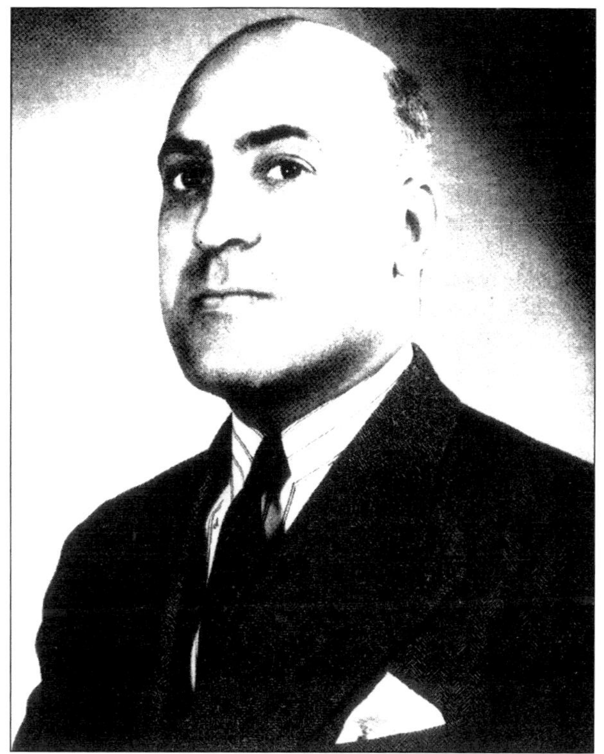

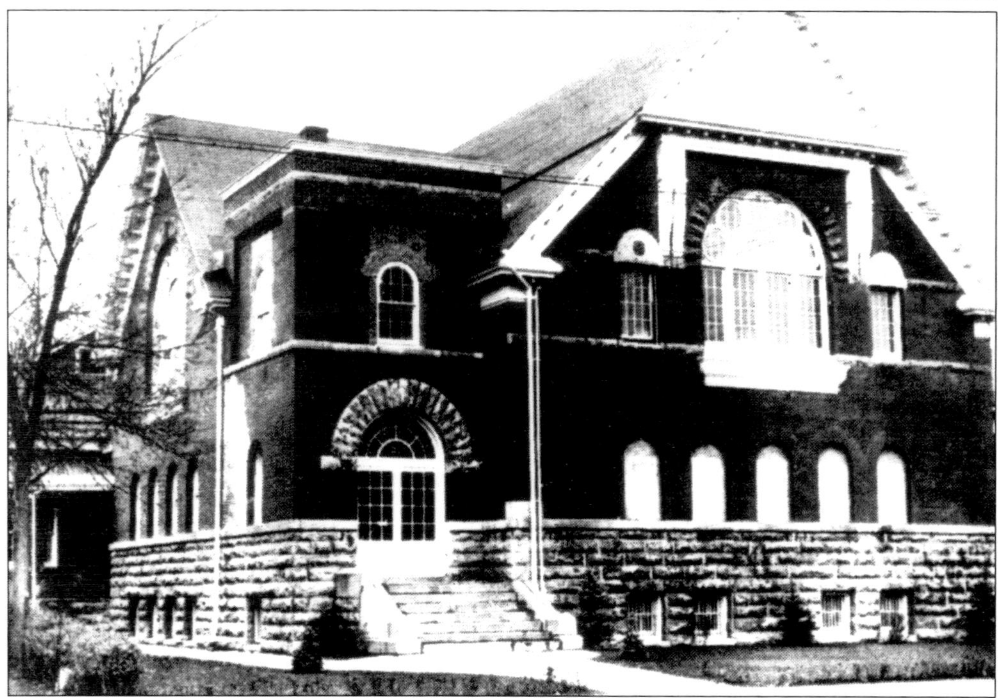

The Dunbar Center helped workers obtain documents required for jobs in defense projects. It intervened whenever possible in cases of racial discrimination and worked steadily, though quietly, to break down long-standing color barriers to employment.

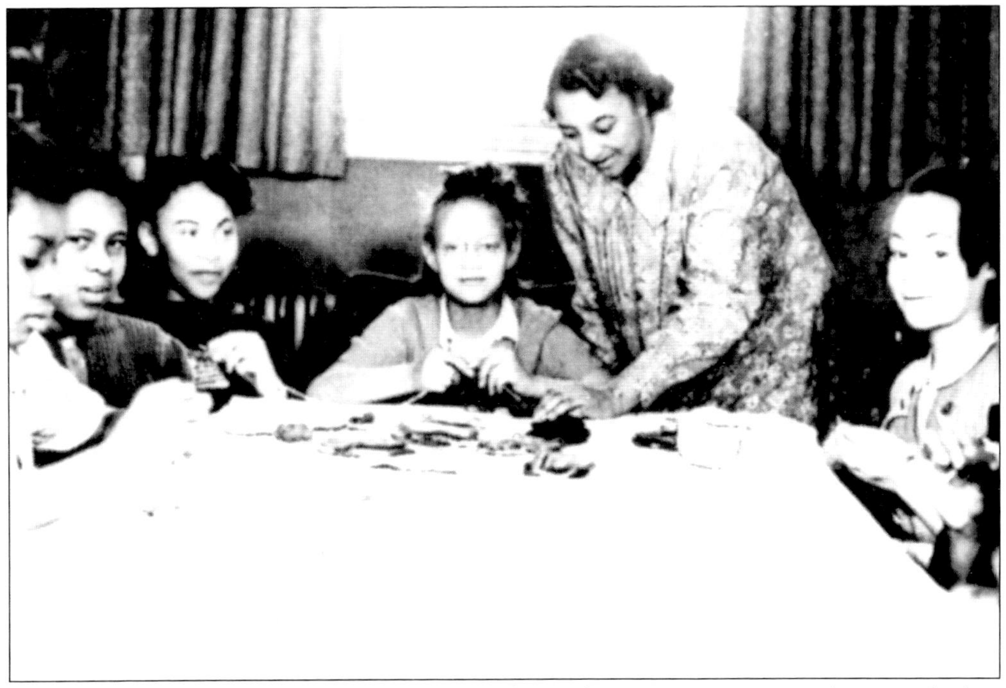

The Dunbar Center provided many essential social services. Its caseworkers worked to help children overcome problems in school, assisted in improving health education and health standards in the African American community, and served as a link to the city's social welfare agencies.

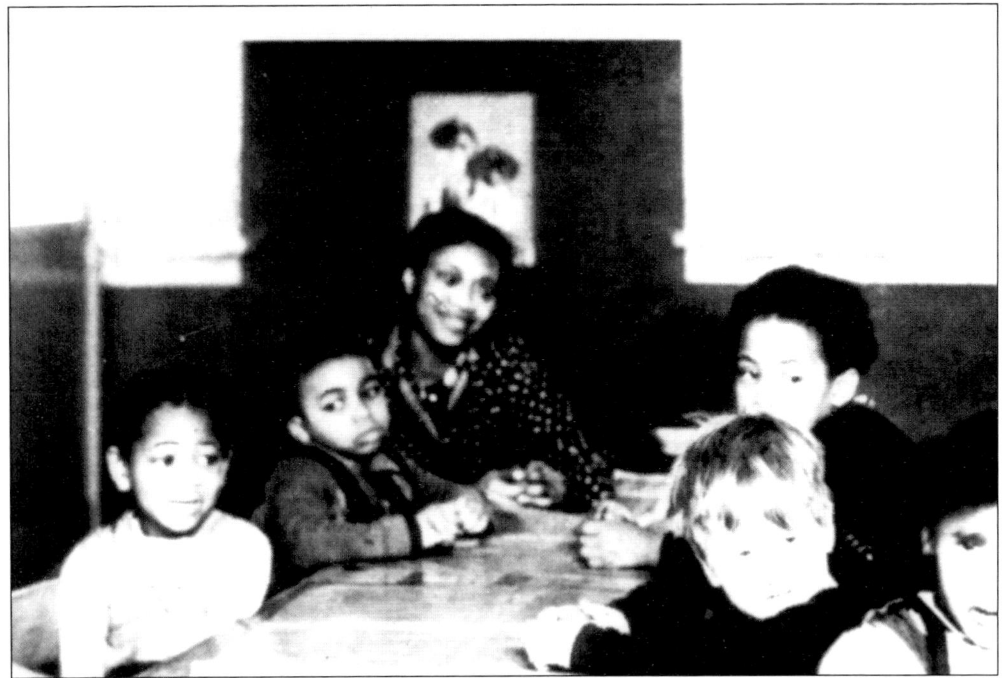

The center ran a Parent Club, which met biweekly to discuss child rearing. Its biracial nursery school was an especially effective program.

A branch of the Syracuse Public Library was established at the Dunbar Center.

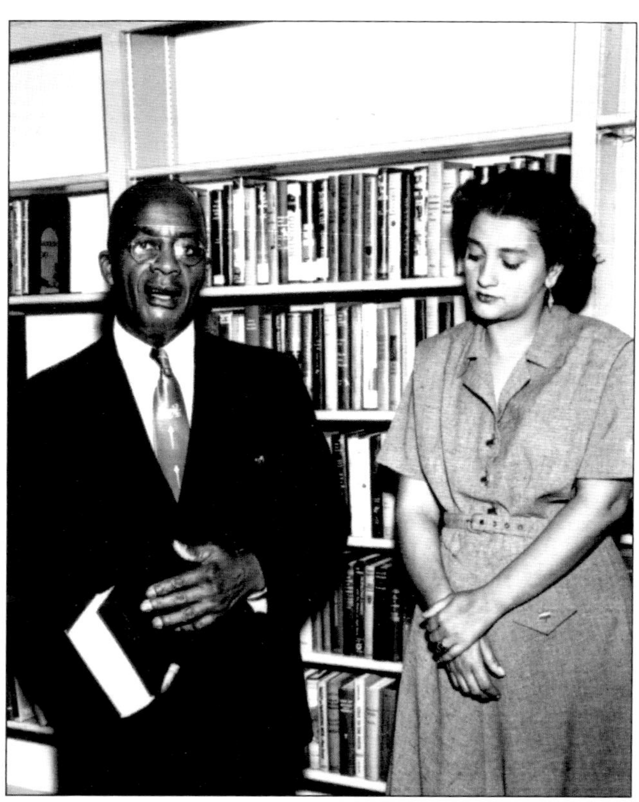

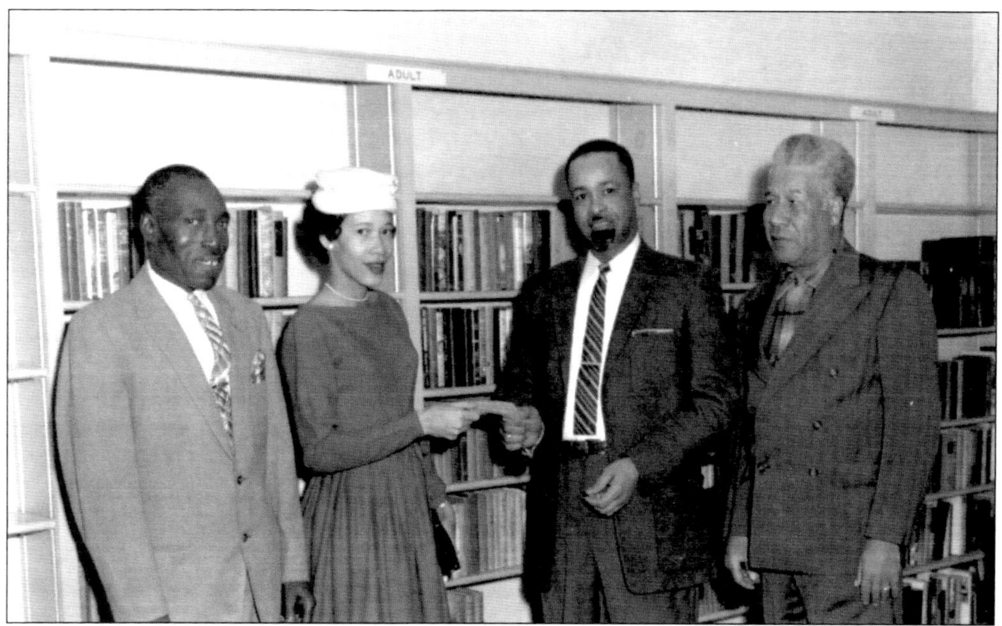


The center provided visibility for the black community. William Chiles described the role of Dunbar as a forum: "Here for the first time the Negro had a non-sectarian, non-political, non-fraternal platform and he was quick to use it. The head of Dunbar became the chief representative and spokesman for the Negro community."

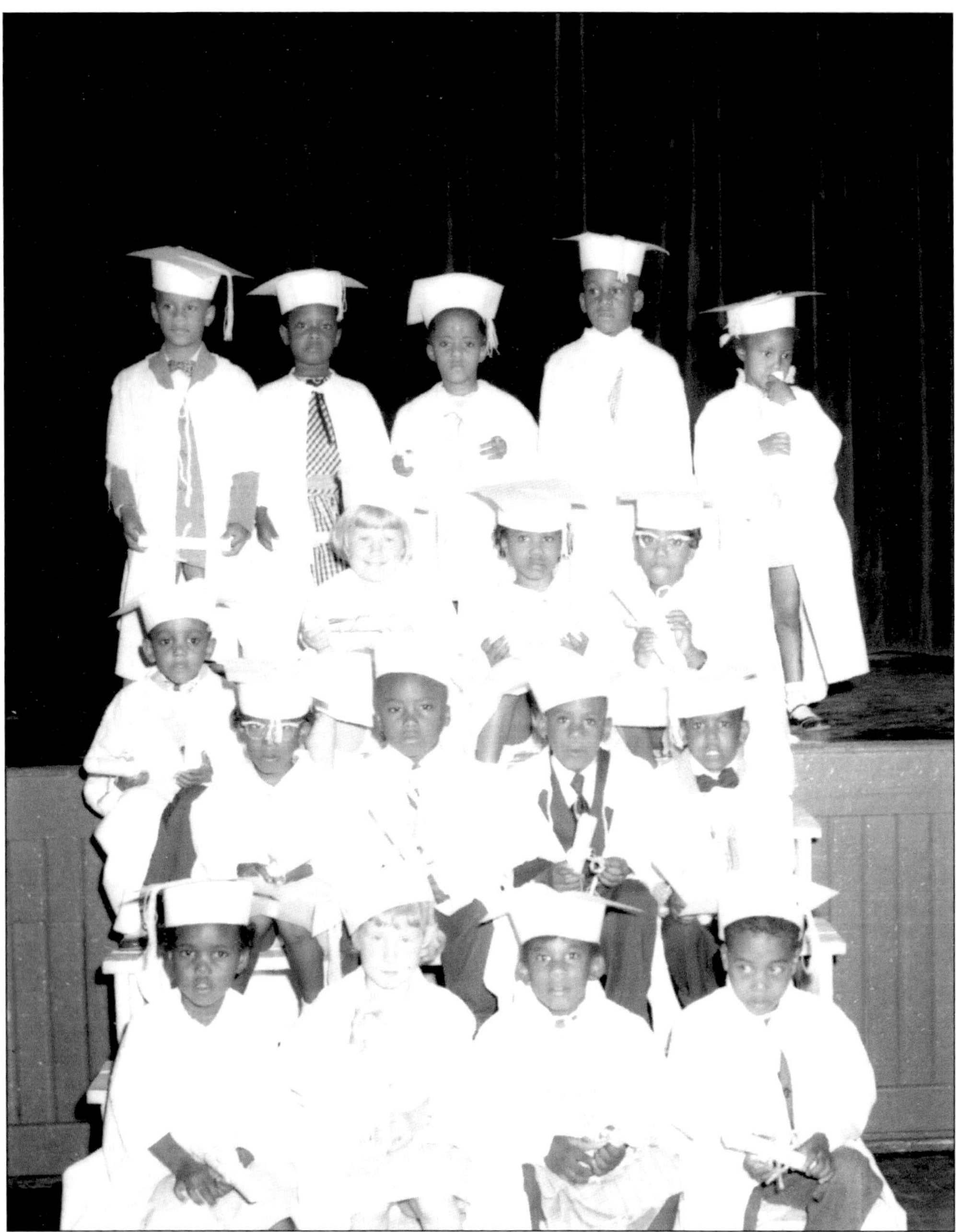

It was in the social area that Dunbar's contribution to community life was most outstanding. Theodore Brown described the restricted recreational opportunities open to the African American community outside of Dunbar: "Besides the tax-supported recreational centers and the theatres, there are but few places where Negroes can find recreational opportunities. Negroes are not welcome in the bowling alleys or skating places. Negro women are always turned down when they go to the riding stables. There are no dancing schools where Negroes can participate. Negroes frequently try to crash into the bars and saloons outside their own area, but they are not served. Service is given all around the Negro, and he is neglected."

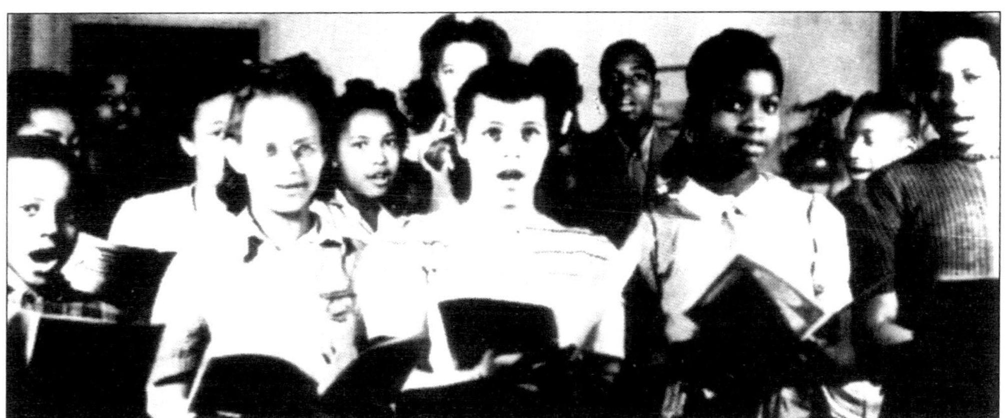

Dunbar's year-round program was essential to the recreational life of Syracuse African Americans. Its activities include scout troops, sports of all kinds, games, craft activities, dances, a glee club, community sings, a drum and bugle corps, dramatic groups, and movies.

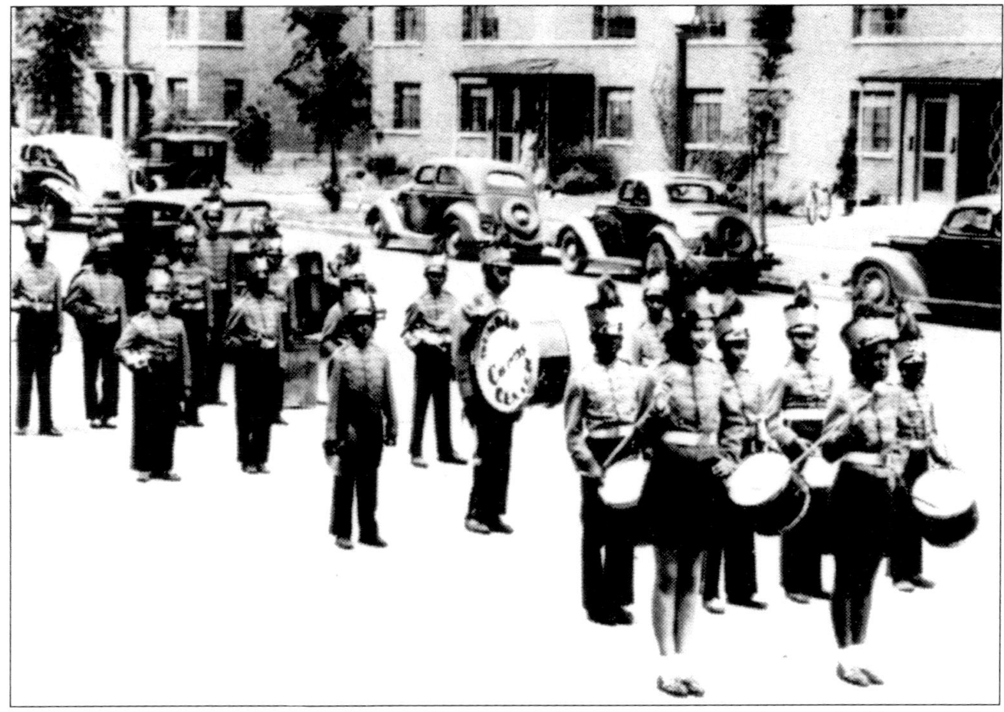

Activities were provided for all ages from preschool to teens, adults, and older people. The chorus and bugle corps were particular showcases for the Dunbar Center.

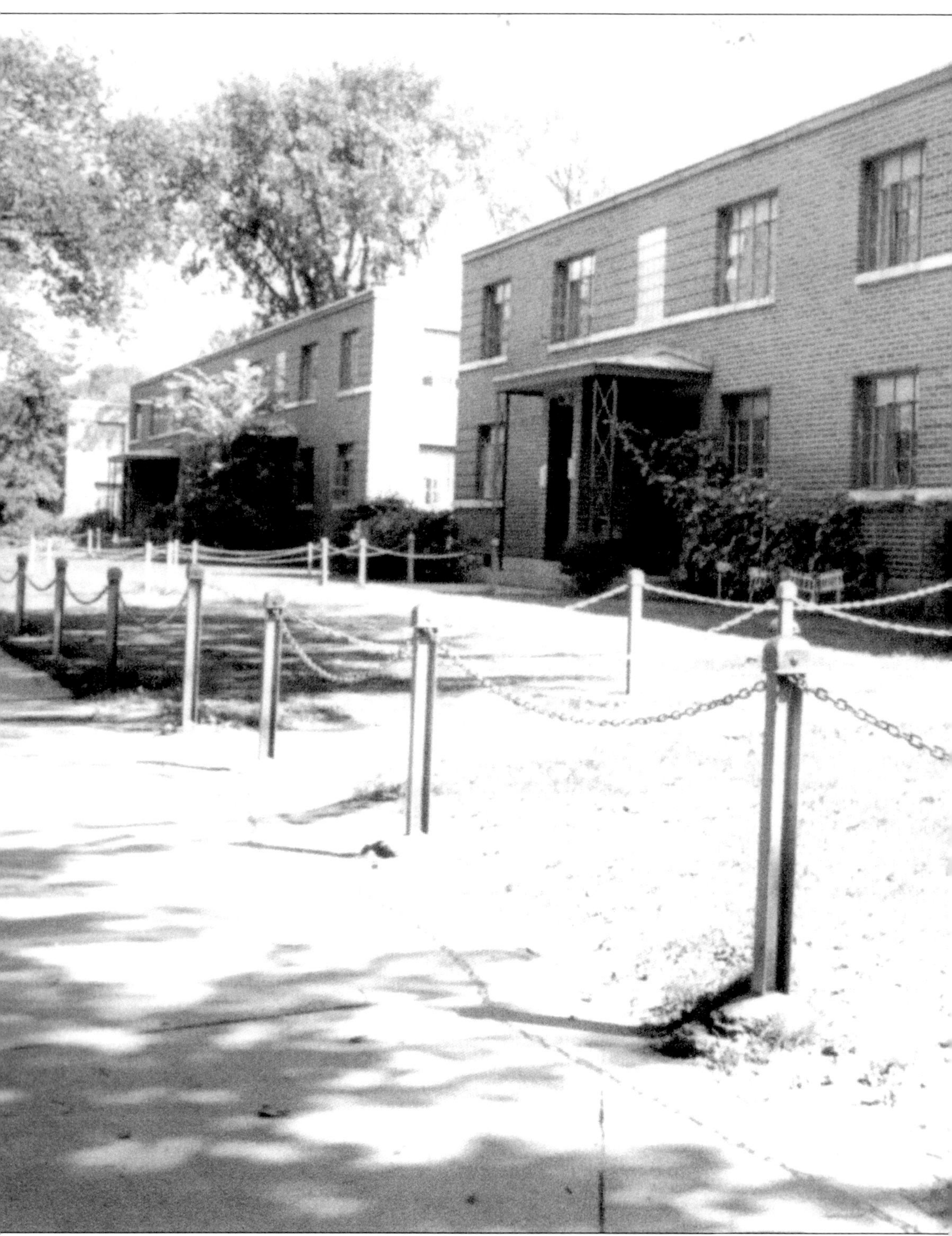

In the housing area, Dunbar worked on the difficult problem of residential segregation. In 1935, when a low-cost housing project was developed for Syracuse due to the efforts

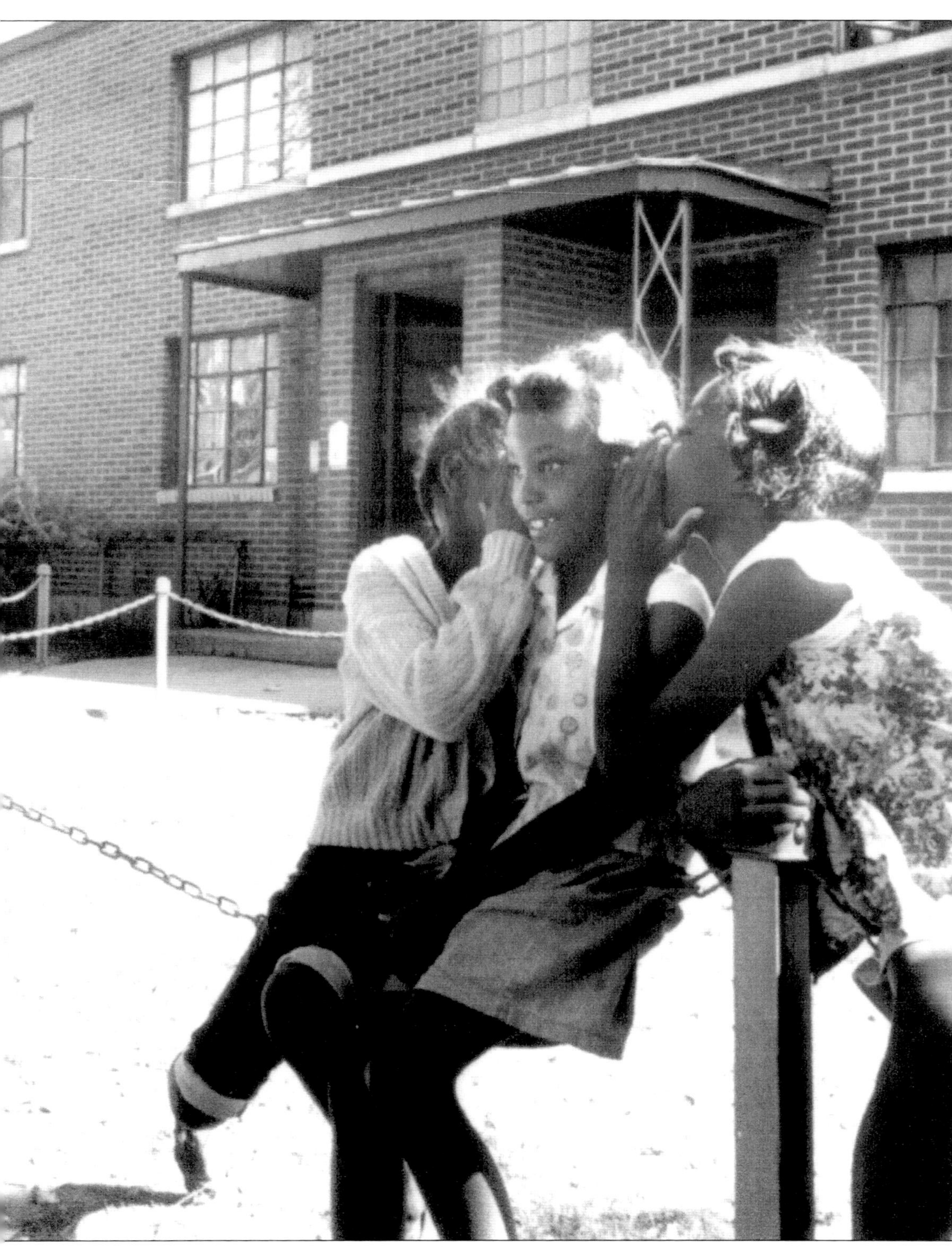

of the Dunbar Center and others, 53 African American families were placed, albeit together, with the 678 white families housed in Pioneer Homes.

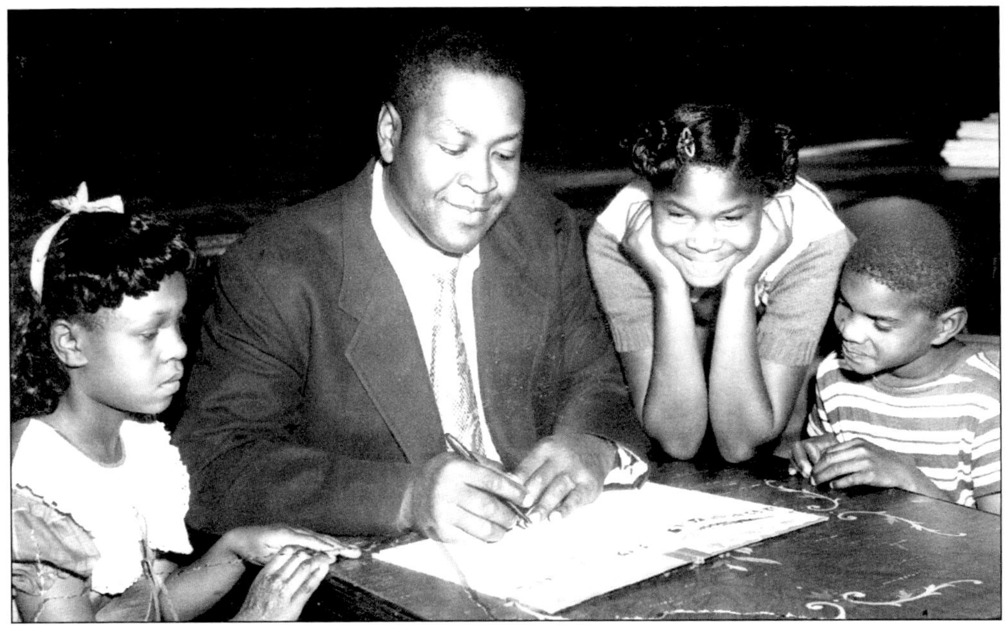

The proximity of Syracuse University provided personnel for Dunbar's early projects and activities. University students were hired to direct athletic programs, chaperone dances, and work with the youngsters. At the same time, however, the relationship between the university and Syracuse's black community was made clear by Dunbar. Both the first and second directors of the Dunbar Center were quick to point out the paucity of local blacks at Syracuse University. Theodore Brown found that during the period 1921–1928, black enrollment in all schools of the university averaged 25. Ike Harrison is shown here with a group of children.

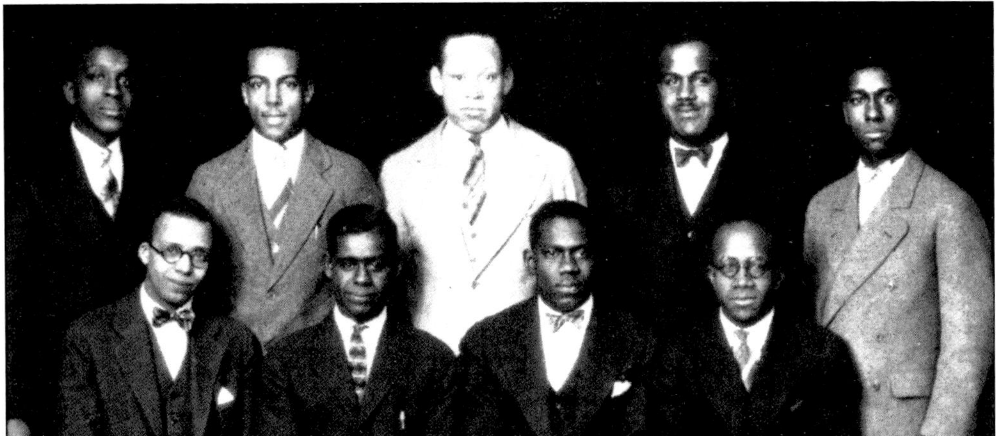

Most of these students, the men belonging to the Alpha Phi Alpha fraternity, established in 1926, were from out of town. Brown wrote that "there have been but few local Negroes attending . . . and to the best of my knowledge, there have been but two graduated." In his pioneering survey of the Syracuse African American community in 1937, Golden Darby also noted that "during the last decade only three Negroes from the local community attended Syracuse University . . . while none attended college elsewhere." He cited economic conditions as the main cause of this low enrollment but also mentioned that black women were not permitted to live in the university's dormitories.

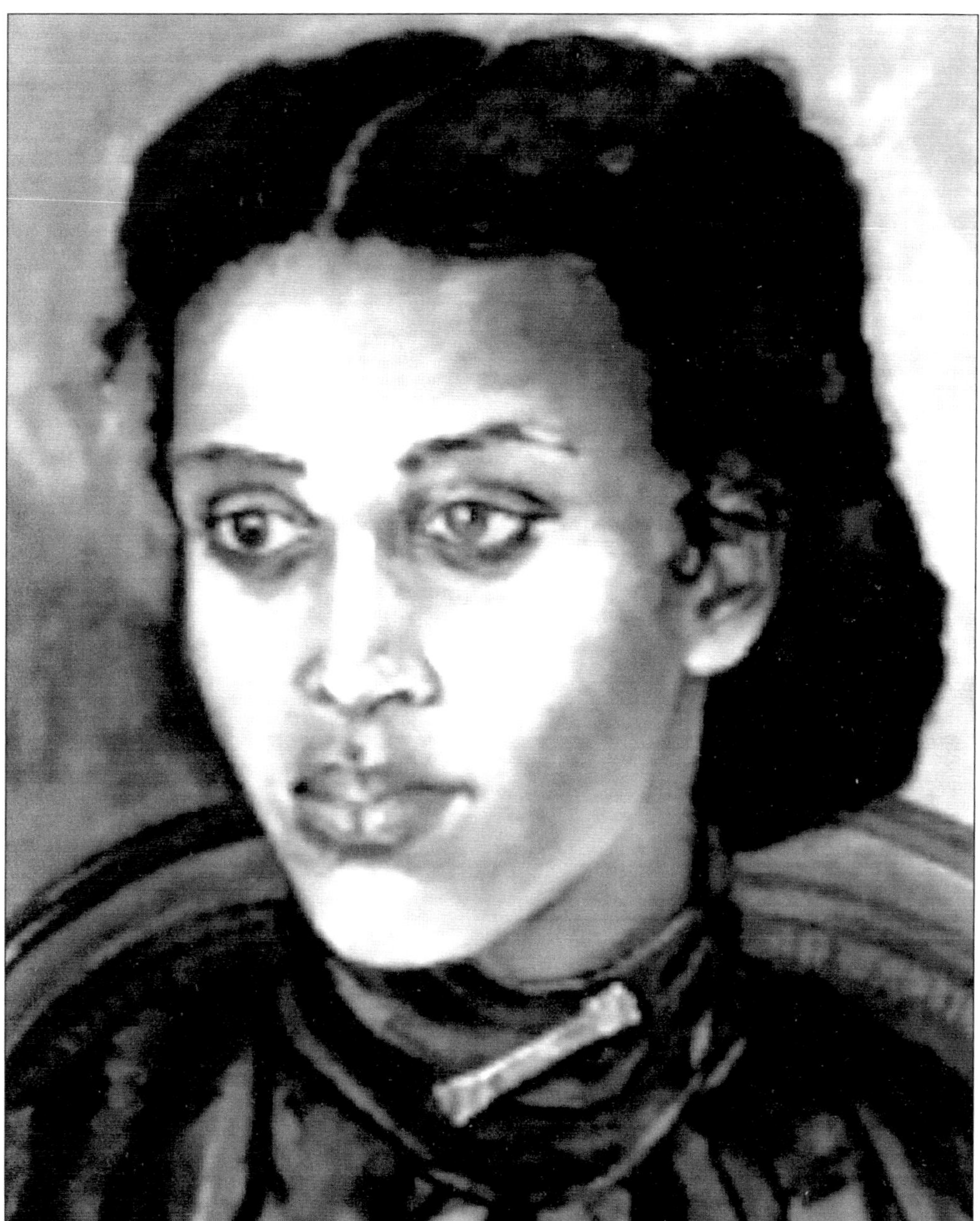

Another important reason why Syracuse's African American youth did not seek admittance to the university was the lack of employment opportunities in Syracuse even for college graduates. Brown noted that "of those few who did make a beginning in college, normal school, or other school of higher education, some saw the way ahead blocked by employment barriers growing out of the color question and considerations of this kind probably held them back." This consideration was quite realistic. Sarah Loguen Fraser, daughter of Jermain Wesley Loguen, was the first African American woman to graduate from Syracuse University's College of Medicine; she had to go elsewhere to practice. This portrait of Dr. Fraser by Susan Keeter now hangs at Syracuse's Upstate Medical University.

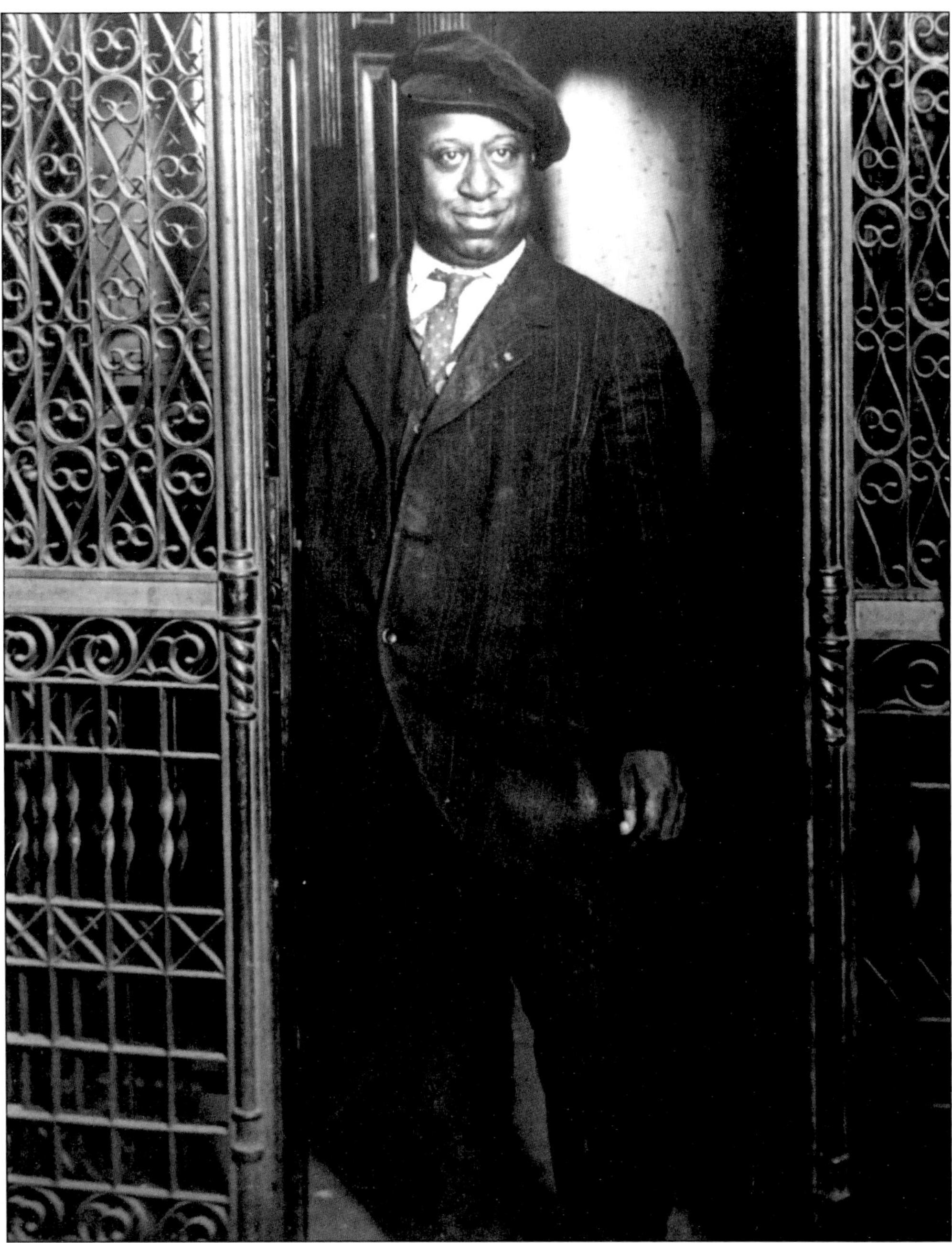

Similarly, William Johnson, the first African American graduate of Syracuse University's College of Law, could not obtain employment in that profession. He remained in Syracuse, but he had to accept a clerk's job instead of the attorney's position for which he was qualified. His brother Edwin, seen here, did not attend the university and became an elevator operator.

Another important institution of the black community in this period was the *Progressive Herald,* founded in 1933 and published weekly by J. Luther Sylvahn, seen on the right, for about 30 years.

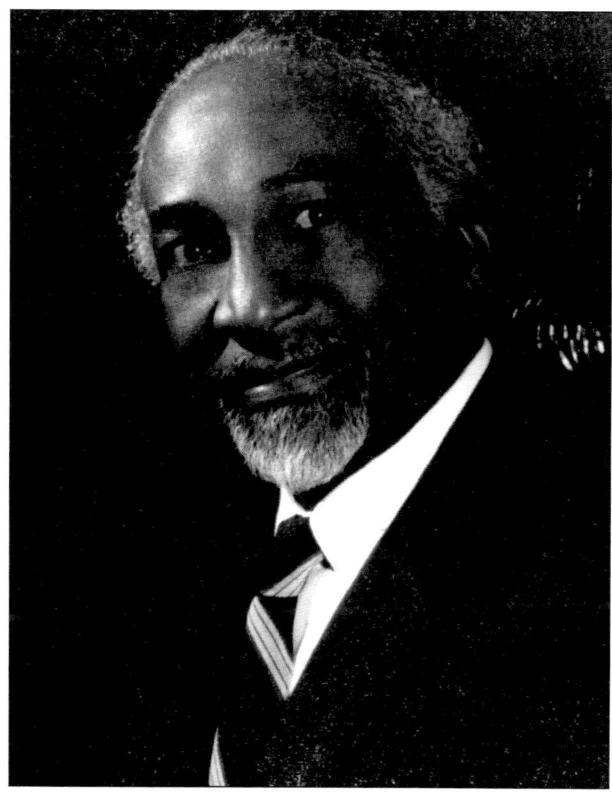

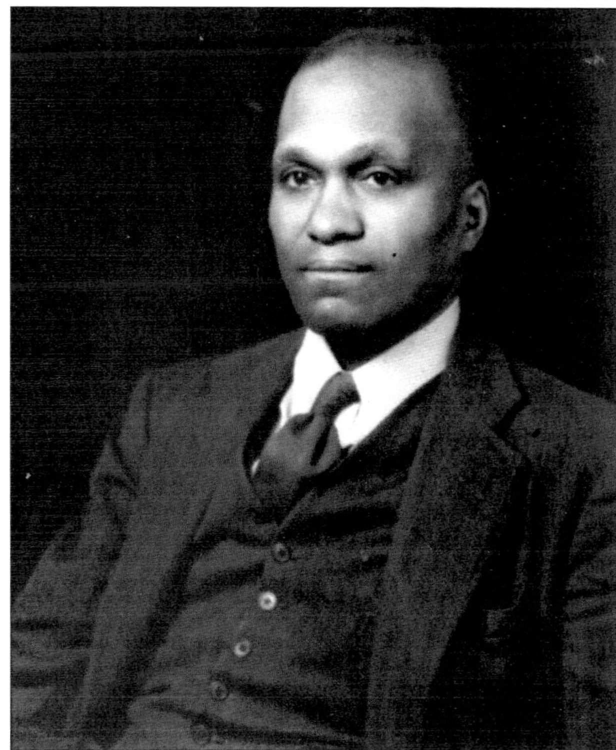

The short-lived *Chatscript* was published for about a year in the 1920s by James Foy and Falstaff Harris (shown to the left), a local artist, whose murals enhanced the Syracuse Savings Bank building.

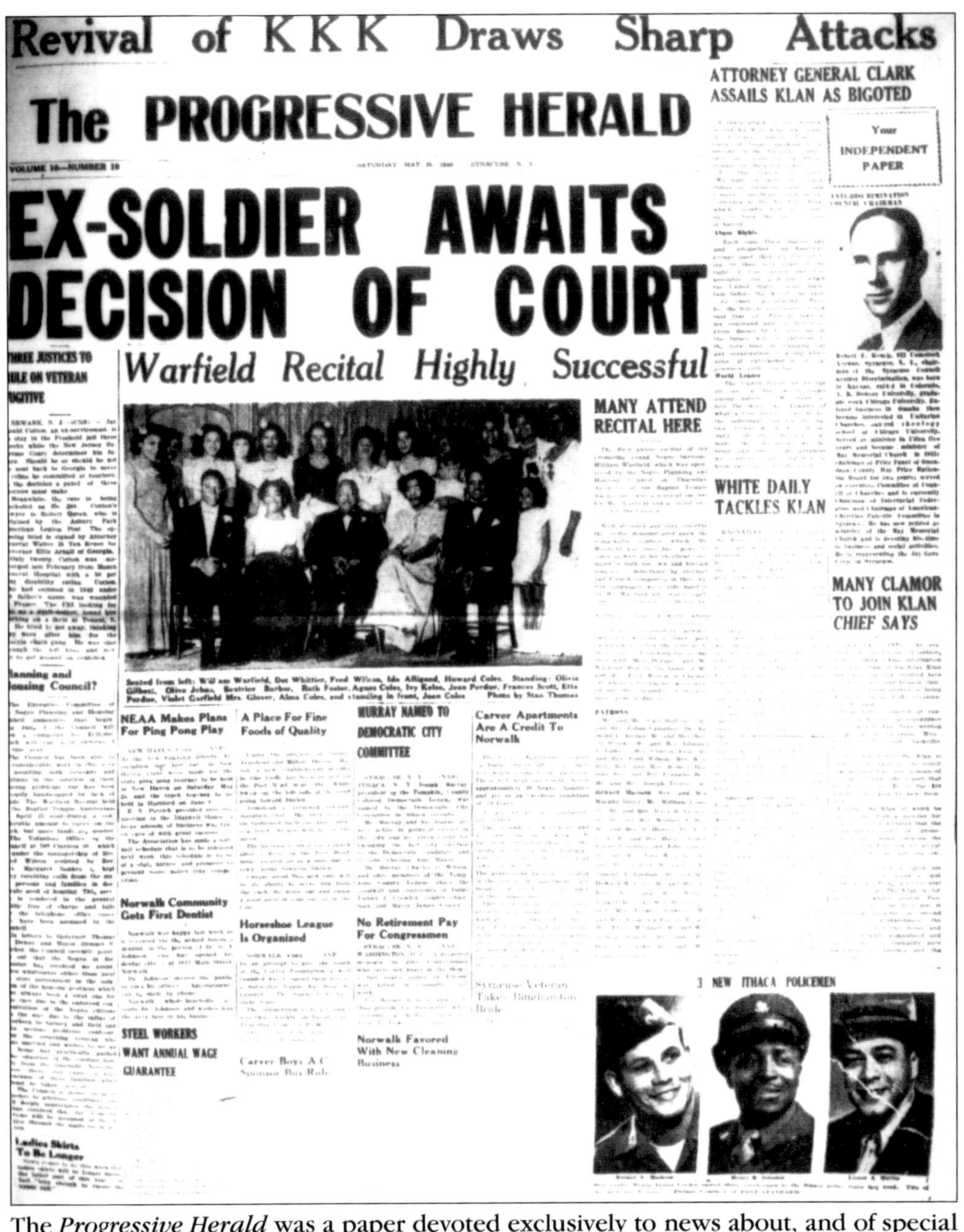

# Revival of KKK Draws Sharp Attacks

# The PROGRESSIVE HERALD

Your INDEPENDENT PAPER

VOLUME 10—NUMBER 19

## ATTORNEY GENERAL CLARK ASSAILS KLAN AS BIGOTED

# EX-SOLDIER AWAITS DECISION OF COURT

## THREE JUSTICES TO RULE ON VETERAN FUGITIVE

## *Warfield Recital Highly Successful*

Seated from left: William Warfield, Dot Whittier, Fred Wilson, Ida Alligood, Howard Coles. Standing: Olivia Gilbert, Olive Johns, Beatrice Barber, Ruth Foster, Agnes Coles, Ivy Kelso, Jean Perdue, Frances Scott, Etta Perdue, Violet Garfield Mrs. Glover, Alma Coles, and standing in front, Joan Coles Photo by Stan Thomas

## MANY ATTEND RECITAL HERE

## WHITE DAILY TACKLES KLAN

## MANY CLAMOR TO JOIN KLAN *CHIEF SAYS*

## Planning and Housing Council?

## NEAA Makes Plans For Ping Pong Play

## A Place For Fine Foods of Quality

## MURRAY NAMED TO DEMOCRATIC CITY COMMITTEE

## Carver Apartments Are A Credit To Norwalk

## Norwalk Community Gets First Dentist

## Horseshoe League Is Organized

## No Retirement Pay For Congressmen

## STEEL WORKERS WANT ANNUAL WAGE GUARANTEE

## Norwalk Favored With New Cleaning Business

## Ladies Skirts To Be Longer

3 NEW ITHACA POLICEMEN

The *Progressive Herald* was a paper devoted exclusively to news about, and of special interest to, Syracuse's black residents. It highlighted the achievements of individuals: Grace Wilson, "the only negro in Syracuse's Teacher's Normal"; Ada Knight, the only black registered nurse in Syracuse; and Helen V. Smith, the "first colored woman given a city or county post." It chronicled the doings of the Dunbar Center, the fraternal organizations, the churches, and the political clubs and gave particular attention to national news of interest to African Americans. Special features included a black heritage column, a Syracuse society section, sports stories, and a "Kollege Kampus Korner," as well as reports of the activities of the African American communities of Detroit, Cleveland, St. Louis, and New York City.

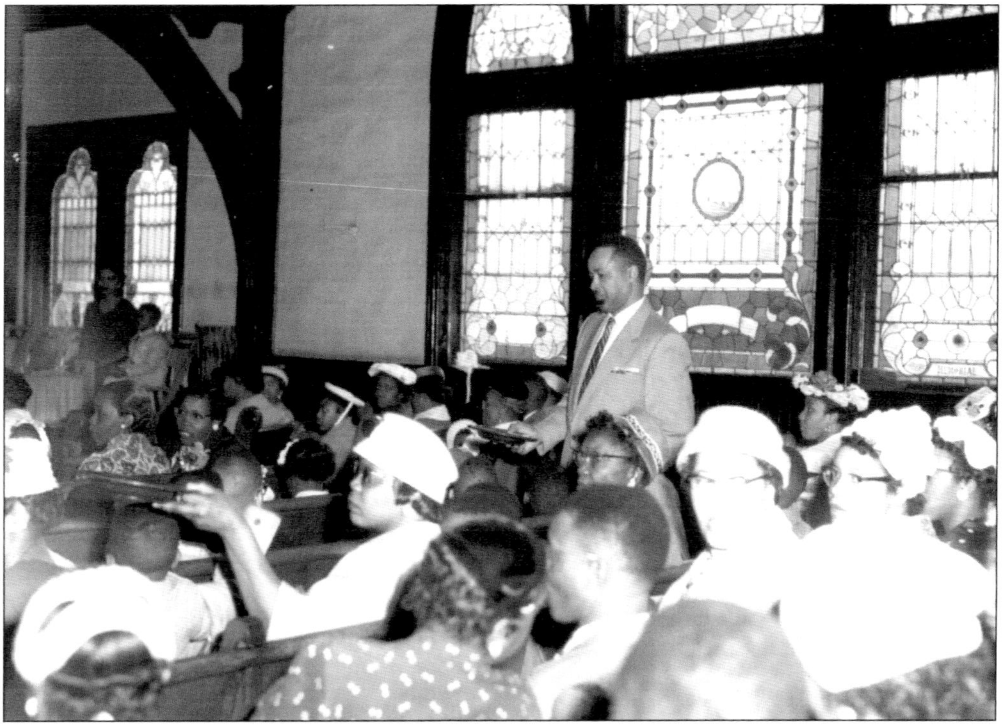

In the 1940s, life in the African American community revolved primarily around church, home, and neighborhood.

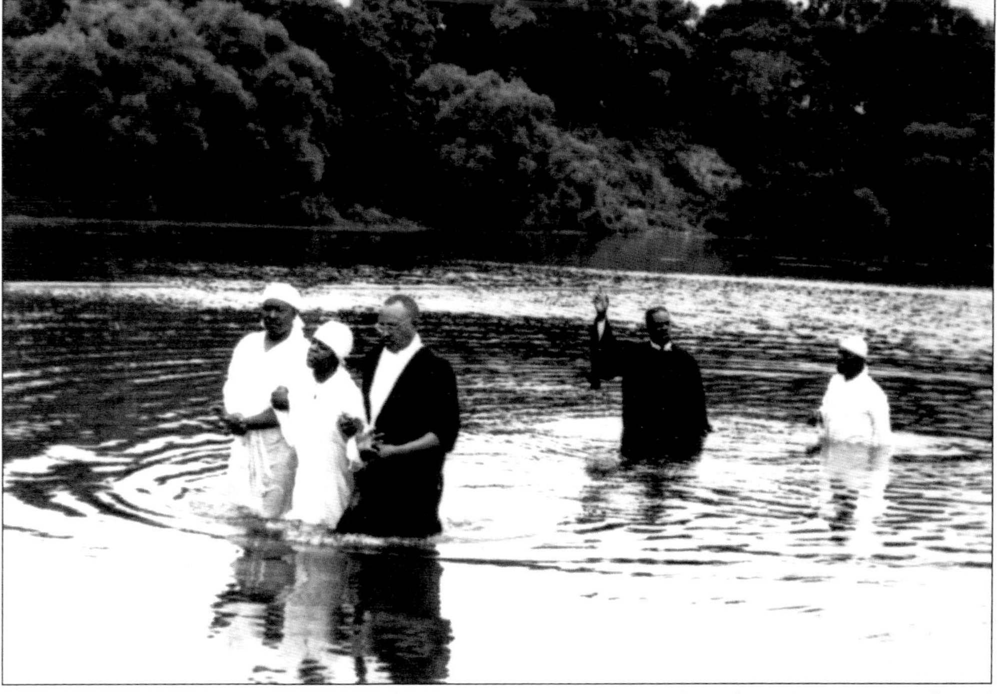

Two new churches were organized in this era, the Church of God in Christ, in 1924, and Hopps Memorial Methodist Episcopal Church, in 1929.

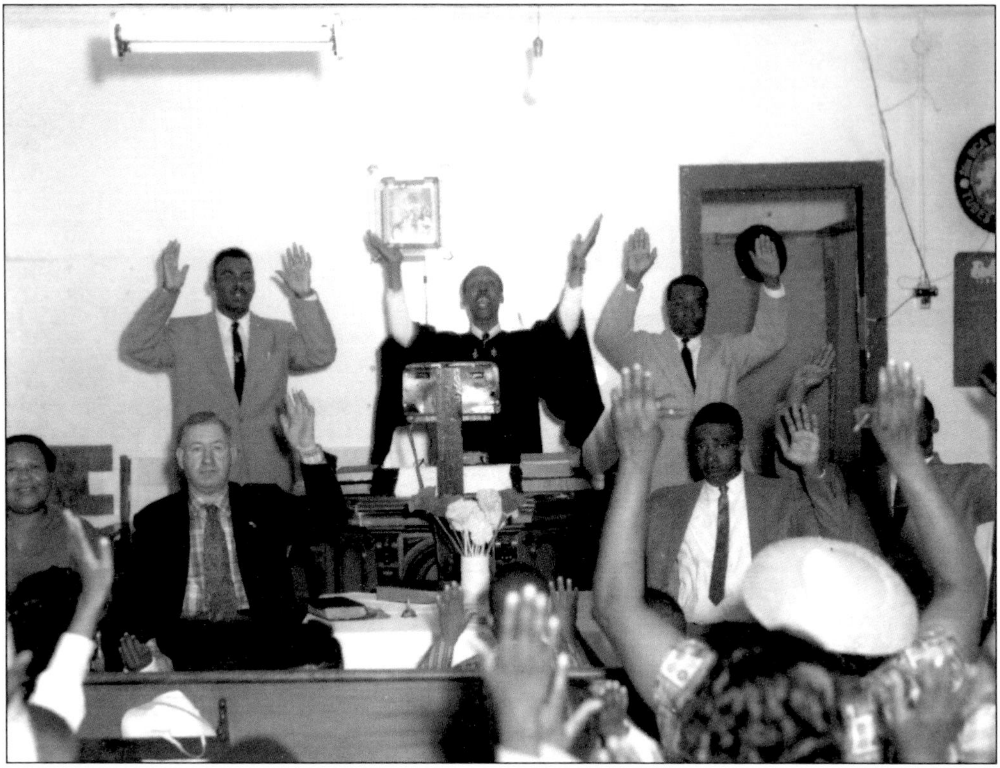

Storefront churches were also formed. These community-based churches offered social and spiritual support for many African Americans, especially those coming from the South.

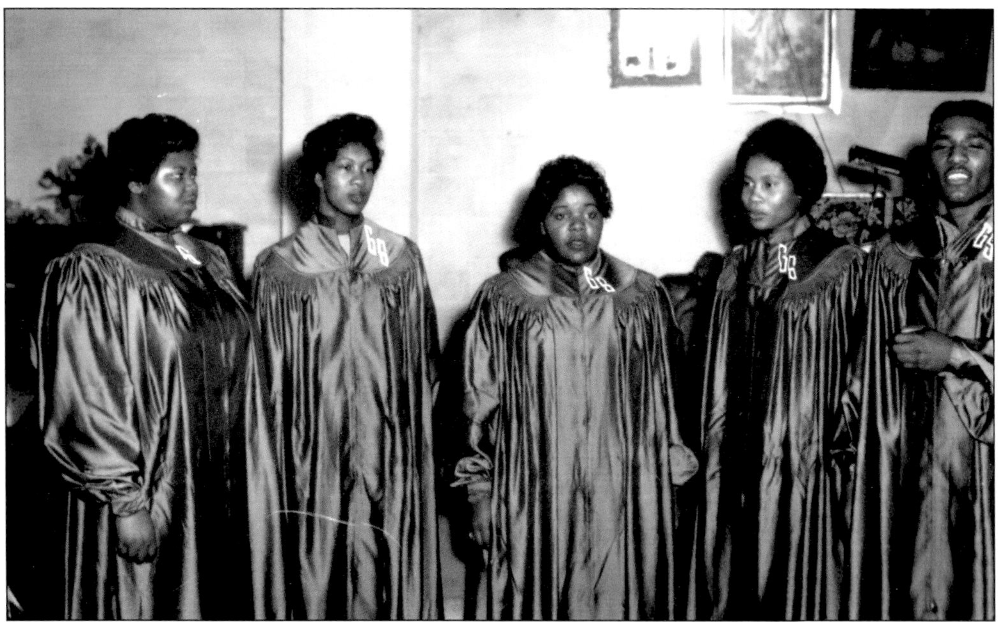

The choir served as a source of cultural identity and a means of artistic and spiritual expression for the African American community.

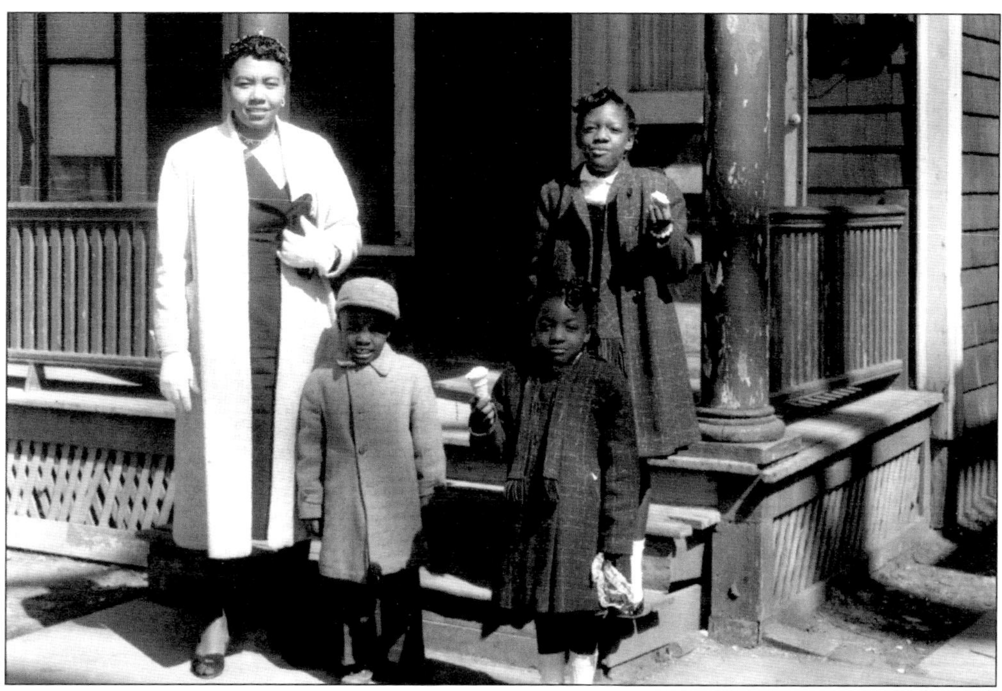

Going to church was as much a social, as it was a religious, experience for the African American community and was a significant aspect of community life.

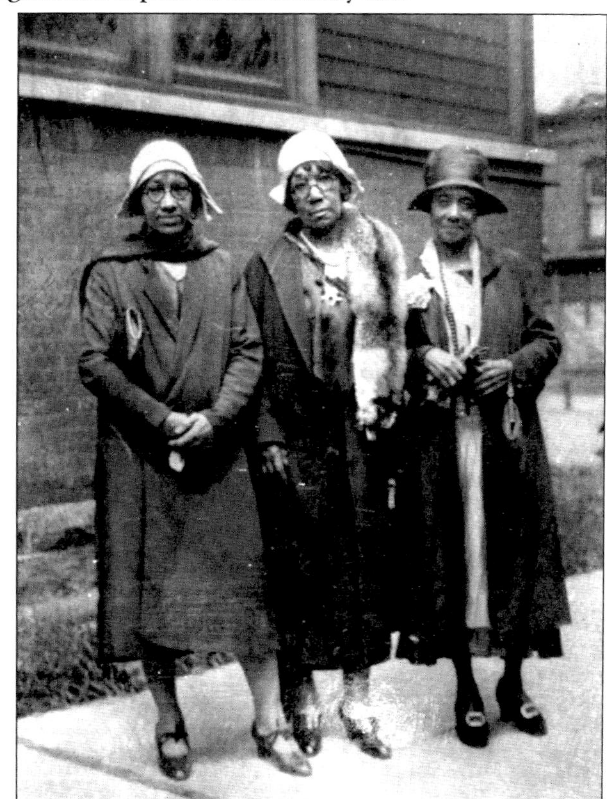

The National Association for the Advancement of Colored People chapter was active, as were the black Veterans of Foreign Wars and American Legion posts. There were also some small, strictly social clubs, such as the Clock-watchers, U-Like-It, Esquires, and Pandora.

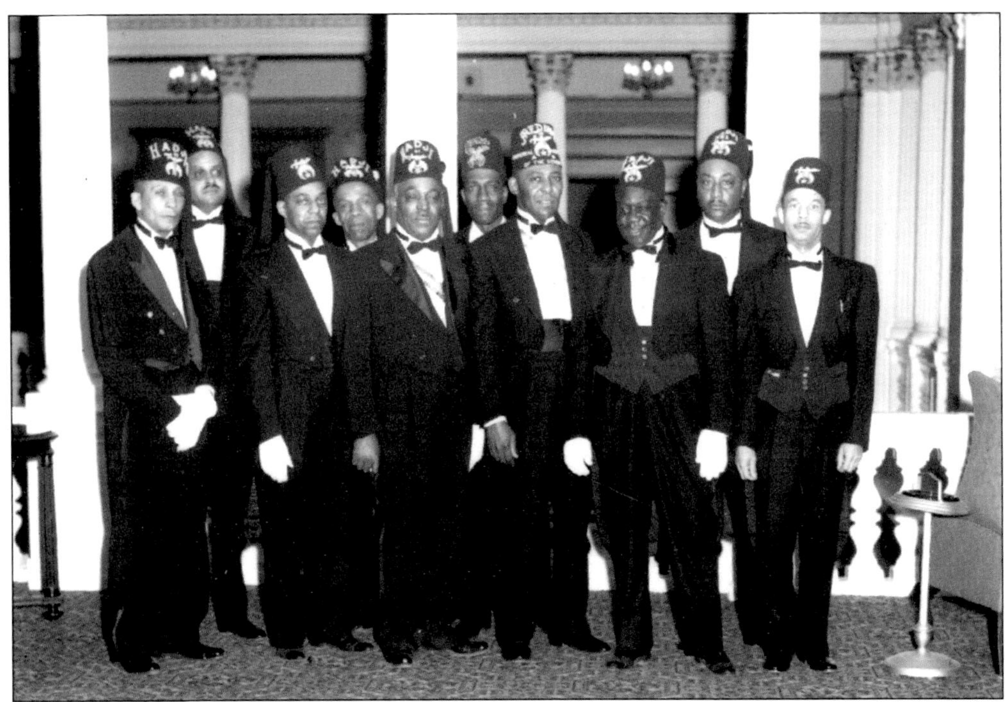

Social events were provided by Dunbar, the Elks chapter and other fraternal organizations including the Masons, Eastern Star, Court of Calanthe, Knights of Pythias, Odd Fellows, and Household Ruth.

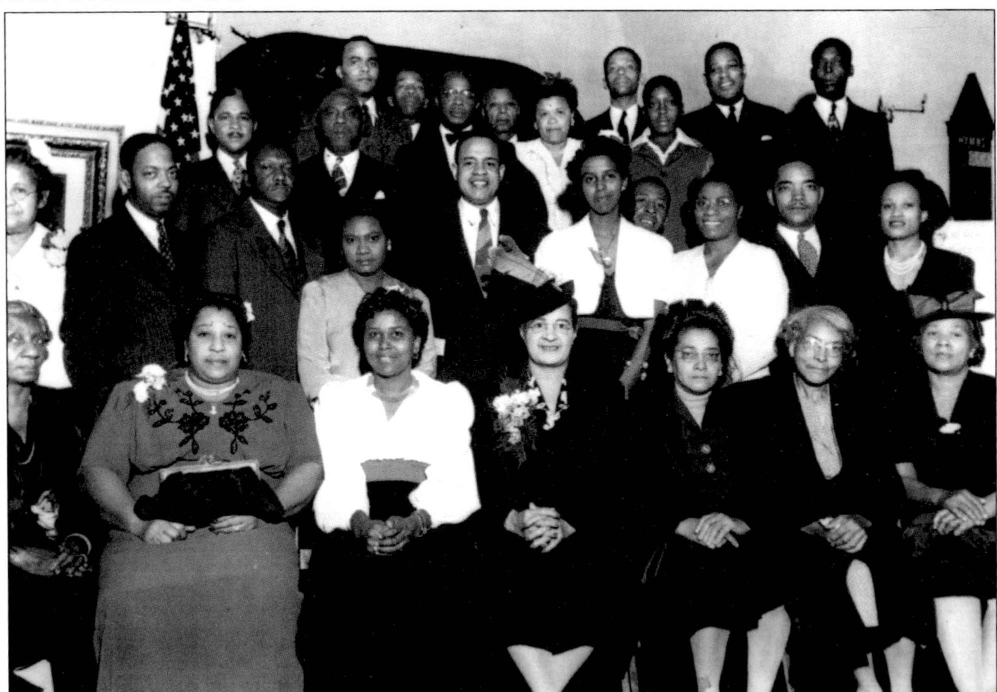

The Court of Calanthe was an early organization of African American women. This photograph dates from 1916.

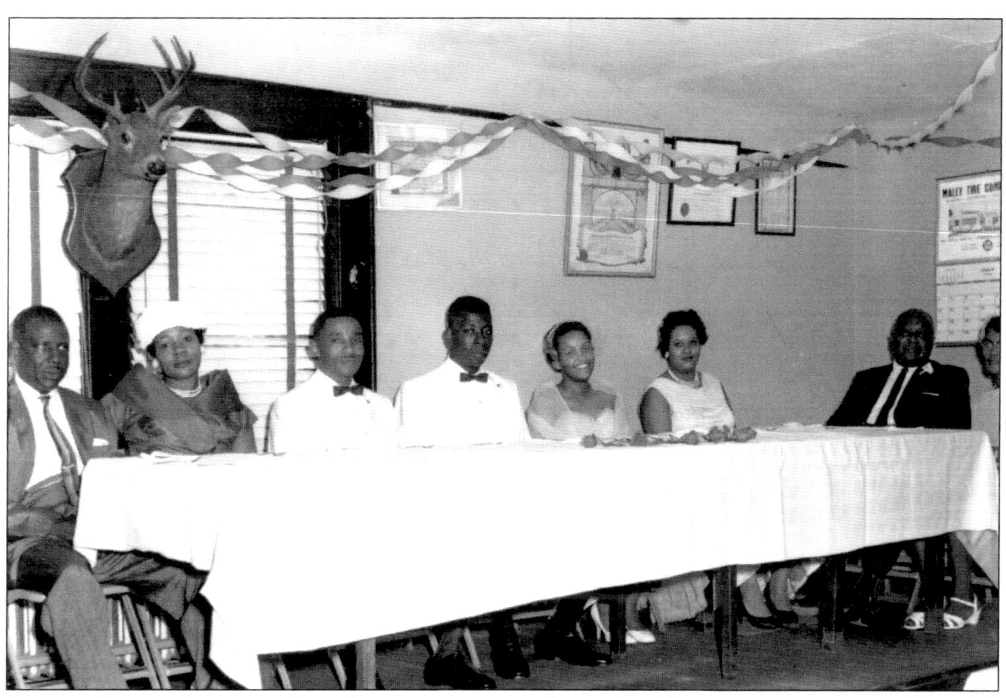

Fraternal organizations played an important role in the African American community.

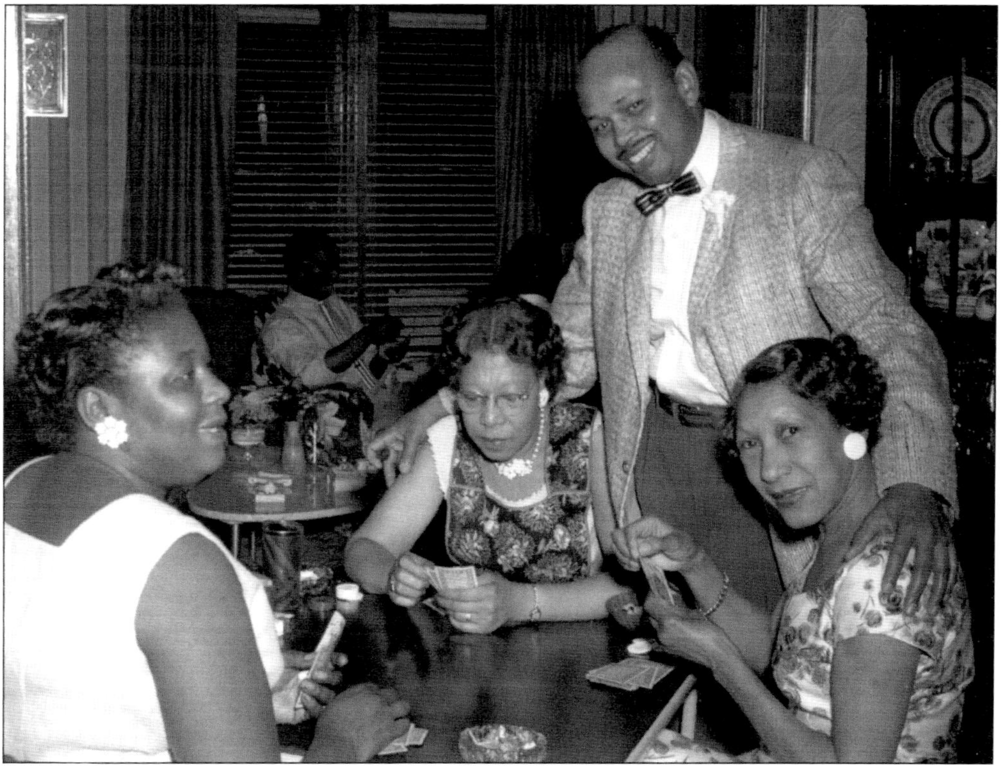

Despite external barriers and pressures, there were good times in the life of the community.

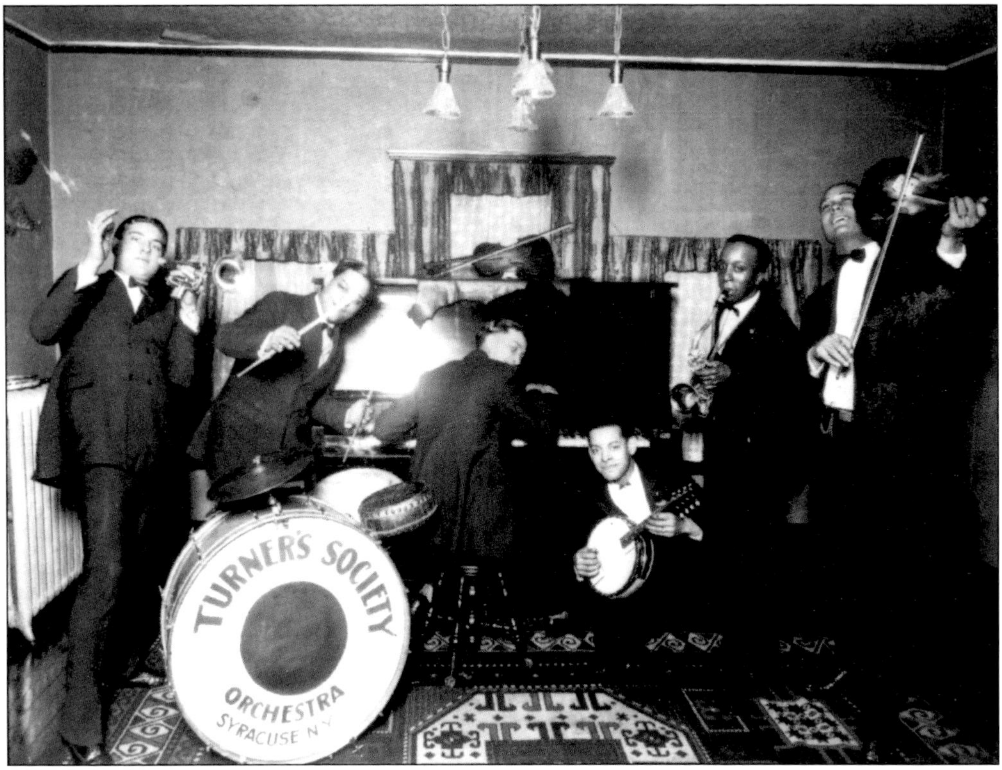

Turner's Society Orchestra was a popular jazz band, one of several, that played in private clubs.

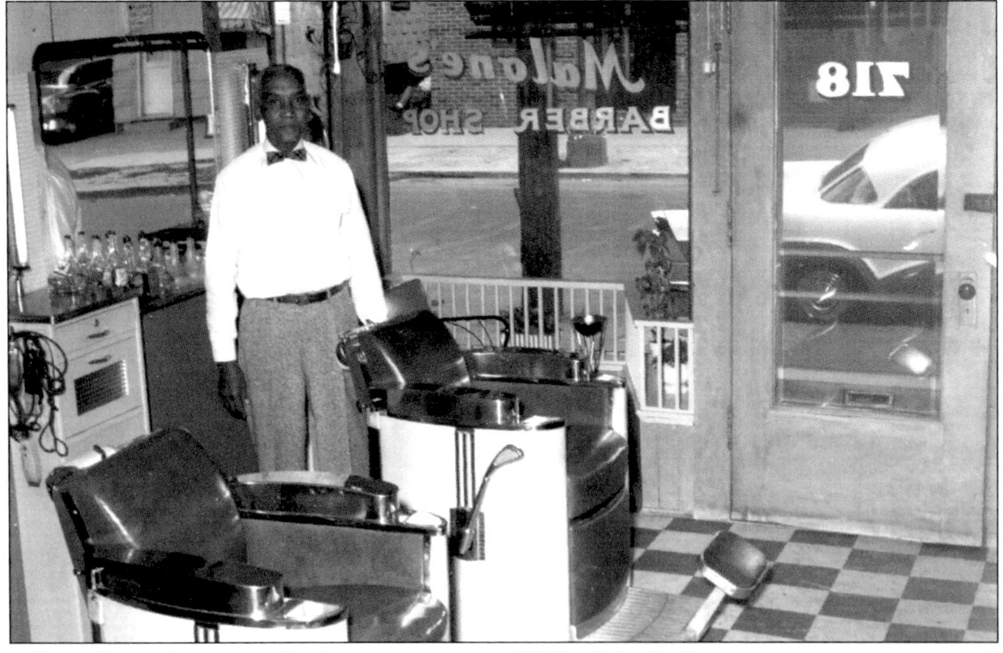

A few African American businesses were established, including a grocery store, several barbershops, beauty parlors, restaurants, bars, and a hotel.

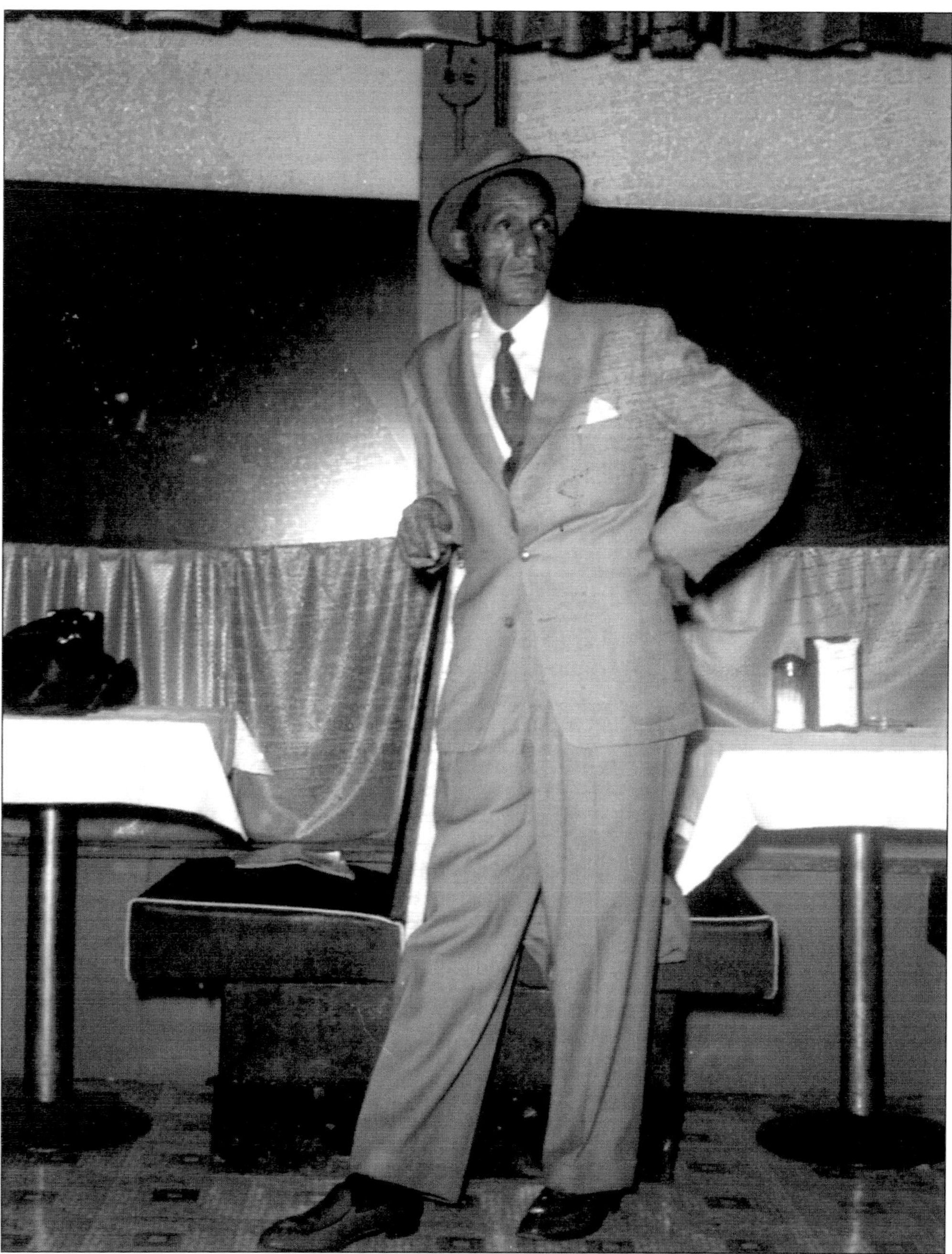

One of the most important visual chroniclers of the African American community in the mid-20th century was photographer Damon Presley who is pictured here. "Here comes Damon with his camera" was the call that went out whenever he appeared. His photographs captured the joys and sorrows of everyday life in the African American community of Syracuse in which he lived.

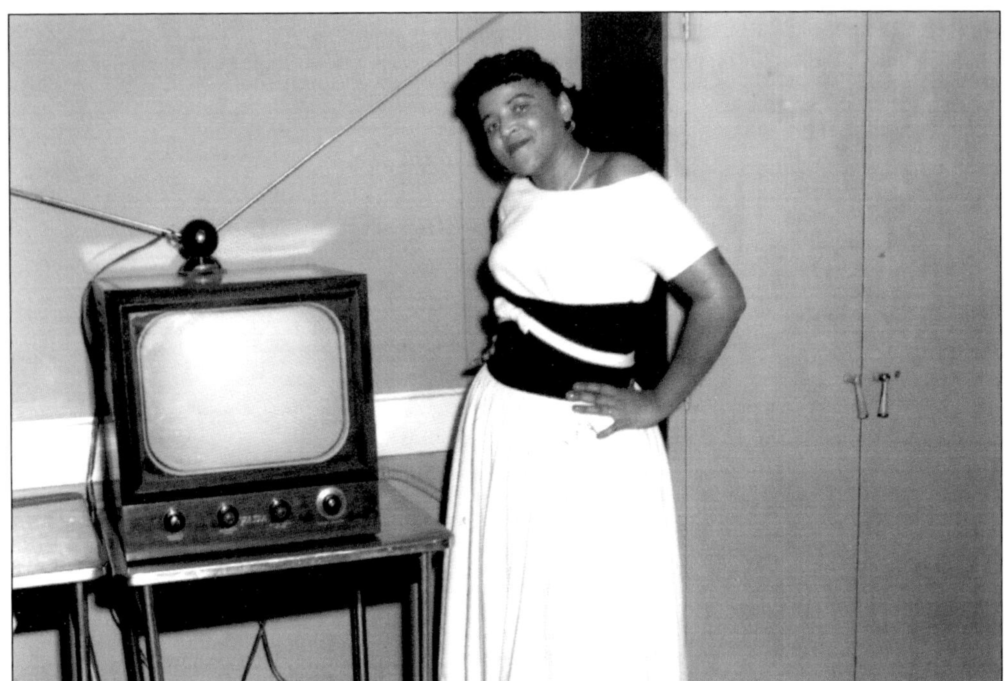

Photographer Damon Presley had a keen eye for the relationship between people and objects in their lives. The pride of ownership in a new television shines in this woman's face.

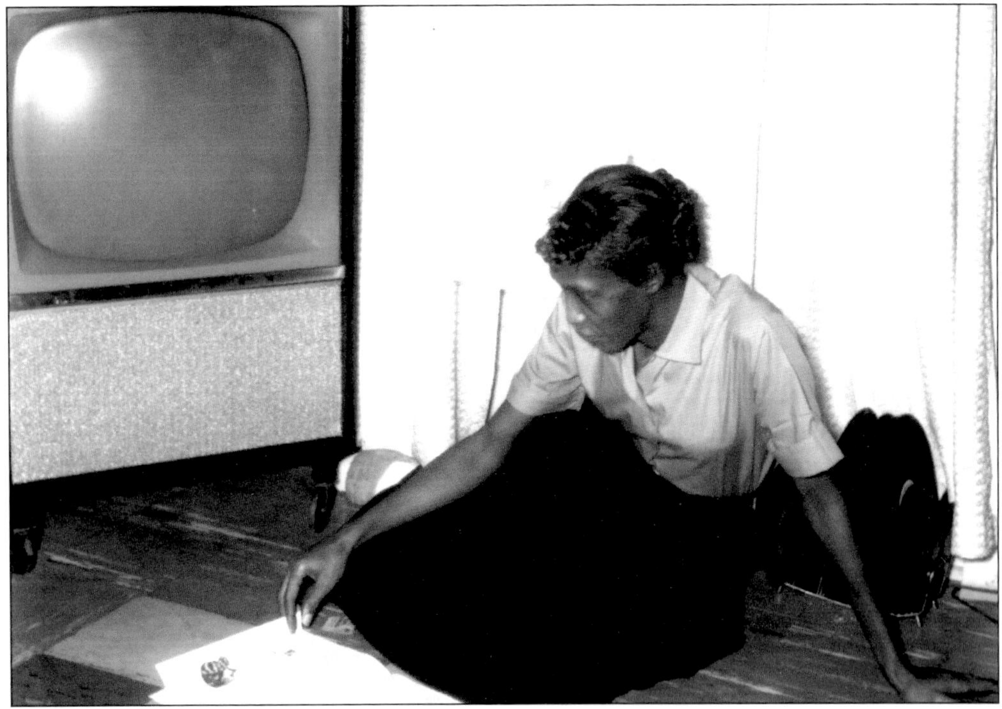

Contrast the first subject with this woman, who is pointedly ignoring her old television as she thumbs through a magazine.

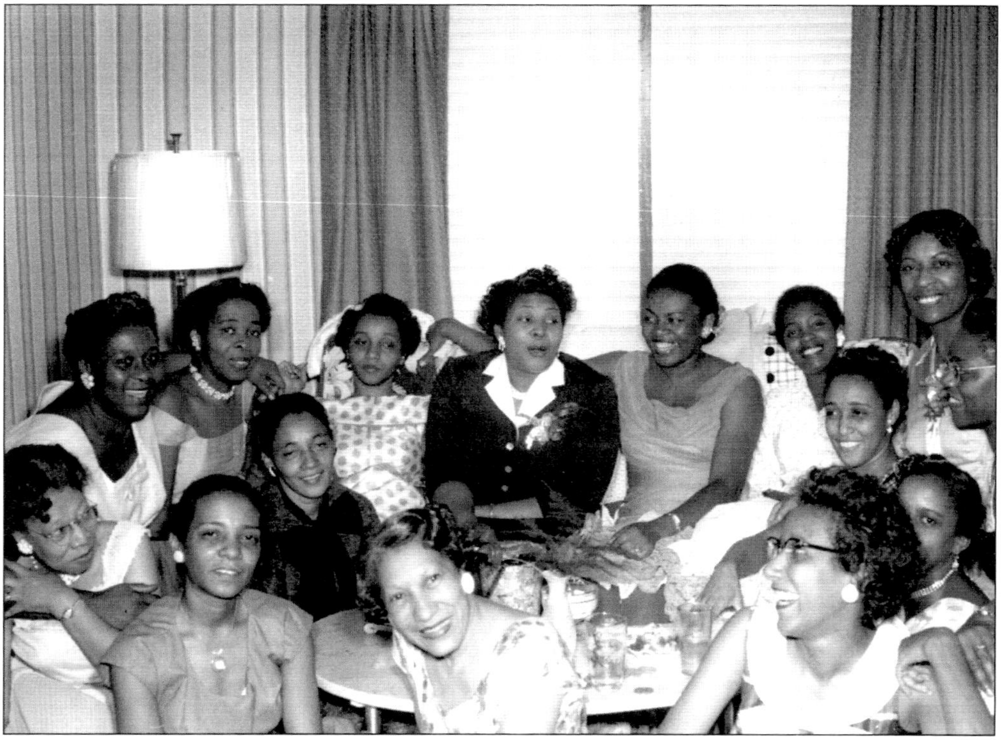

Damon Presley documented gatherings in the African American community in a way that no one else did. He captured people at moments of great pleasure, as in this group shot.

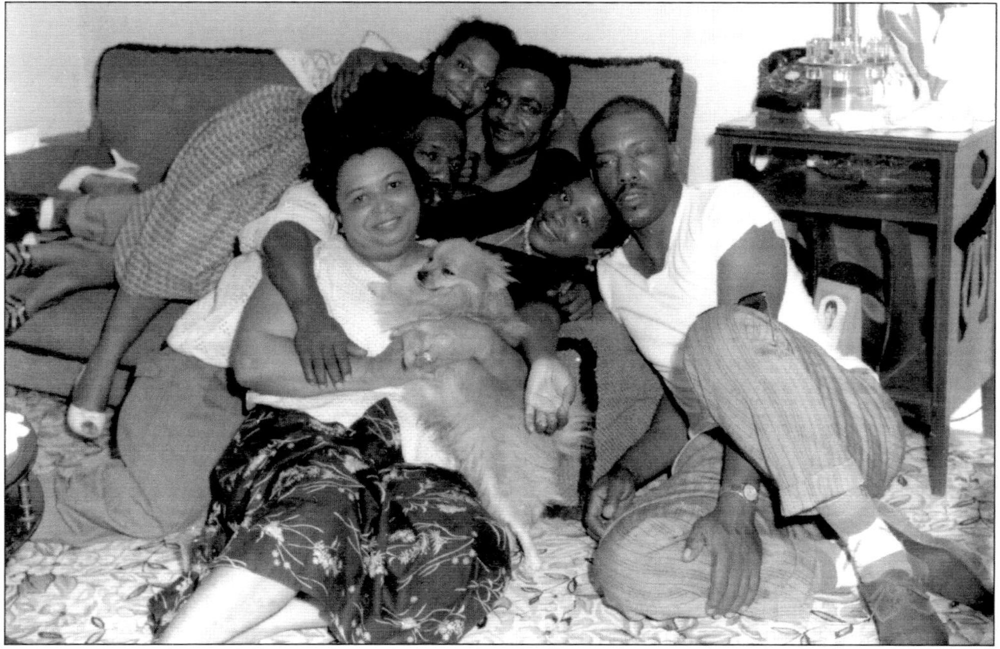

Presley's photographs make the viewer want to know more about his subjects and about the moments in their lives that he chose to capture.

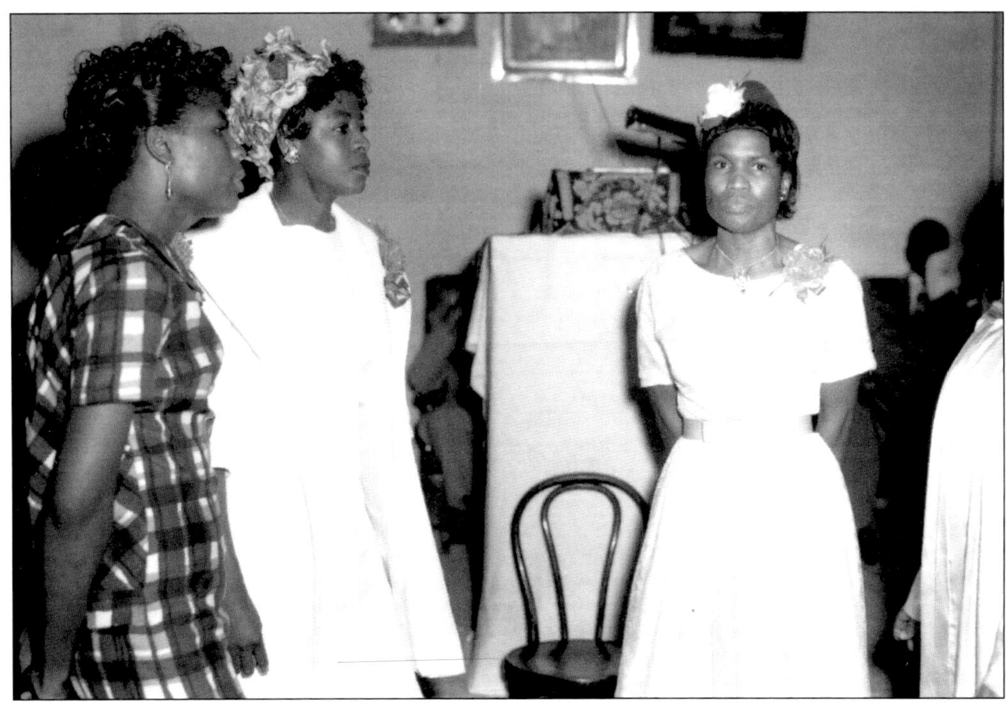

These sullen churchgoers are surely experiencing a less than spiritual moment, and Damon Presley was there to enshrine it photographically.

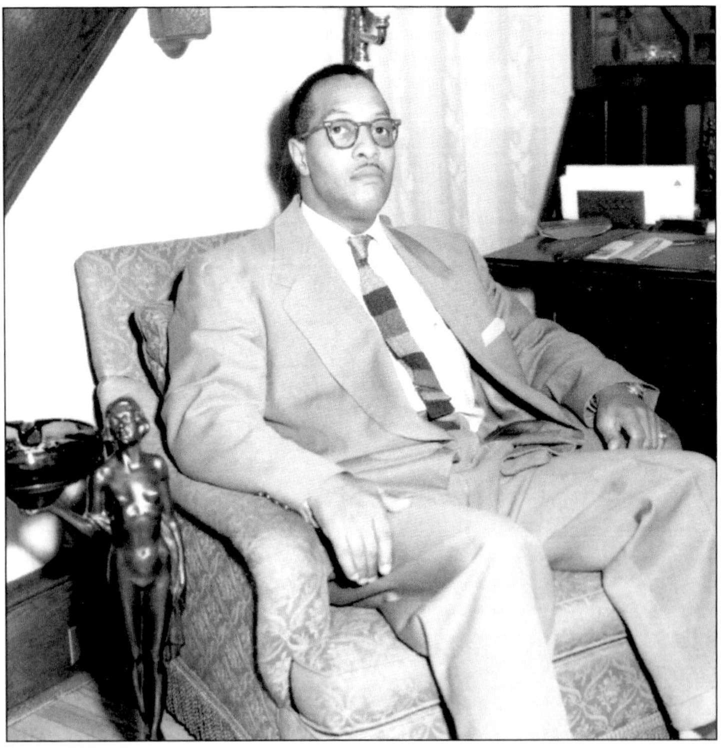

Juxtapositions of people and their positions in ways that bring out their similarities are part of the artistry of Damon Presley's photography. The ashtray and the man capture the viewer's eye and raise interesting questions.

Damon Presley caught the relationship between this couple with his camera. Their stance hints that they are close, but not too close.

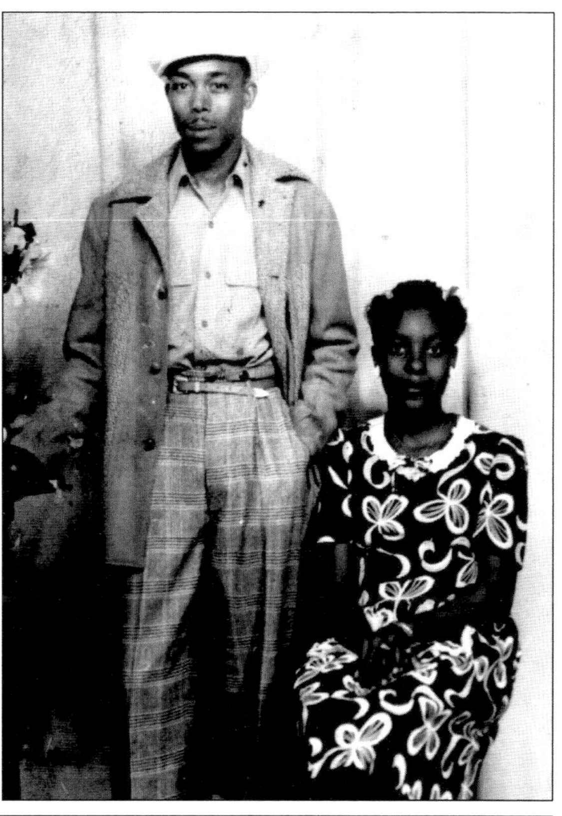

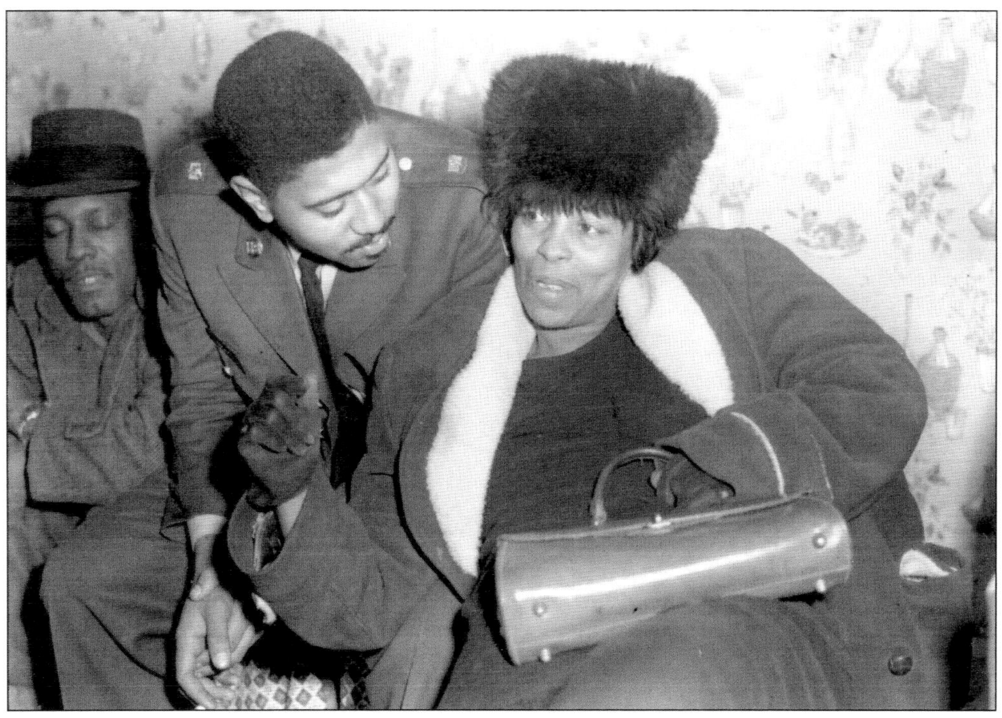

This couple clearly has a more comfortable and open relationship with one another.

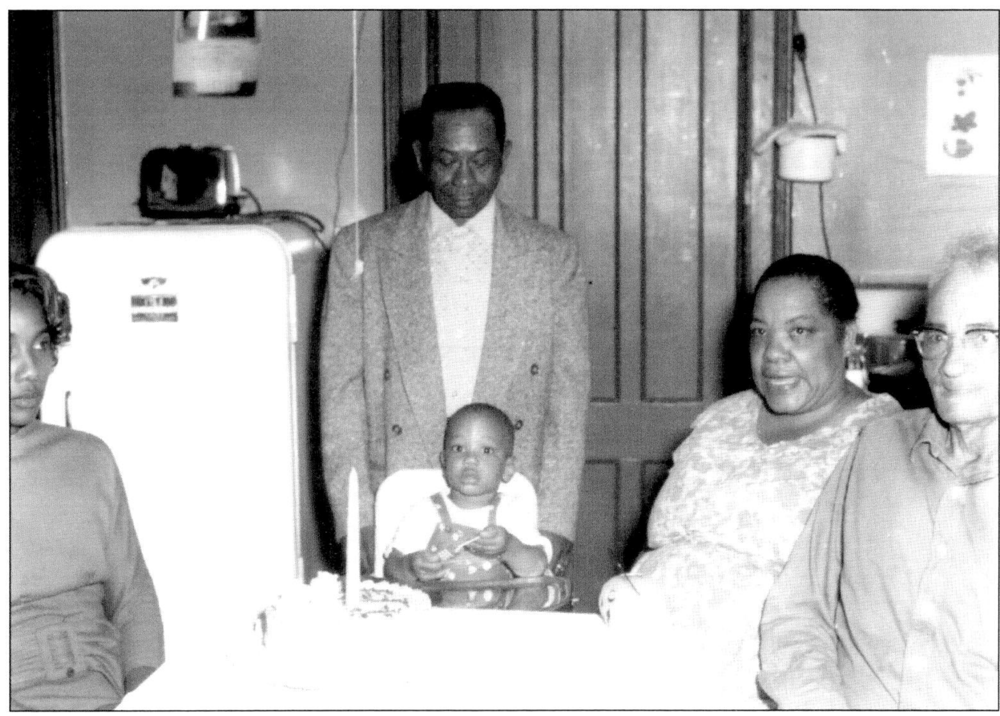

There is great poignancy in this photograph of a first birthday, with its intergenerational attendees and its revelation of a family that does not have much materially.

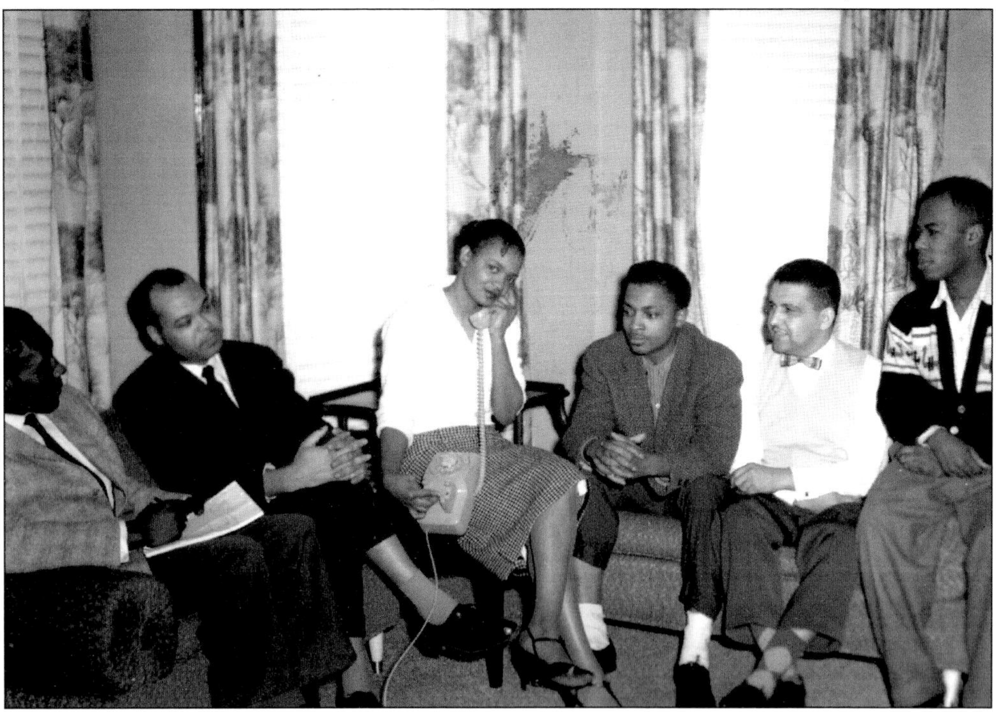

This photograph of a telephone call raises many questions as to subject, circumstance, and context.

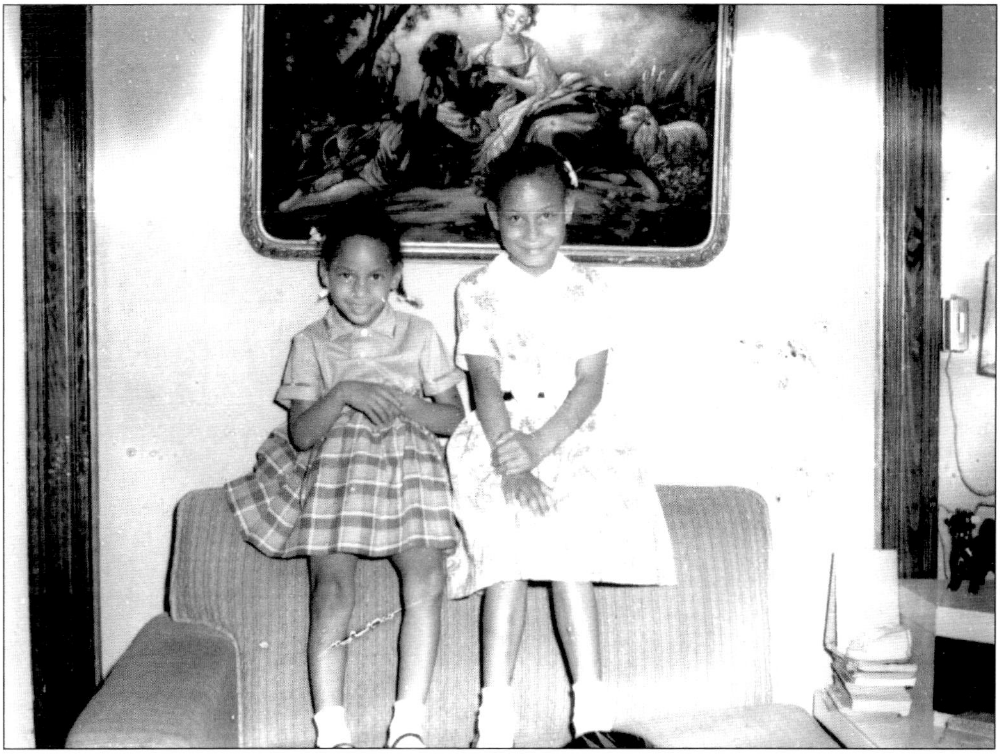

Damon Presley loved children. In his later years, he was honored as a foster grandfather. In this portrait, his affectionate portrayal of the girls is juxtaposed with the stilted elegance of the picture behind them.

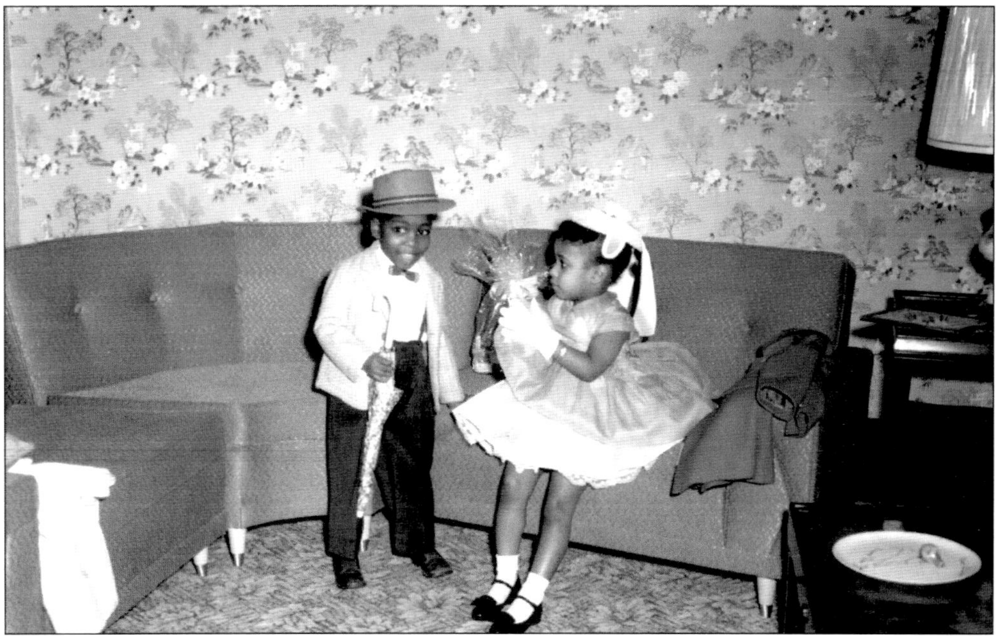

The exuberance of children dressed for a party comes across clearly in this photograph.

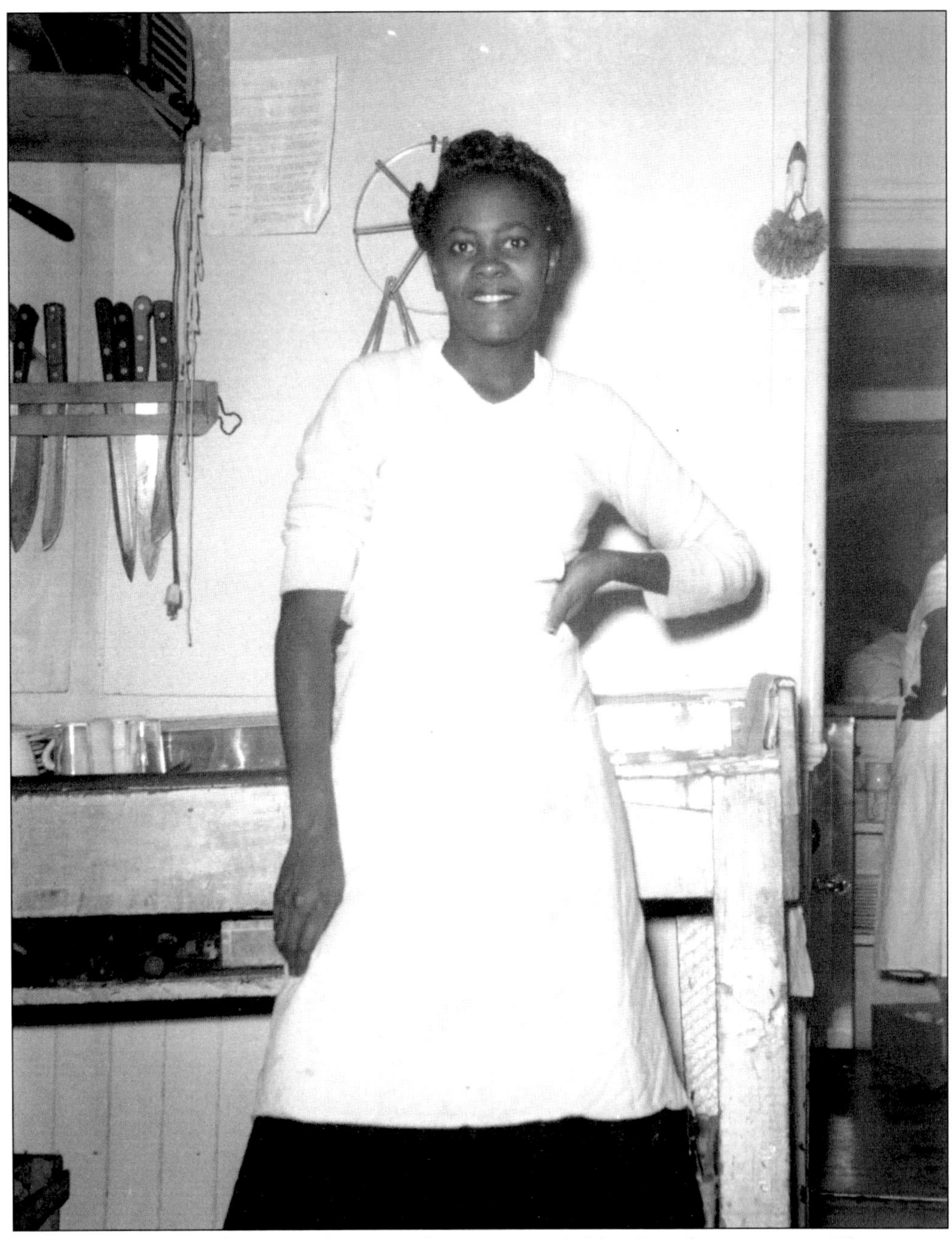

Damon Presley took many photographs at one neighborhood restaurant. They are a treasure trove of glimpses into daily life. This picture of the cook bestows dignity and beauty upon her.

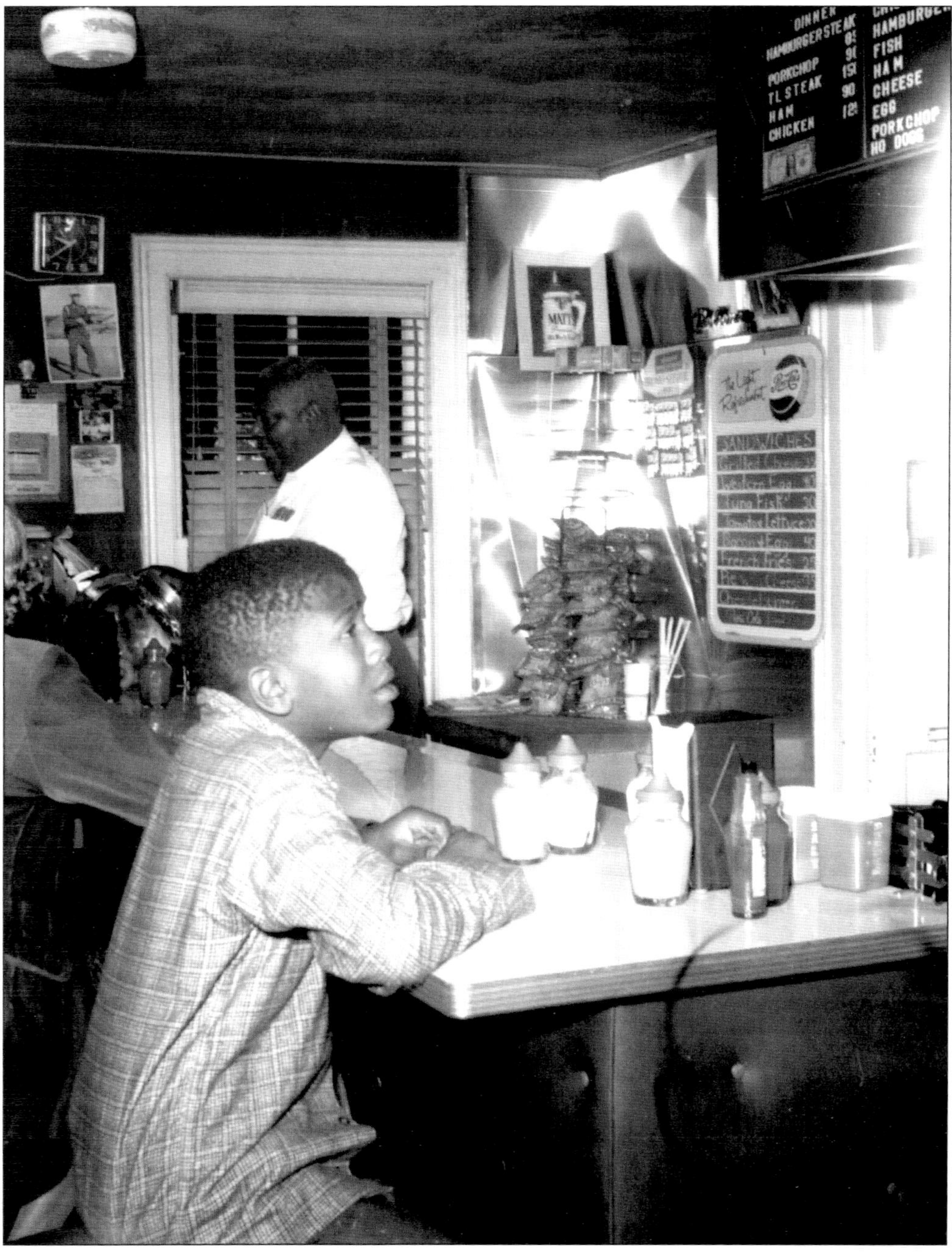


This portrait of a hungry little boy, unable to make up his mind on what to order—or perhaps fearful of not having enough money—captures a poignant moment in time.

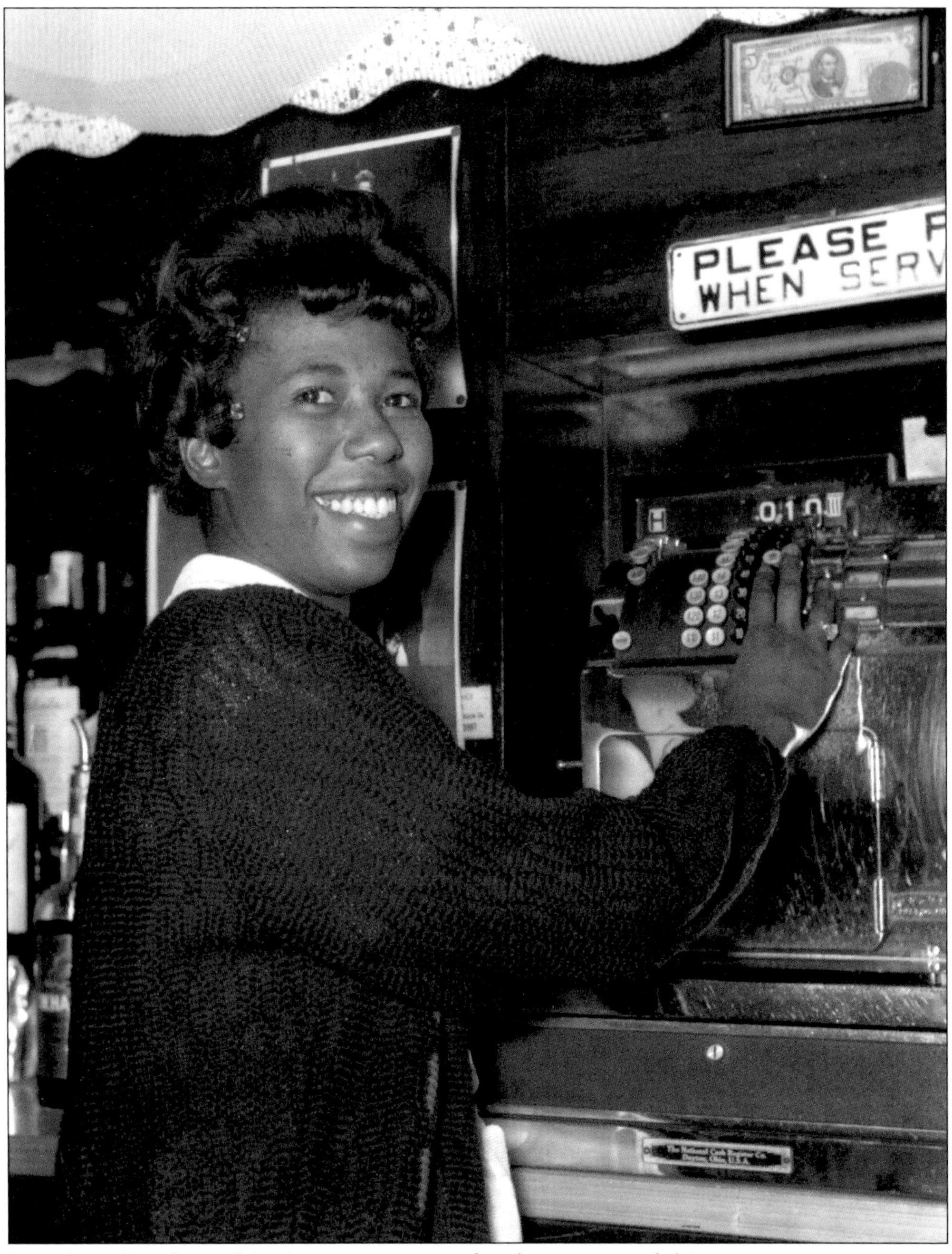

It is clear that the cashier is a great reason for the success of this restaurant.

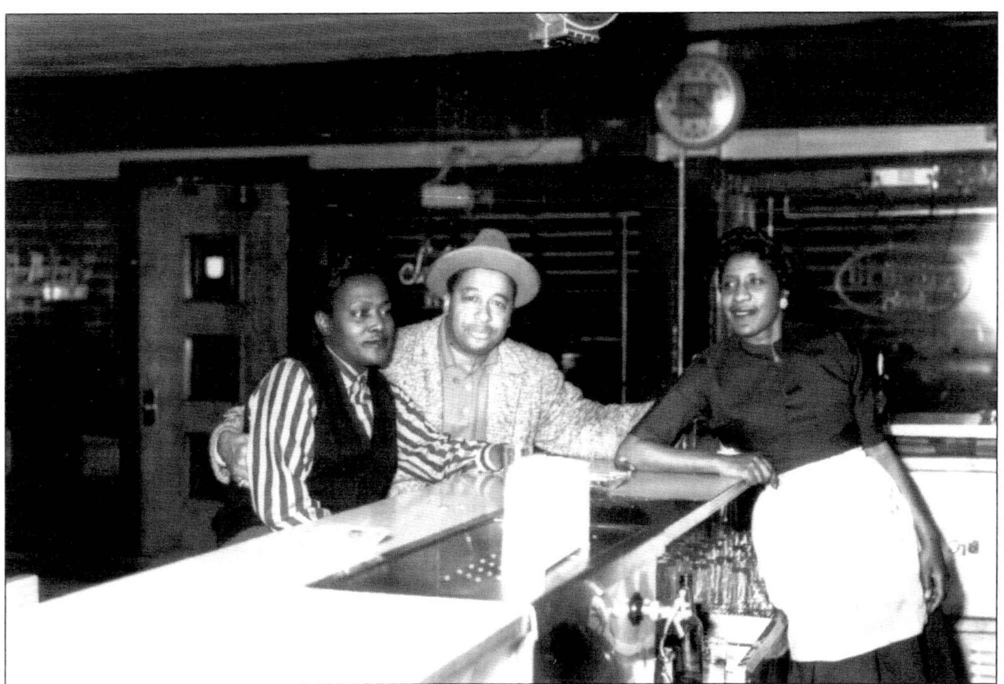

Damon Presley's photographs in a local bar show his keen understanding of human nature, as well as his sense of humor and his empathy with his subjects. This series of four photographs depicts archetypical relationships. The first is a portrait of relaxed contact and communication.

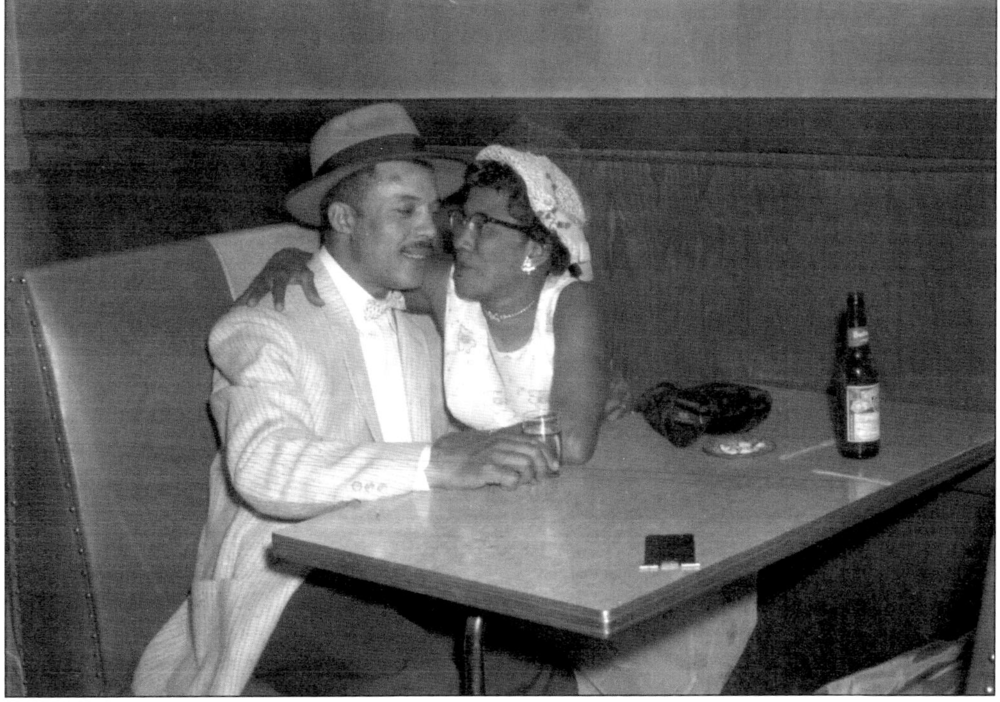

The second photograph portrays a moment of comfort and closeness.

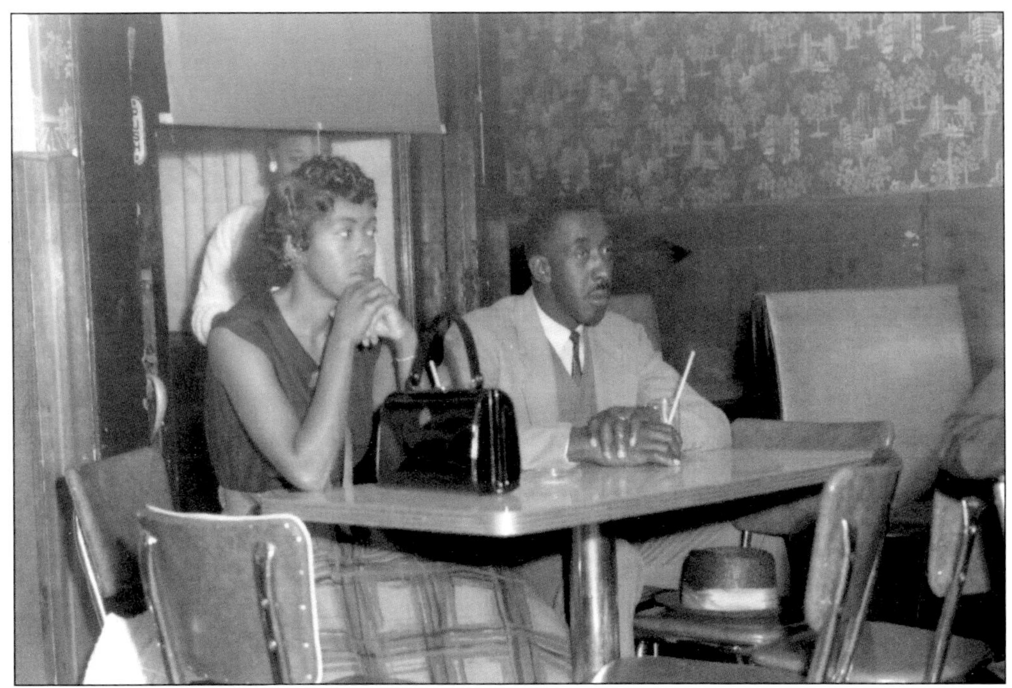

The third photograph clearly displays the discomfort of a less than happy couple whose relationship is undergoing some stress.

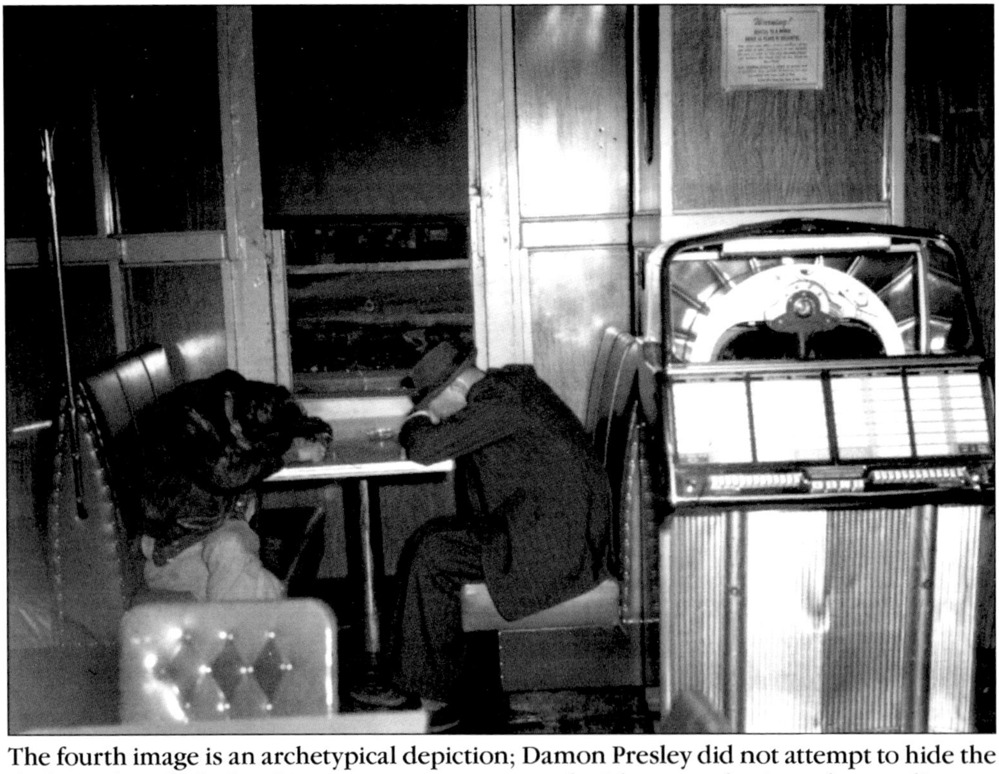

The fourth image is an archetypical depiction; Damon Presley did not attempt to hide the darker sides of life, but his pictures are composed with sympathetic understanding.

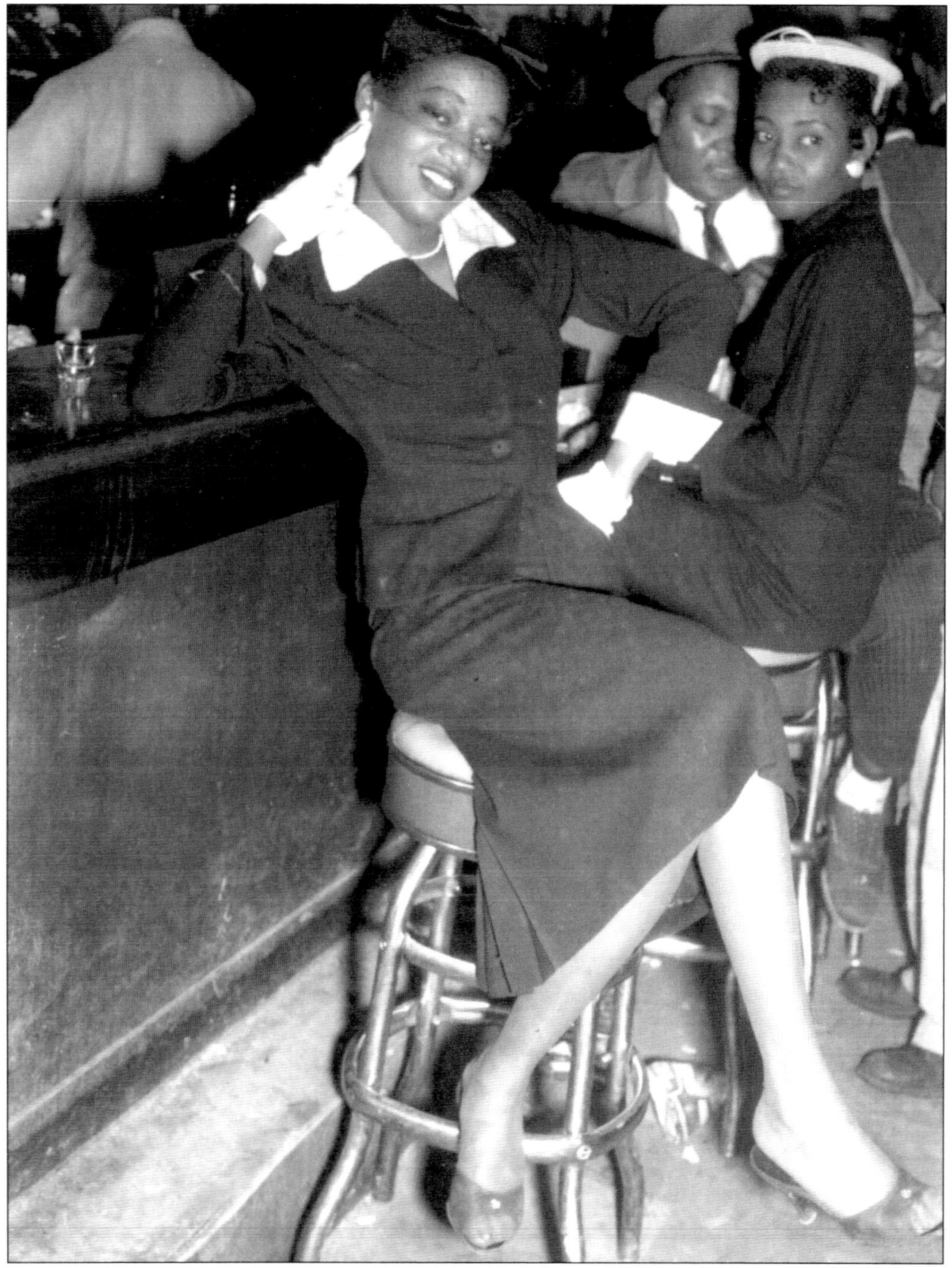

Young Janice Mitchell's pose and poise establish just the right note of flirtation.

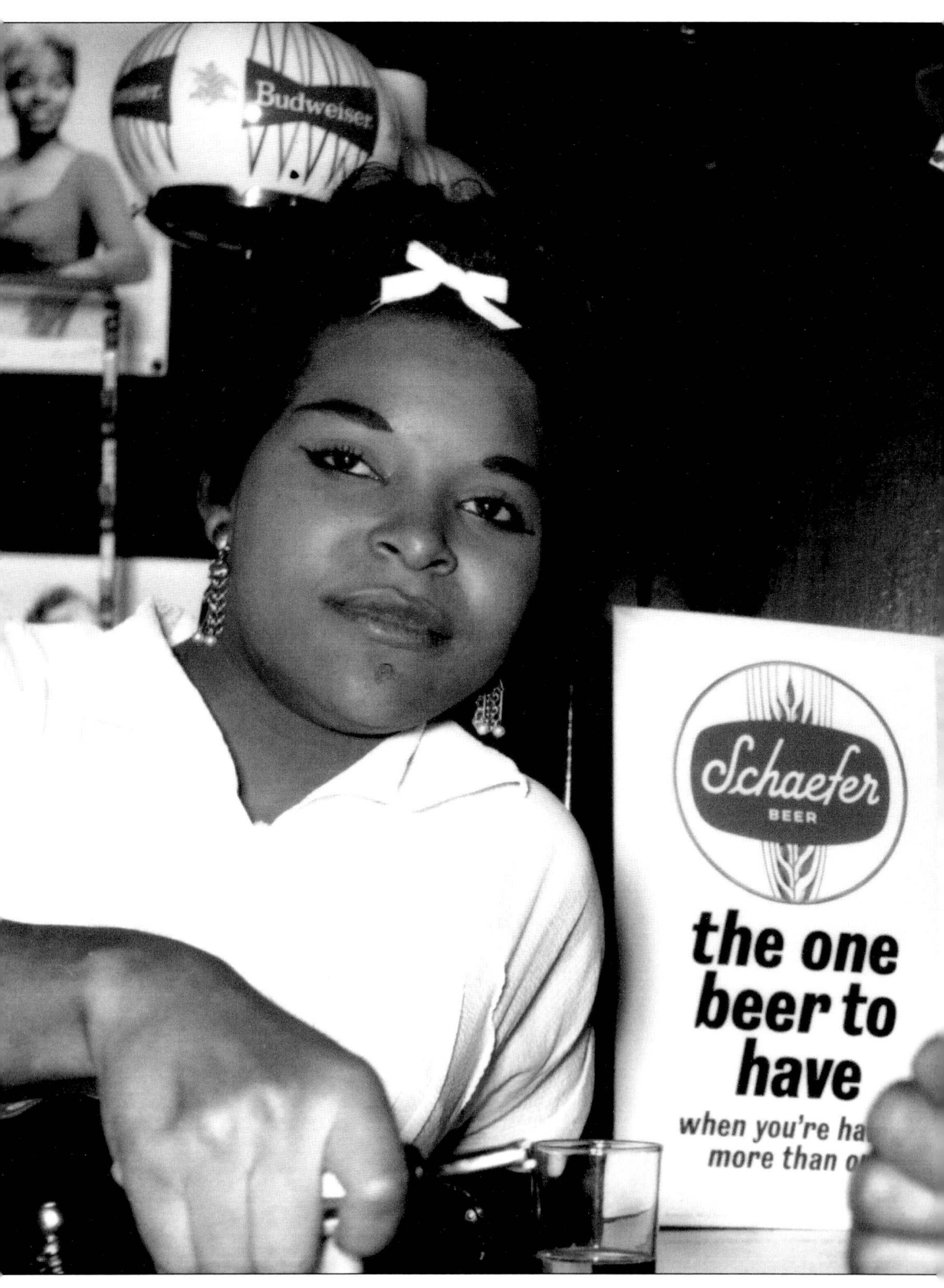
Budweiser
Schaefer
BEER
the one
beer to
have

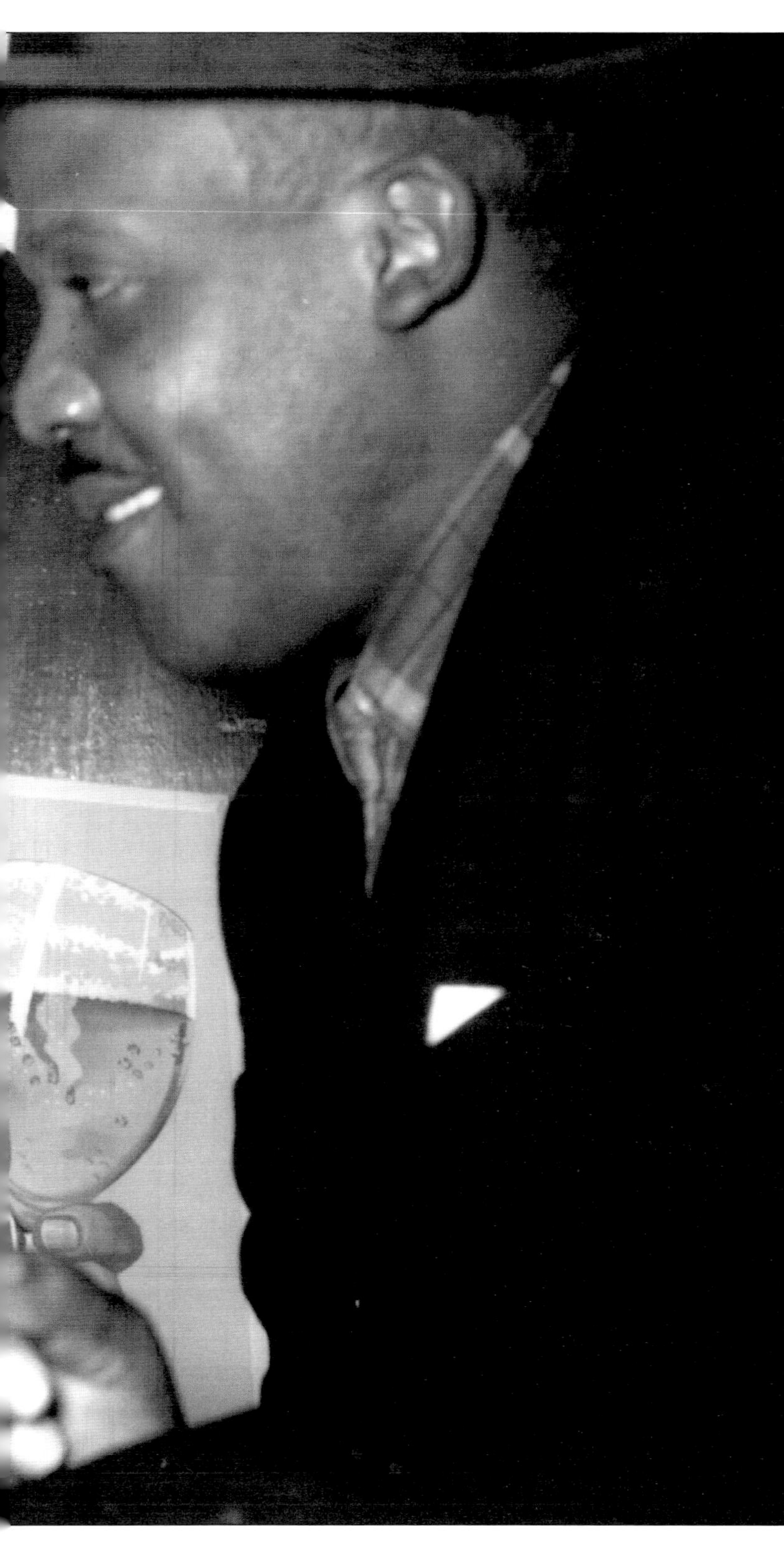

This photograph is a delight of trompe l'oeil, as the glass of beer in the advertisement seems to reside in the hand of the bar customer. The fact that the waitress is looking at the camera, while the customer only has eyes for her, further clarifies the situation.

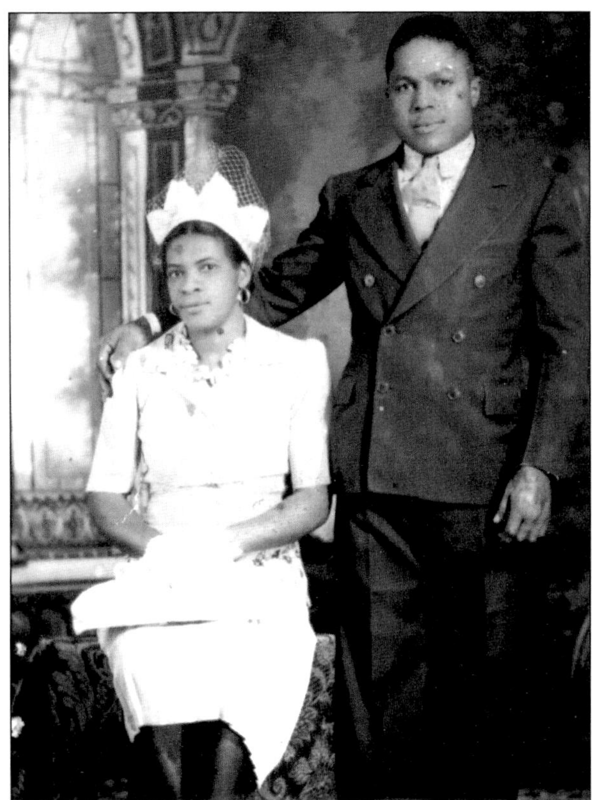

Damon Presley's empathy for relationships made him an excellent wedding photographer, as this formal studio portrait shows.

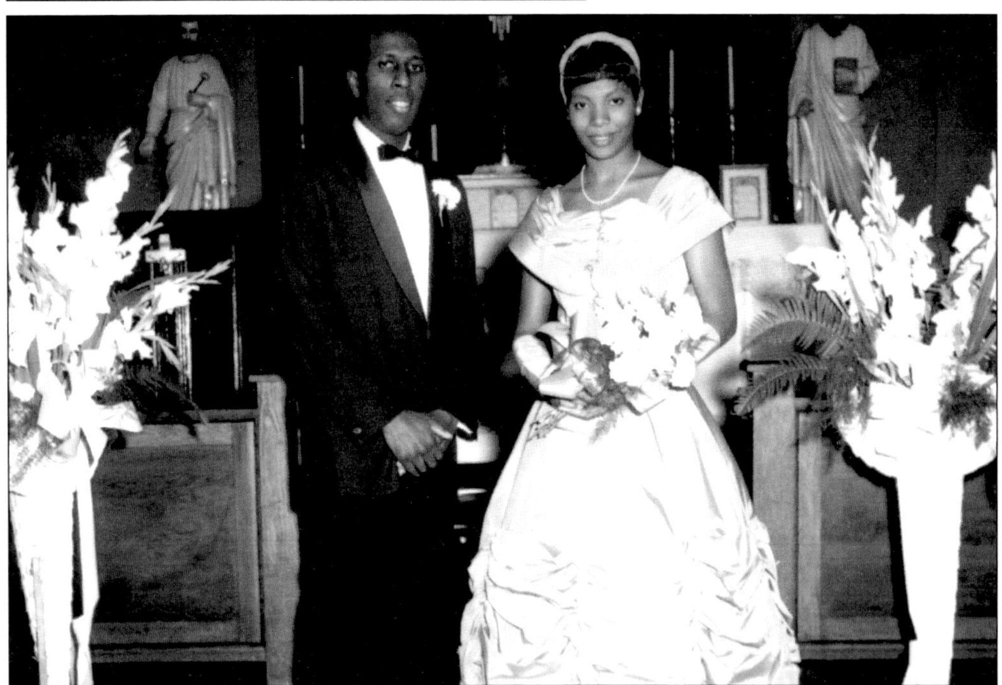

This church photograph, likewise, bestows a benevolent blessing on the happy couple.

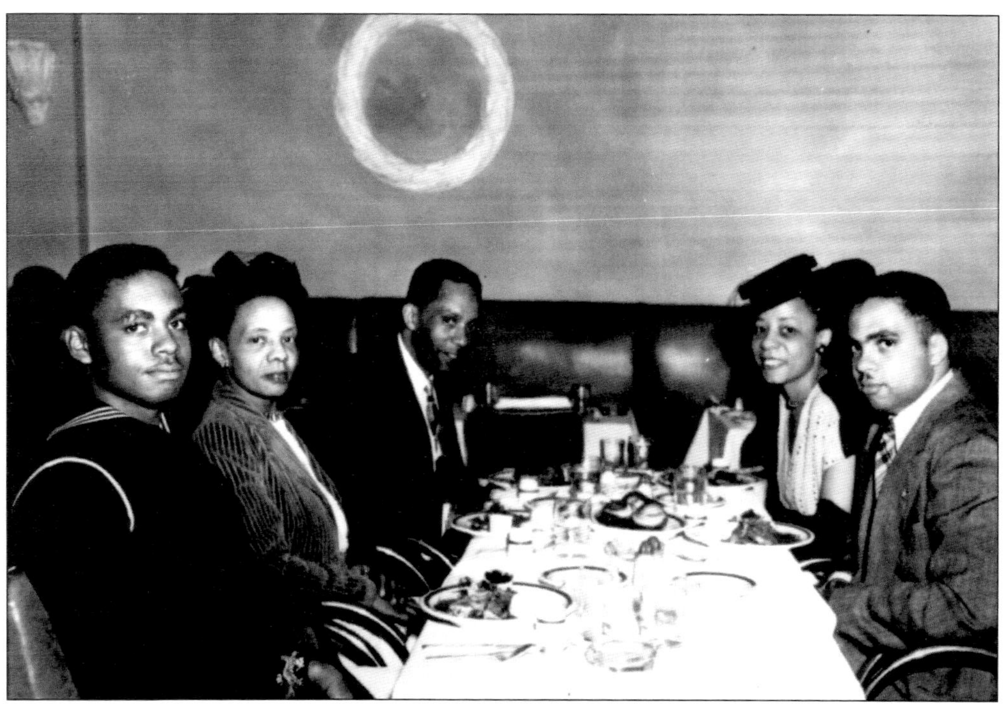

Damon Presley's subjects sometimes regard his interruptions with a mixture of hostility and welcome, as this dinner photograph demonstrates.

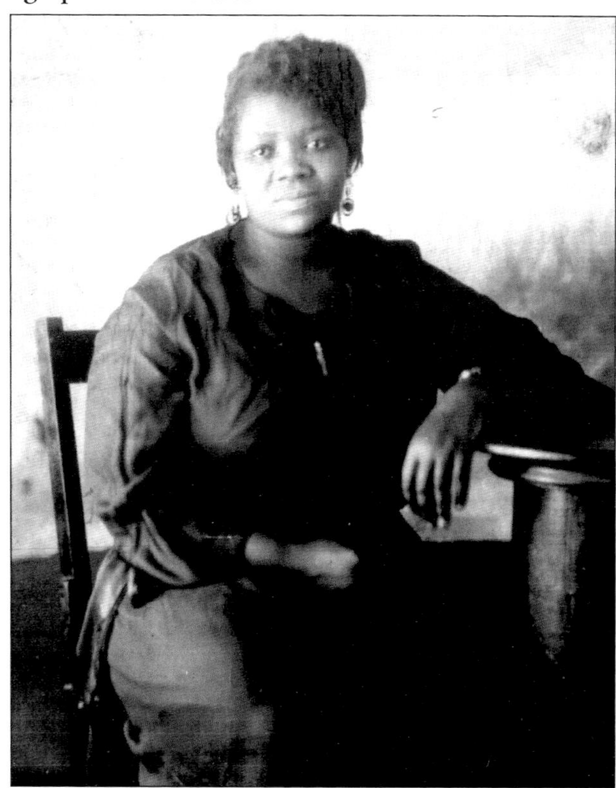

Likewise, this study captures an enigmatic expression on the subject's face.

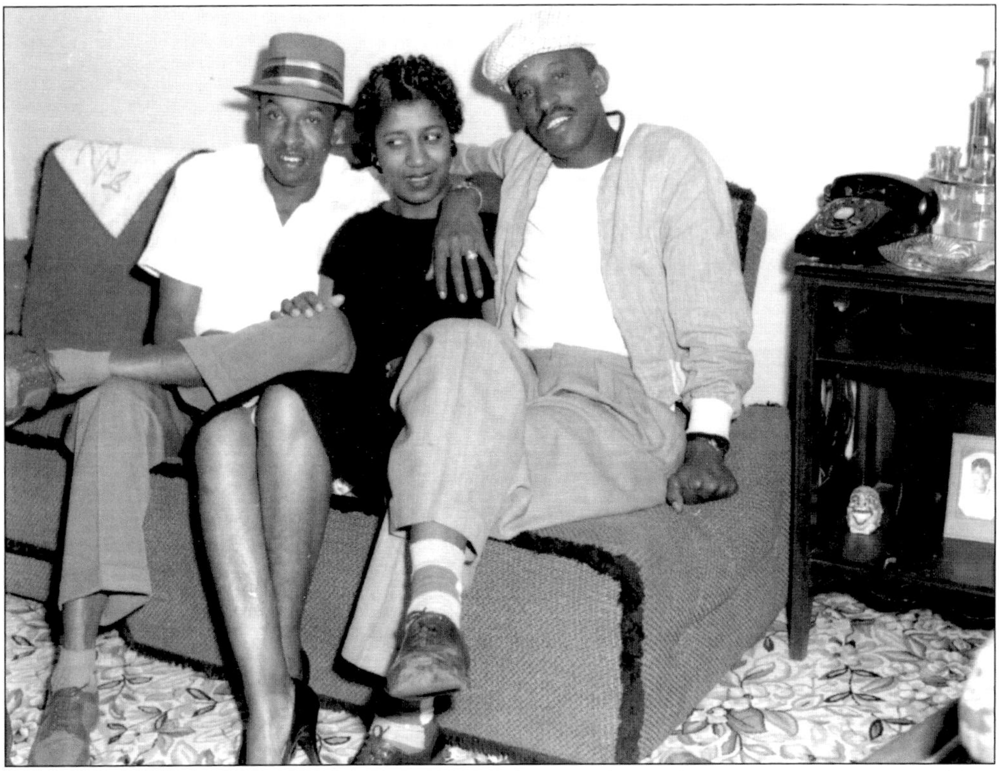

It is hard to tell which gentleman the lady prefers, as both show possessiveness and her eyes are turned away from the camera.

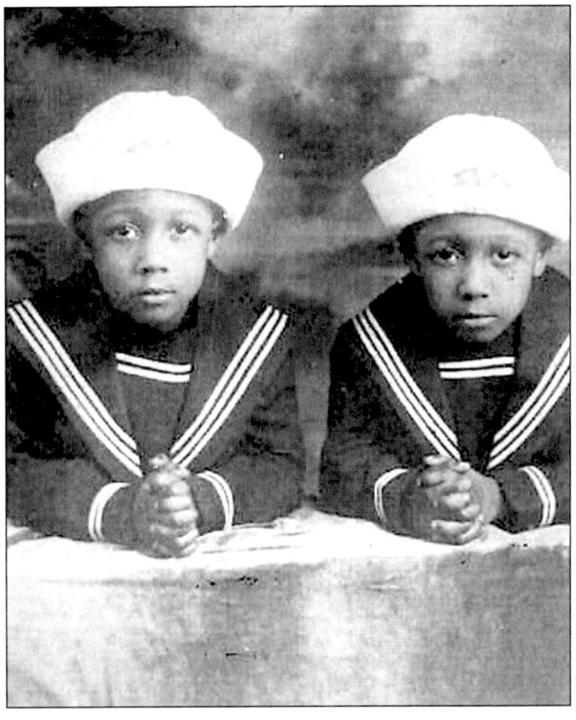

There is no question where these two pairs of eyes are focused, although there may be some doubt about how happy they are to have their portrait taken.

The benevolence of this woman is clear in Damon Presley's portrait of her.

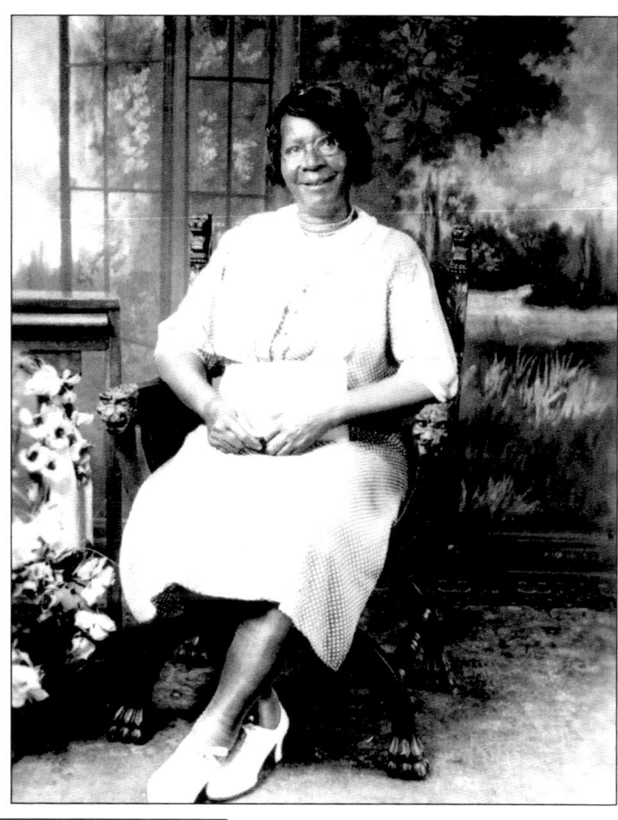

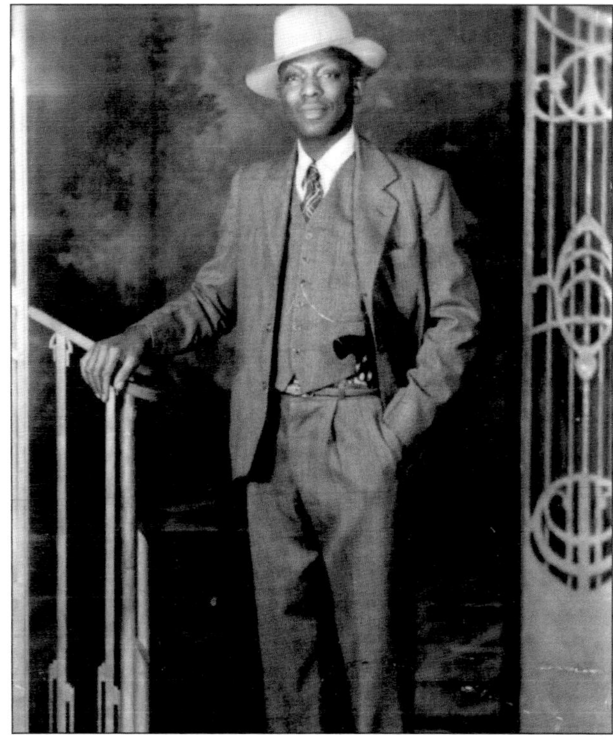

Whereas in this portrait, the stance is relaxed, but the gun appears quite boldly.

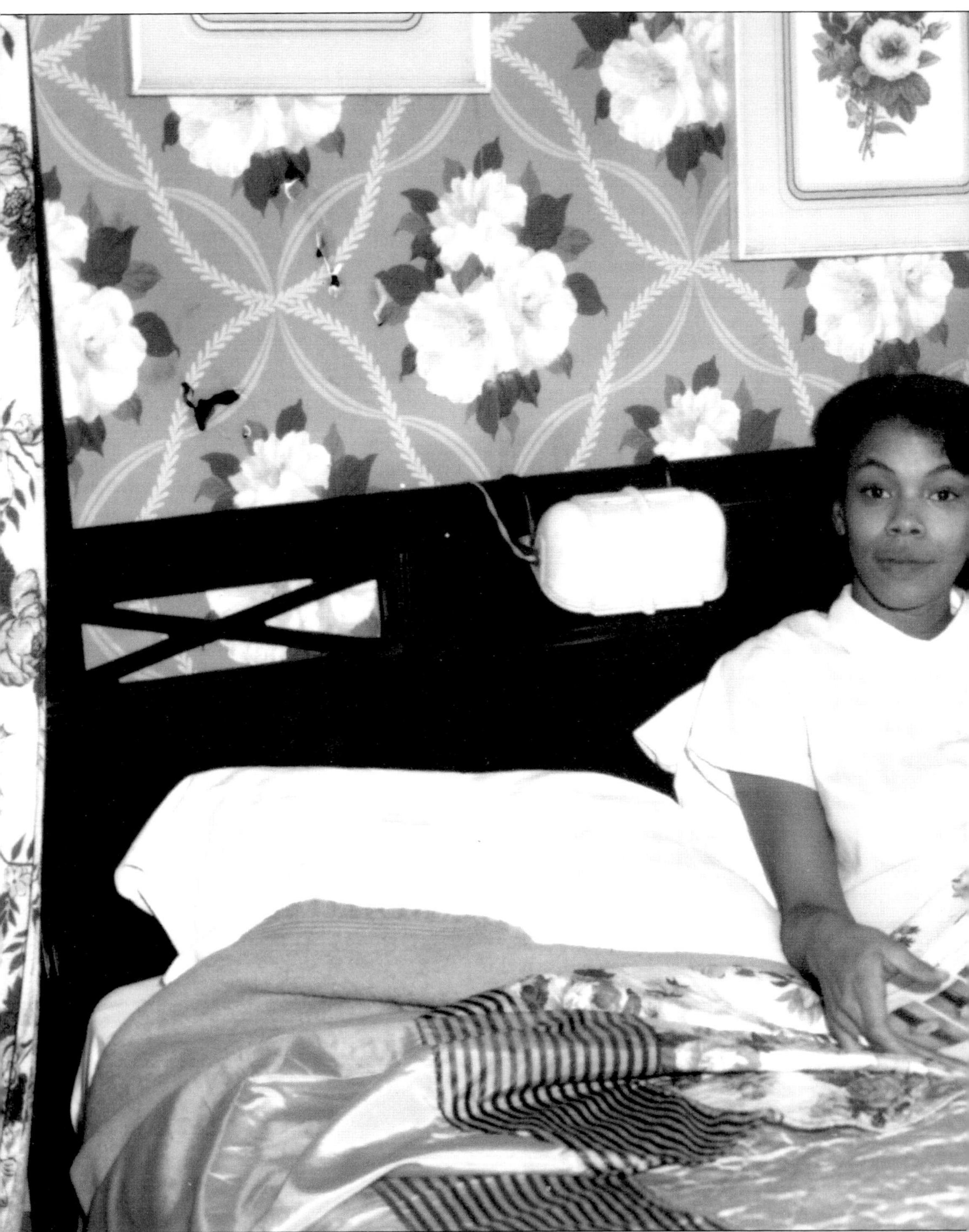

Damon Presley's unique visual chronicle of the lives of everyday people extended from the barroom to the boudoir. The visual contrasts and composition of this portrait are astonishing.

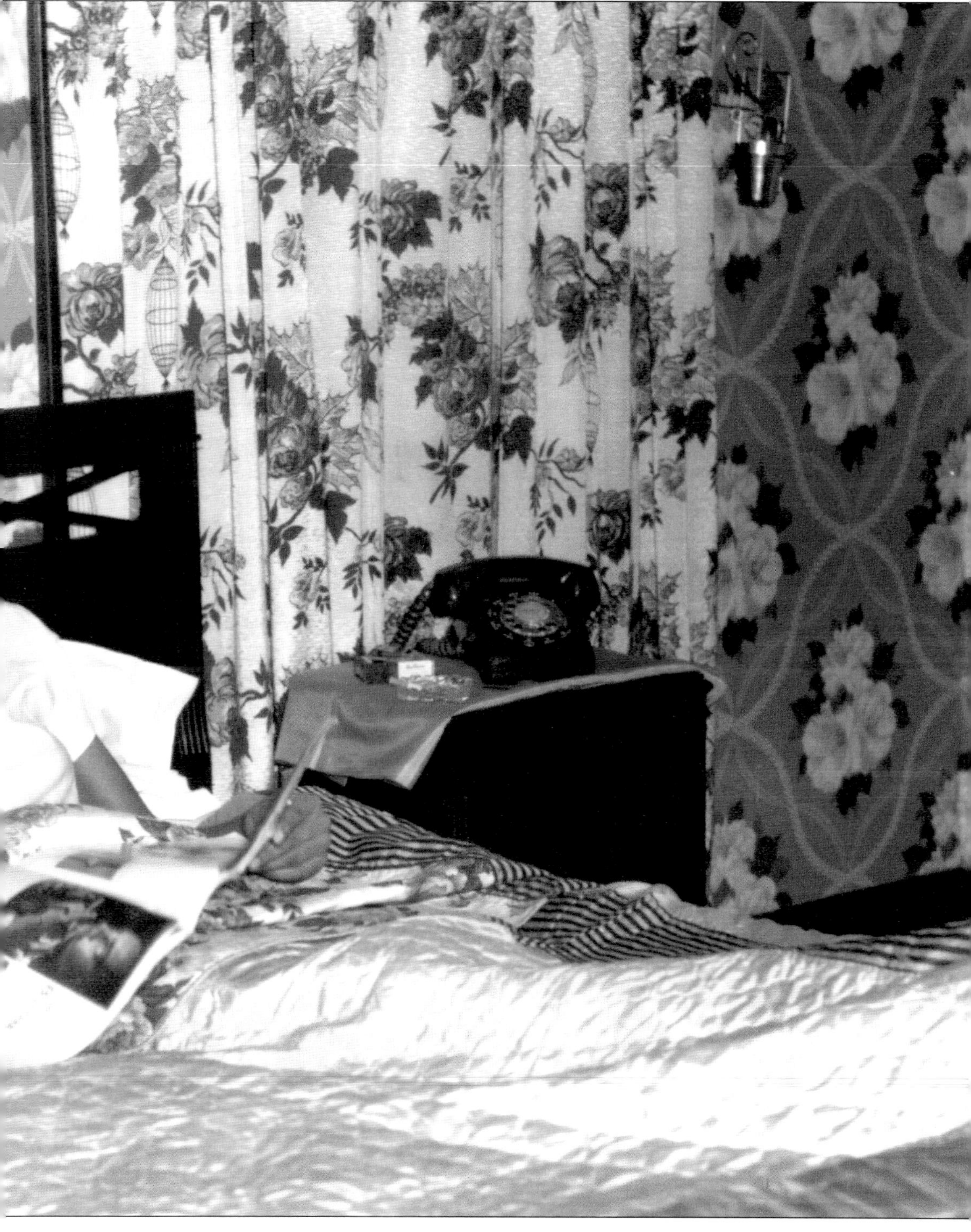

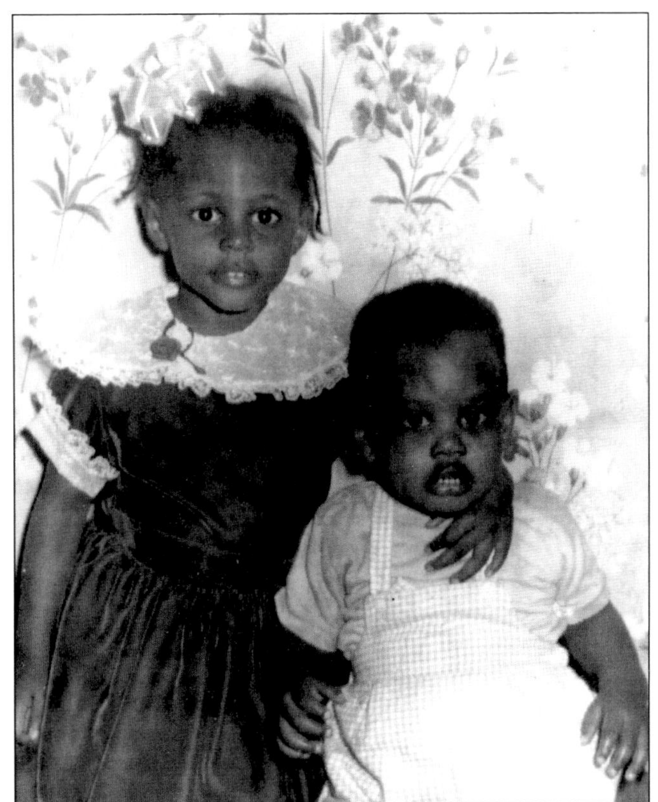

Once again, Damon Presley's love of children shines through in these faces, as does the older sister's protectiveness toward her little brother.

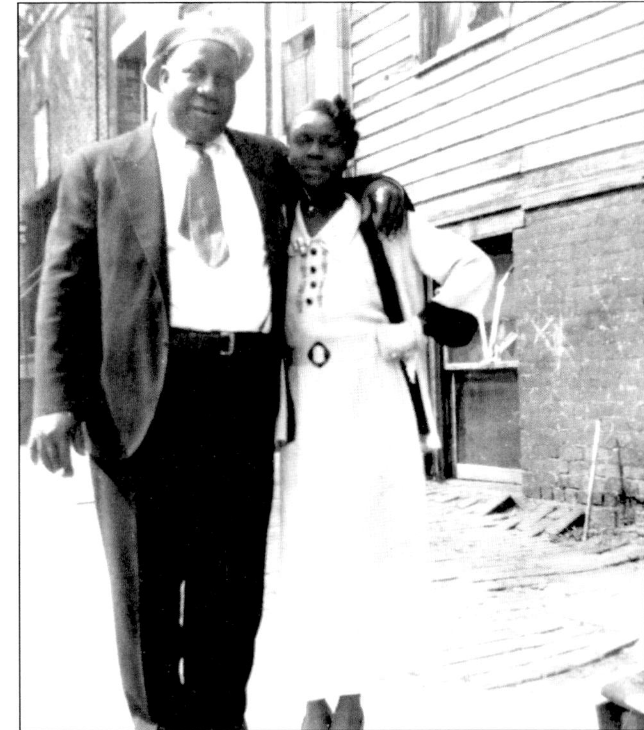

A similar pose, between a very large man and his slimmer girlfriend, carries the same sense of protectiveness.

# *Five*

# THE CHALLENGES OF THE MODERN ERA

World War II, and the social and economic changes it brought about, altered life for Syracuse's African American community more totally and irrevocably than any other event in its history. The war signaled the end of one era and one community and the beginning of another. Census figures tell the story: from 1940 to 1950, Syracuse's African American population grew by 120 percent; in the 1950s, the increase was 144 percent; and between 1960 and 1970, the black population doubled again. The increases resulted from migration; in 1970, it was reported that no other city with the same size black population had as "large a proportion of its population migrating from the South as did Syracuse." The new influx of people meant new needs, new problems, and new challenges. Urban renewal and civil rights came to dominate the community's political agenda from the middle to the end of the decade. Housing, employment, and education were to undergo major changes, though no aspect of the social framework was left untouched.

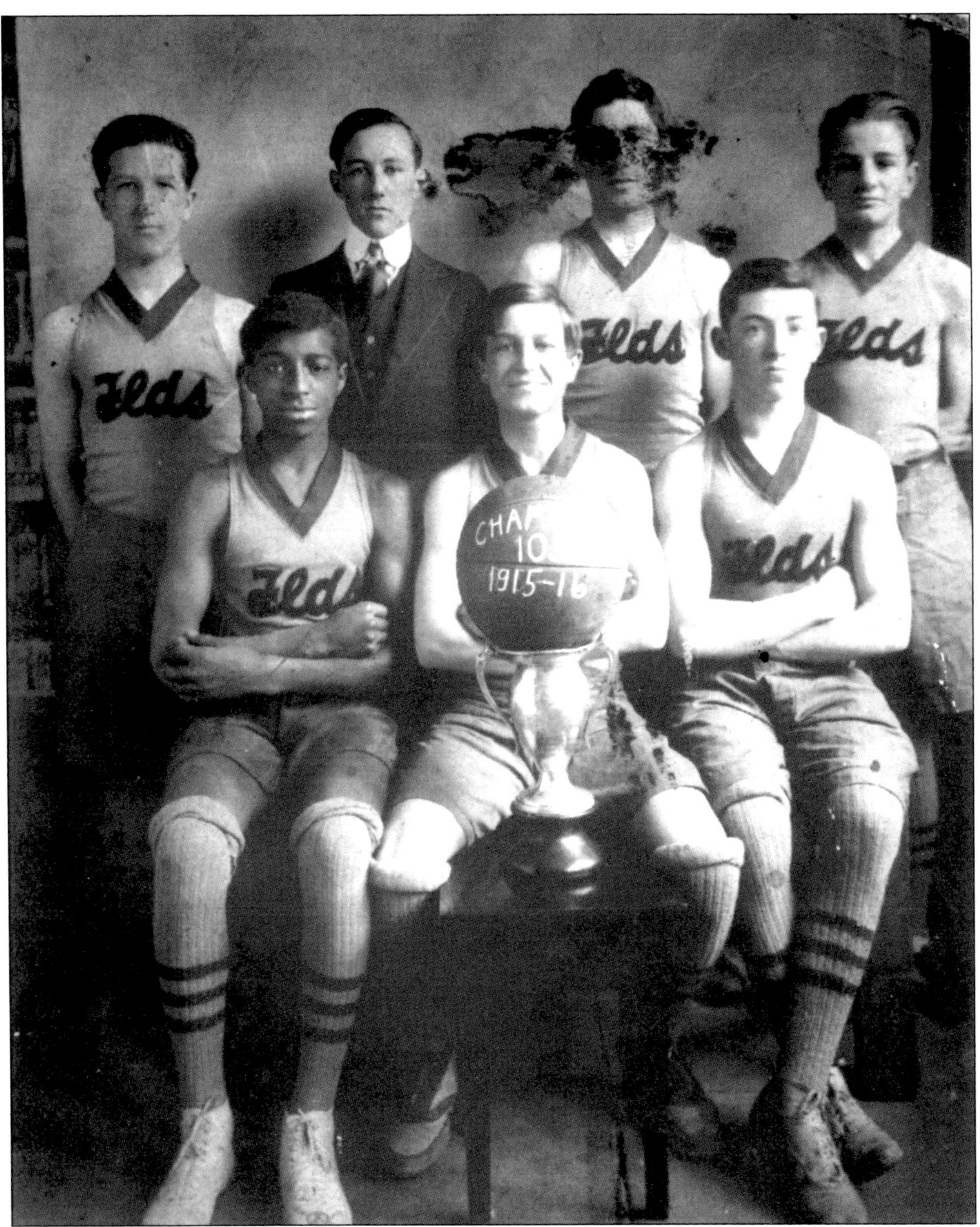


Prior to the 1950s, African Americans were practically invisible within the white majority in Syracuse.

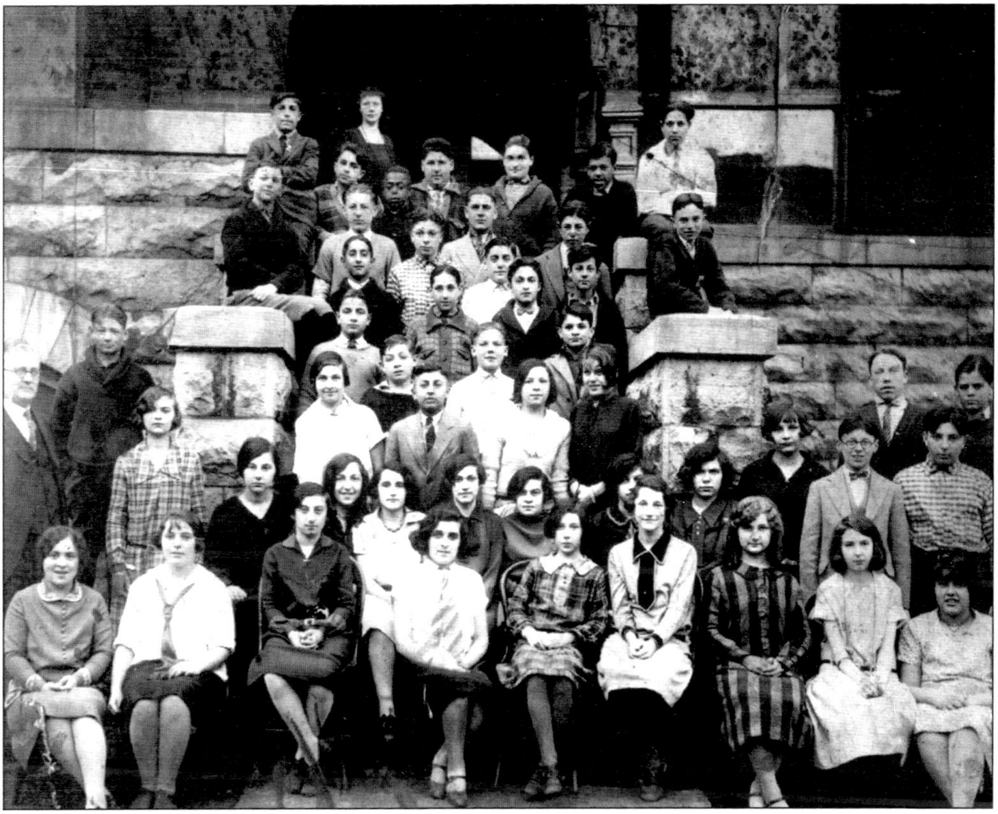

This is the Putnam School in 1928.

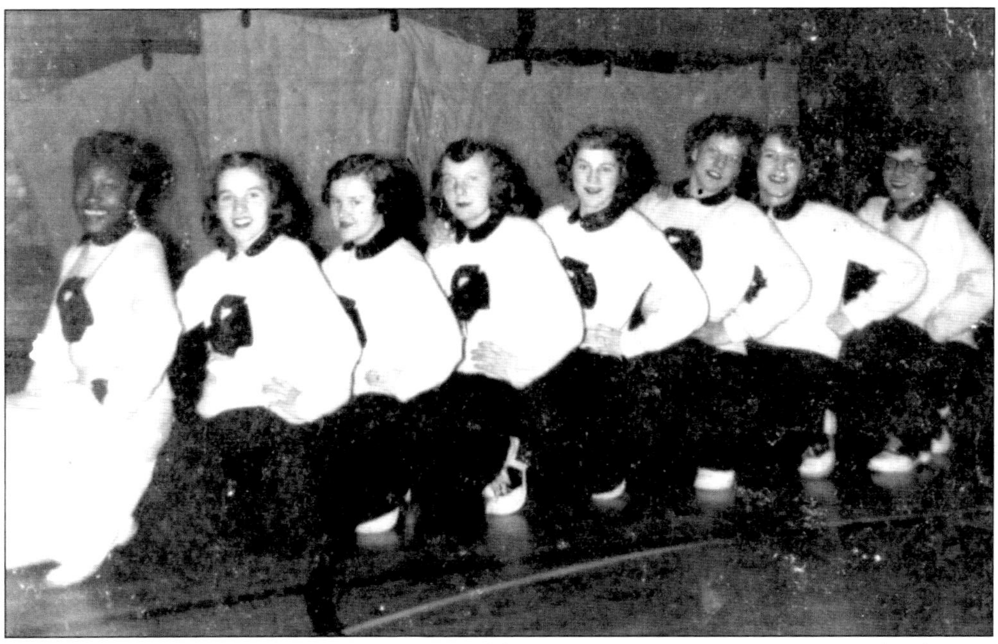

While individual African Americans were able to gain acceptance, they were clearly very much a minority.

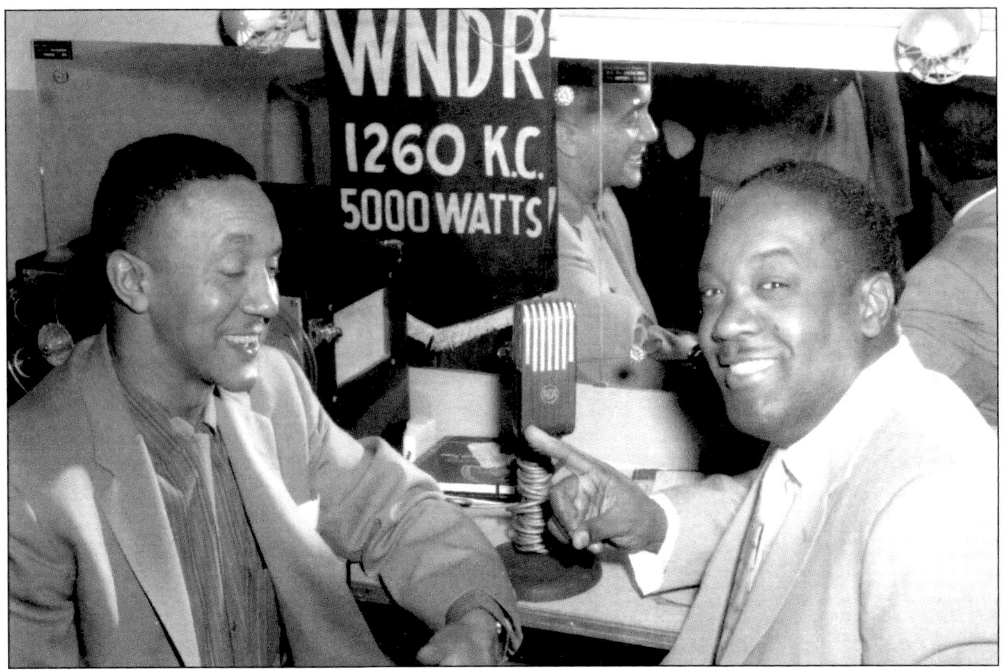


But things were slowly changing, and the community entered an era of firsts. In 1939, Dr. Henry Washington had come to practice general medicine in Syracuse; almost 30 years later, he was still the only African American physician in practice in the city. However, New York laws against employment discrimination based on race were enacted in 1945, and a year later, a branch of the National Association for the Advancement of Colored People was chartered in Syracuse. In 1951, the Syracuse Board of Education hired its first African American teacher, Marjorie Dey Carter, and William Gilbert became Syracuse's first black police officer.

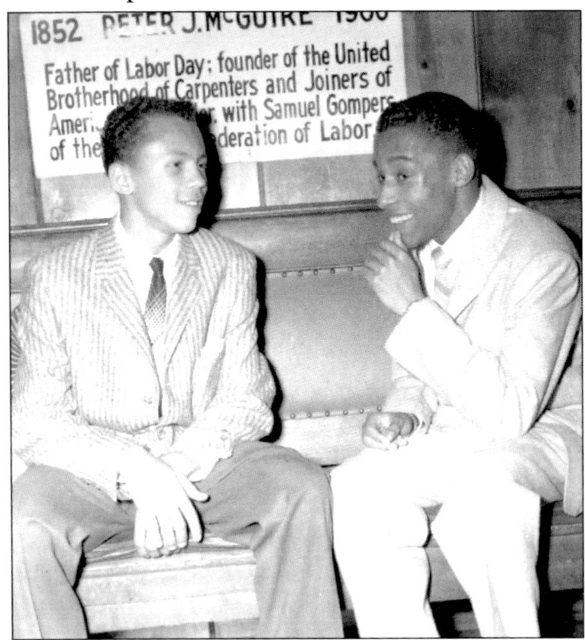


Chester Whiteside, seen in these two images, was the city's first African American disc jockey, working at radio stations 570 WSYR and 1260 WNDR. He also became the city's first black television commentator and its first African American firefighter.

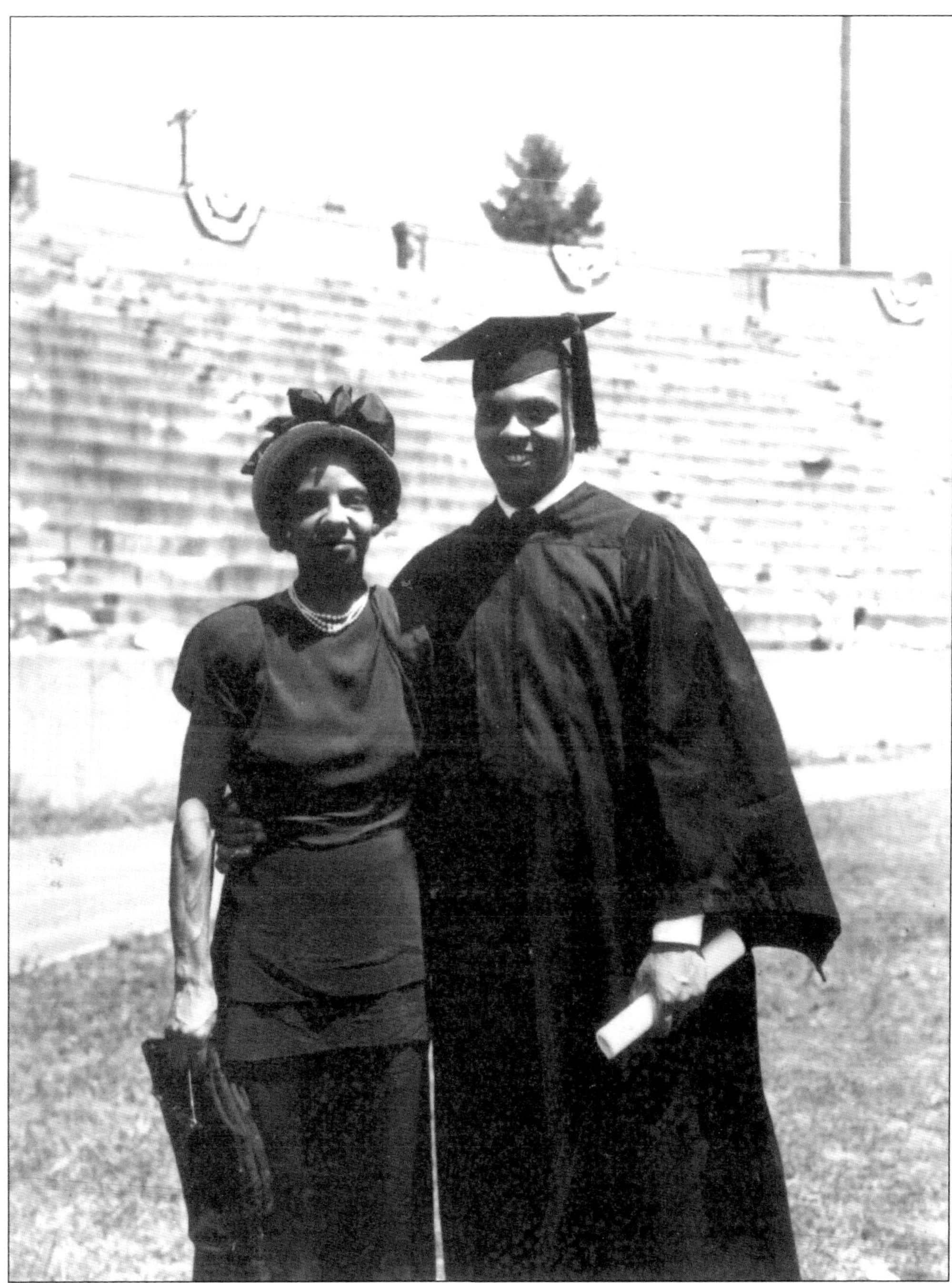

Though inroads were made in higher education, discrimination in employment was still widespread. Daniel Caldwell, shown at his graduation from Syracuse University, was not allowed to attend medical school here because of his race and had to go to Howard. Author John Williams described his employment after leaving graduate school at Syracuse University in 1951: "I left there and became a clerk at Loblaw's supermarket on Adams Street. At that time they must have had the most intellectual group of clerks in the city. All of the black people there had at least a bachelor's degree and some had master's."

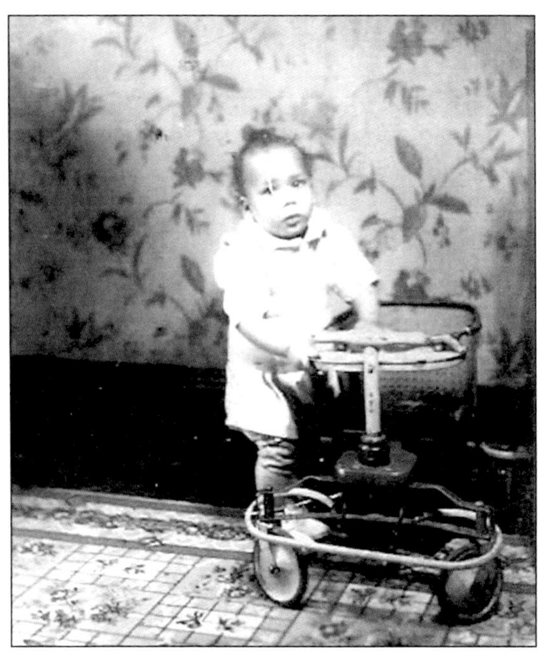

The 15th Ward, where most of the African American population lived, was a lively, racially diverse neighborhood, "our own little melting pot," according to Clarence Dunham. Dunham, seen here, who later became a county legislator, lived as a child first in the downtown area and later in Pioneer Homes.

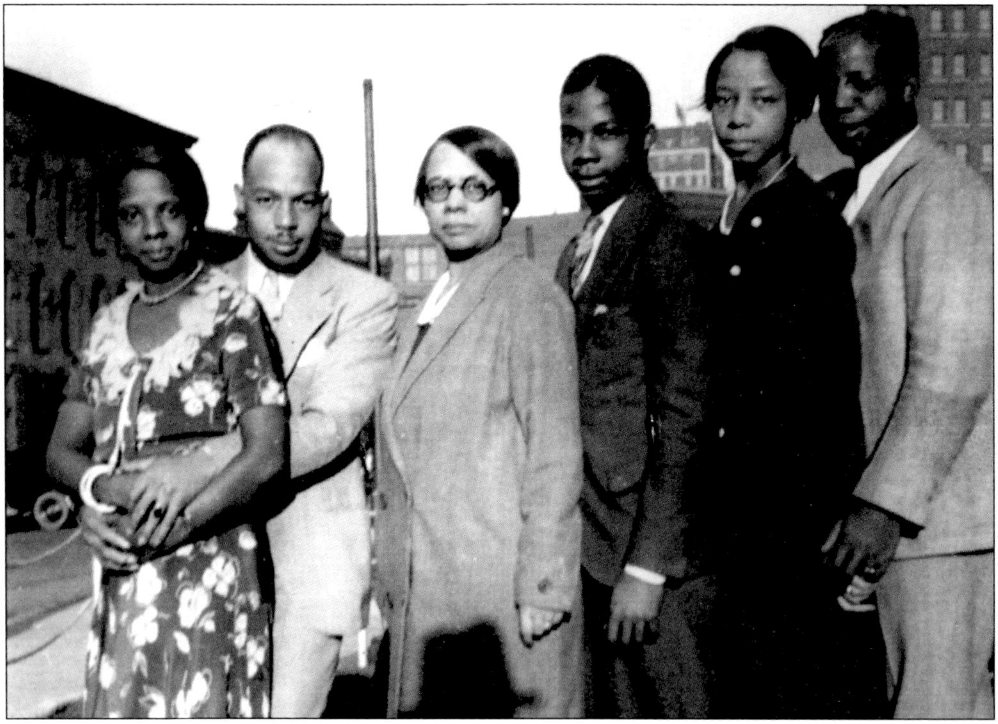

The 9th Ward, known as the "Water-Washington Strip," was the poorer area. "We didn't have the 'pleasantries,'" remembered Donald Caldwell of his childhood in the 200 block of West Jefferson Street, "like indoor toilets or electricity." Shown in their 9th Ward neighborhood are, from left to right, Thelma Caldwell (née Hasbrouck), Homer Hasbrouck, Harriet Smith (née Hasbrouck), Dr. Elsworth E. Hasbrouck, Clarice Williams (née Hasbrouck), and Arthur Hasbrouck.

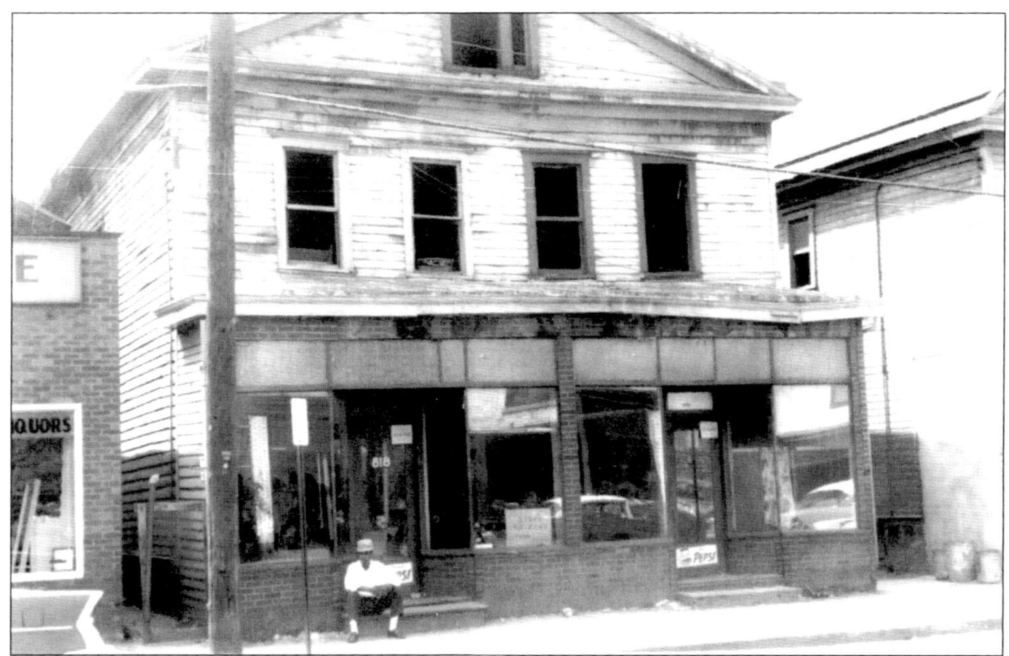

Golden Darby described the 9th Ward in harsher terms: "The houses themselves are hopelessly antiquated and run down, some of them actually falling into the category of shacks, and by far the greatest number of them in desperate need of repair, not to mention installation of baths, toilets and the most elementary sanitary devices."

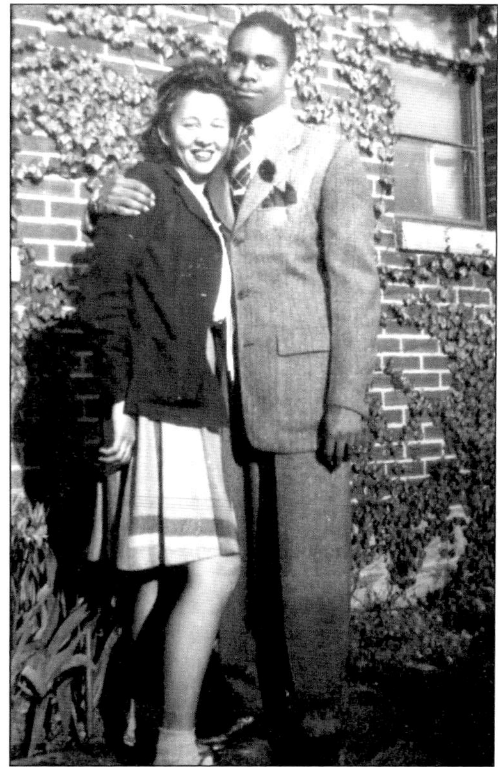

The demolition of the 9th Ward and the move to Pioneer Homes in 1935 was a definite step up for the families involved, even though the housing was segregated. Thelma Tinker Woodley and Daniel Caldwell are shown at Pioneer Homes in 1946.

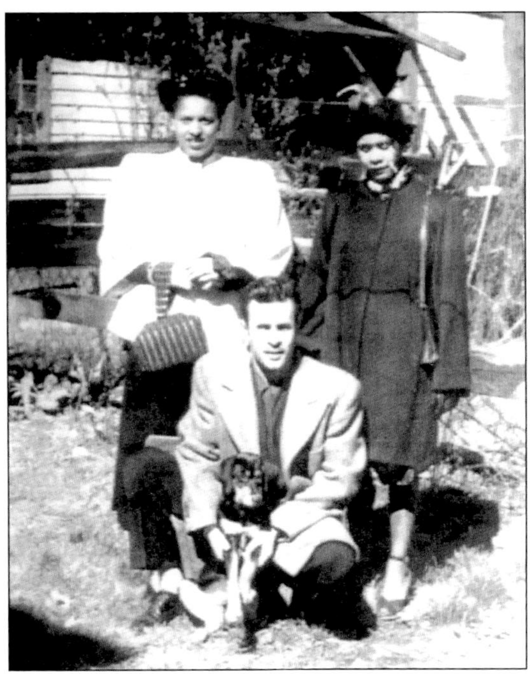

Most frequently recalled about the Ward are strong families and the way people looked out for each other. Emmanuel Breland, the first African American to receive an athletic scholarship to Syracuse University, described his neighborhood in the 400 block of Adams Street as "a close-knit community where parents disciplined each other's children." Emily "Pidge" Miller Hall (left), Bea Vanderpool (right), and Larry Hall (center), with Flip, are shown in the 700 block of Almond Street in 1948.

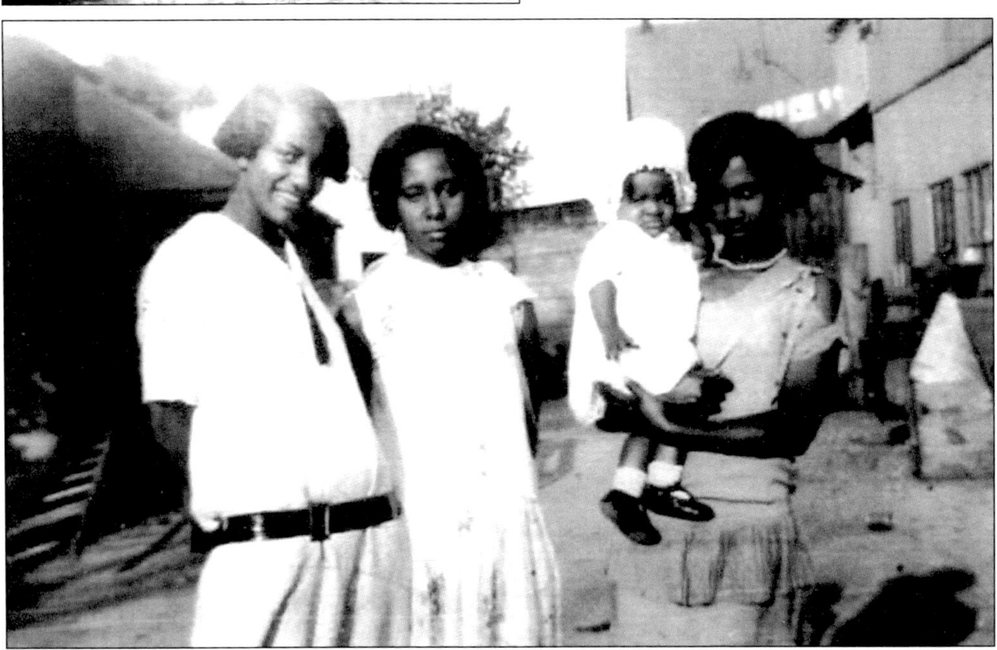

Writer John Williams had similar recollections: "When I was a child, people, Negro or white, in our neighborhood always spoke. It was as though they were glad to have survived the Great War and the Depression, and glad that someone else had survived with them. If both parents were away at work or shopping, you could bet your life that some old biddy or old man whittling on a stick had their eyes on you. If you misbehaved, the folks had the report as soon as their feet hit the steps. Ours was a community, despite everything else, in which survival of the other fellow or his children meant survival for you." Kate and Tootsie Shepard with baby Doris Moore are shown with an unidentified friend.

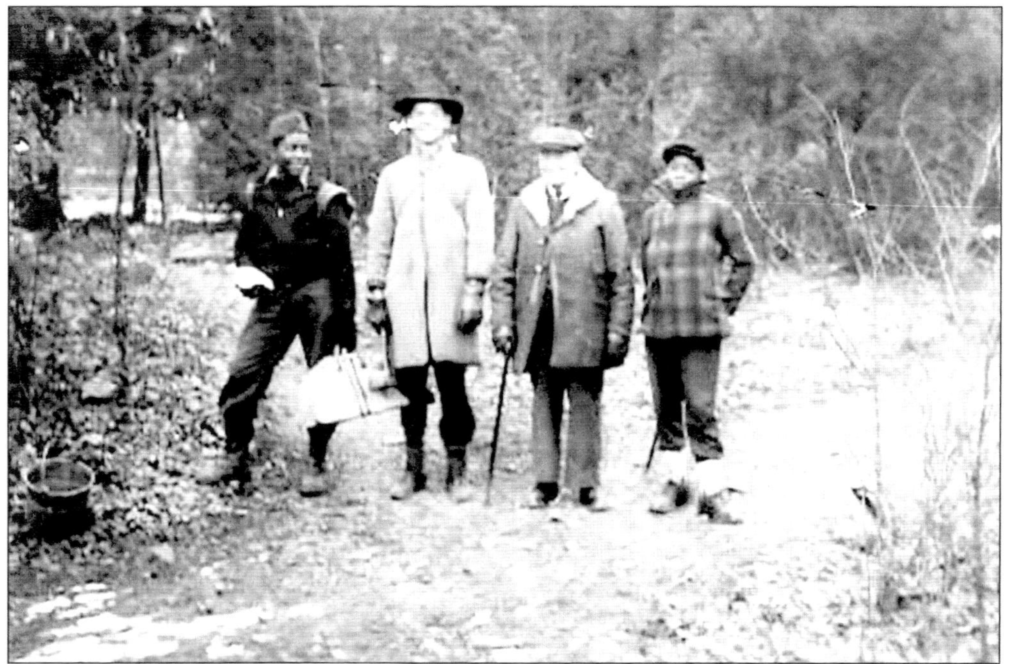

In another place, John Williams wrote, "Many kinds of people lived there, Negroes, Jews, Italians, Irish, Poles, Indians and 'native Americans.' The people shared conversation and other small joys. The religious holidays of all were greatly respected. If your parents were at work or shopping, someone on the block had his or her eye on you."

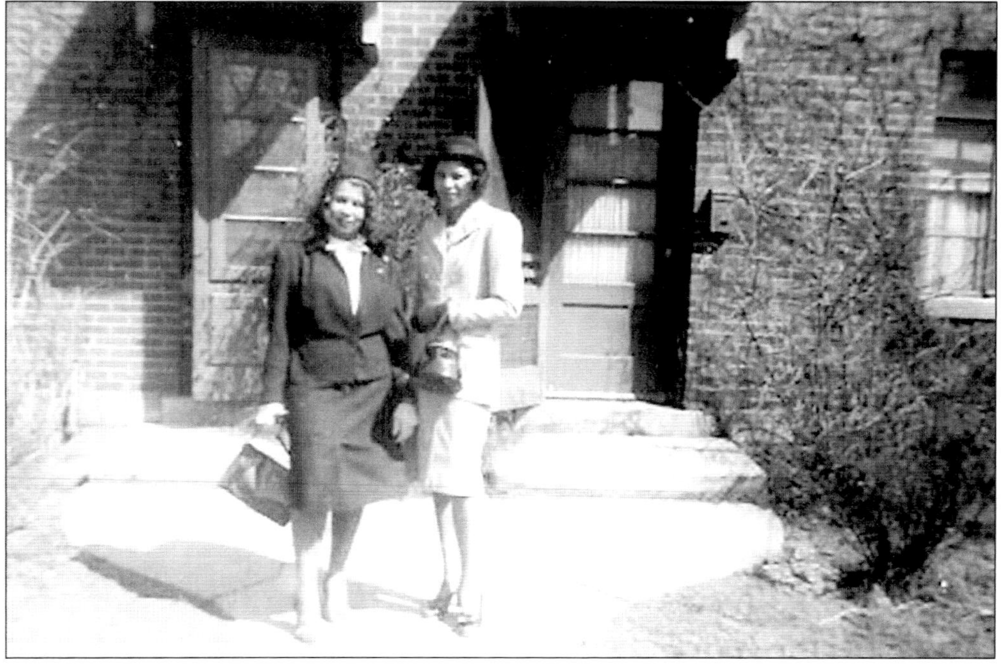

Williams continues: "In the Ward, survival of the other fellow and his children meant survival for you. For me, the Ward was home and the rest of Syracuse radiated outward from it."

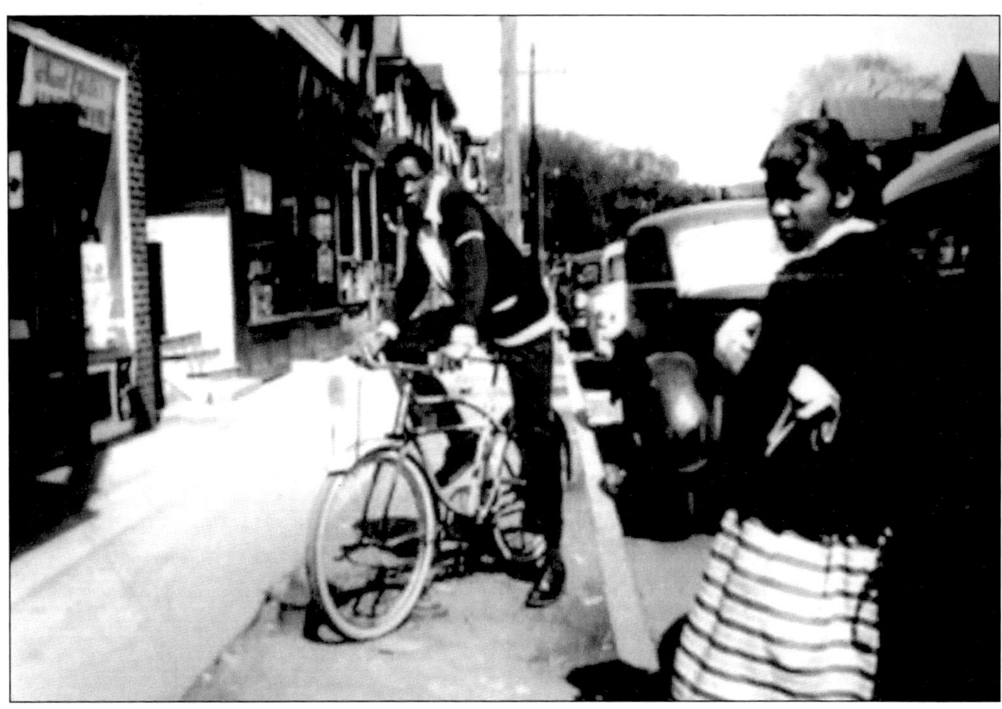

These teenagers gather near a favorite neighborhood candy store.

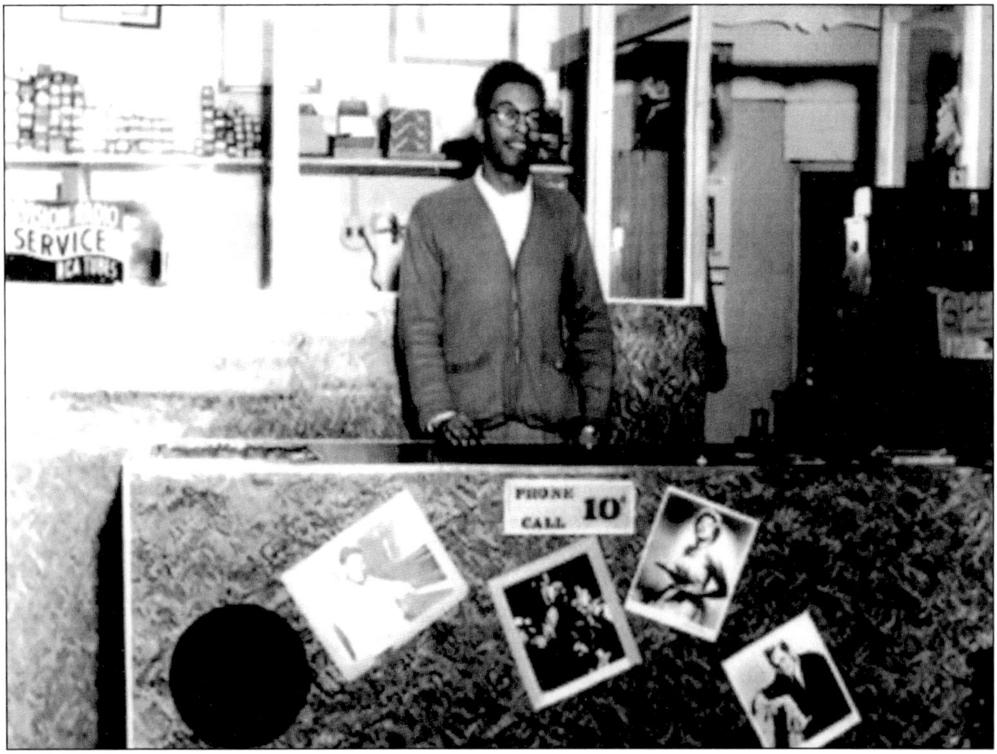

The Ward's stores, churches, clubs, and activities were central to African American community social life.

Scouting was a favorite and positive pastime.

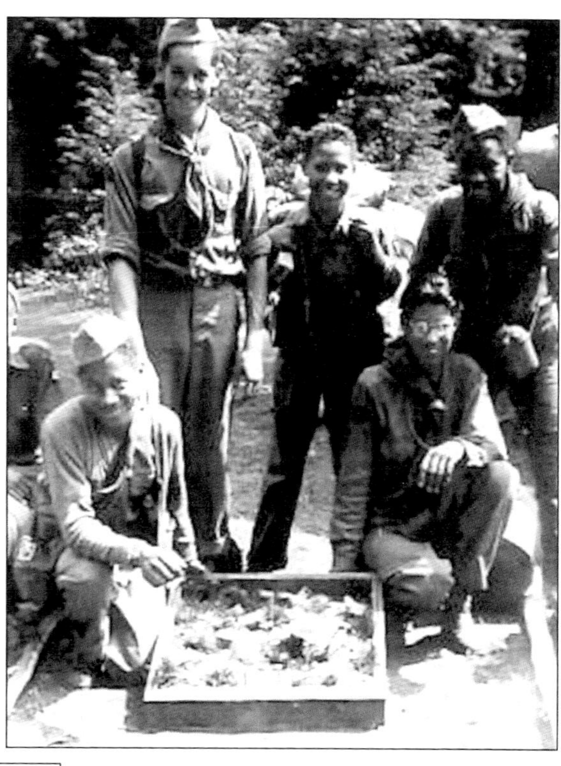

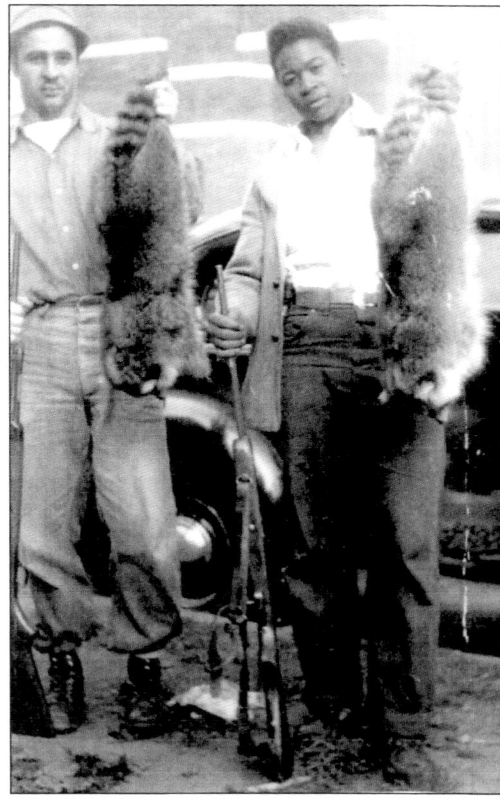

These two hunters, Larry Hall and one of Conrad Vanderpool's younger brothers, from Almond Street had success down in Lafayette.

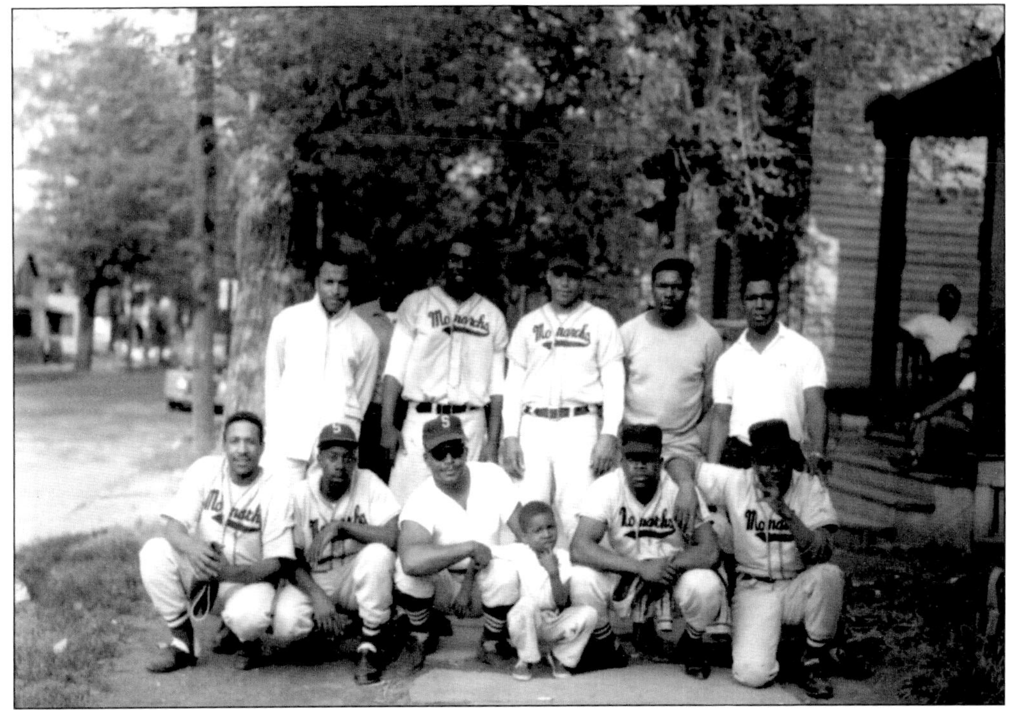


Sports were particularly important to the African American community. The Mohawks pose in the Ward.

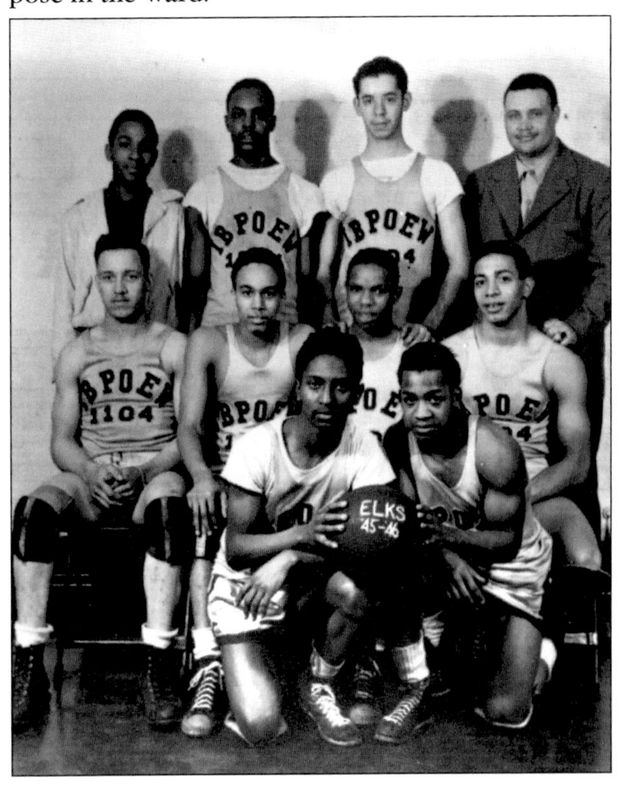


The Elks team was coached by Ernie Powell.

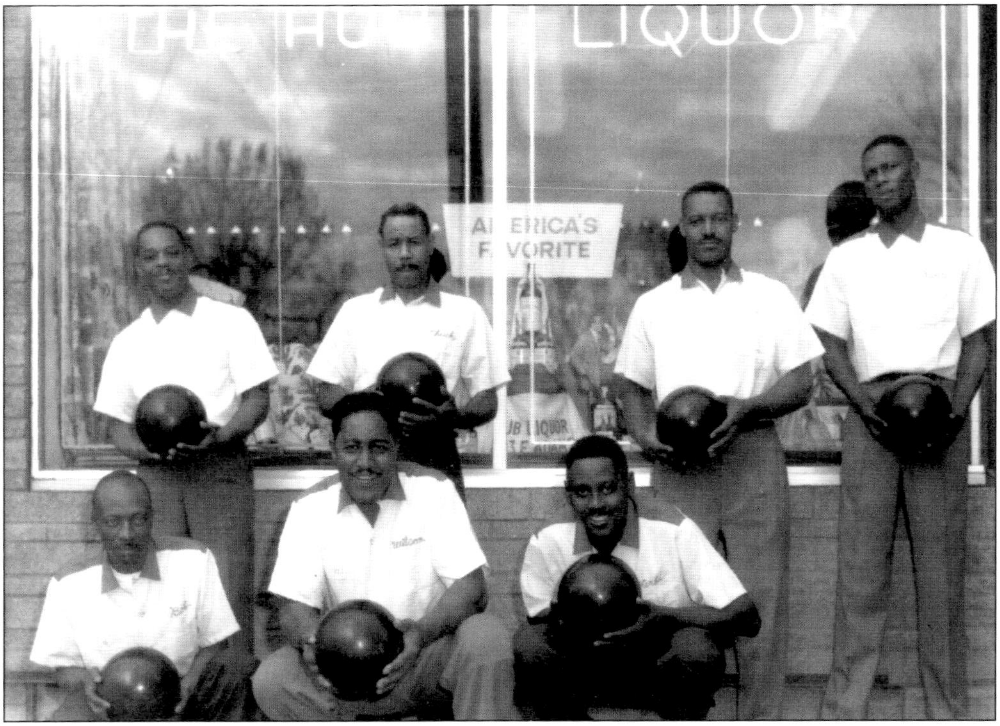

A local bowling group poses in front of their sponsor.

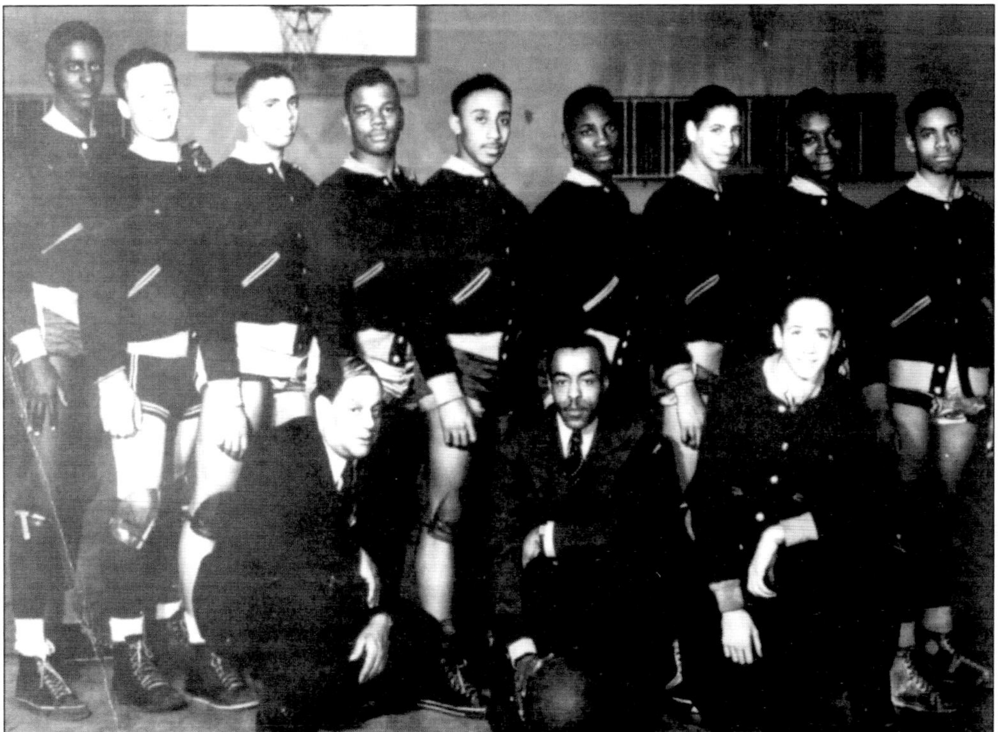

The Dunbar Center's basketball team had a roster of star players.

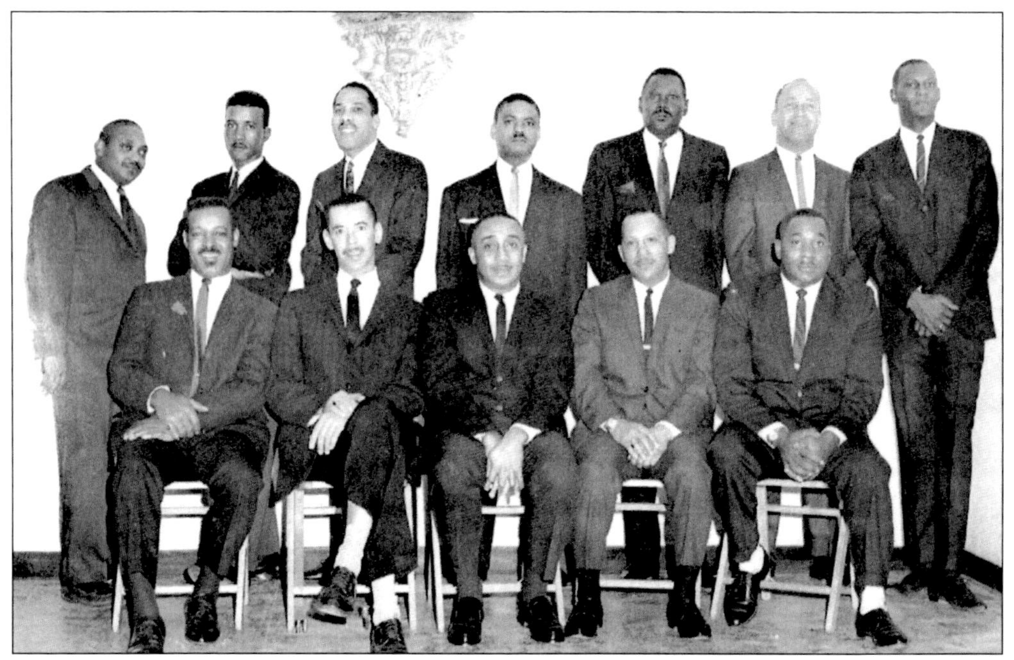

The Grand Street Boys was a social club that recognized the importance of athletics and academics by an annual award to a high school scholar and athlete in memory of Ormond Spencer, a promising athlete who died young.

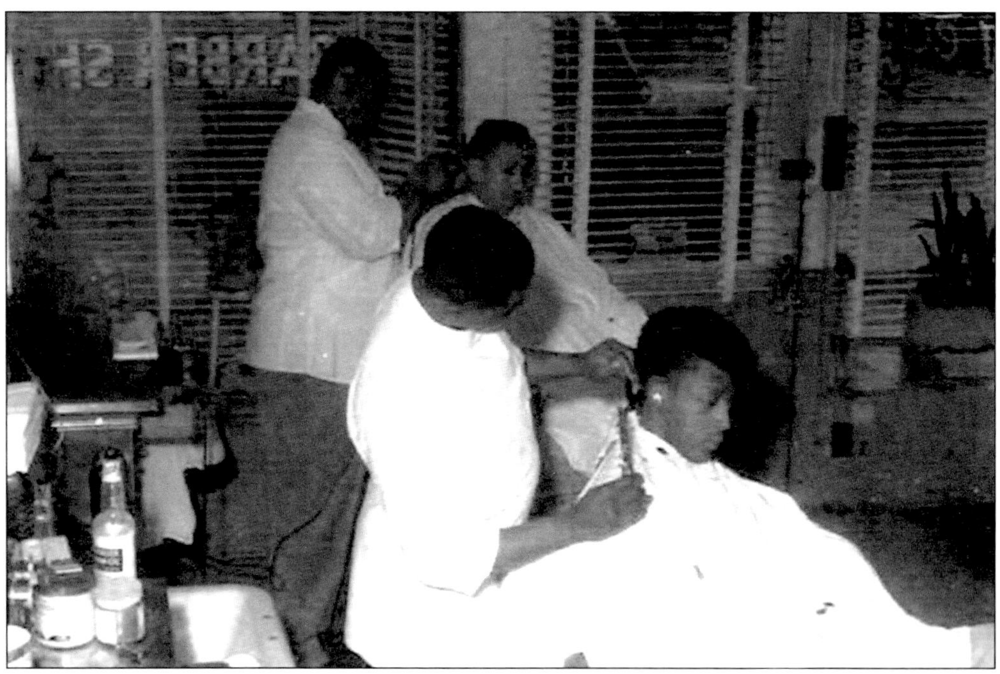

Most business in the African American community was service oriented (barbers, beauty shops, and so forth) and frequently run out of homes.

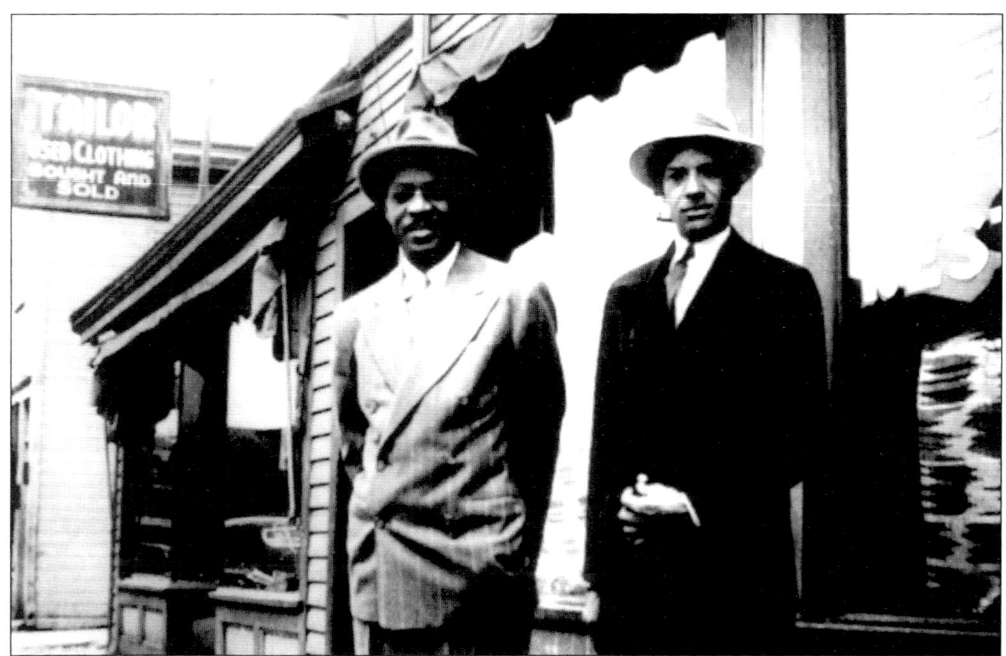


According to the *Post Standard*, "in addition to blacks, there was also a significant Jewish population, and many of the businesses in the Ward had Jewish owners. Discriminated against by the rest of society, the blacks and Jews of the 15th Ward survived with each other's help." Pictured in 1940 are E. Kemp Jr. and Bob Werts.

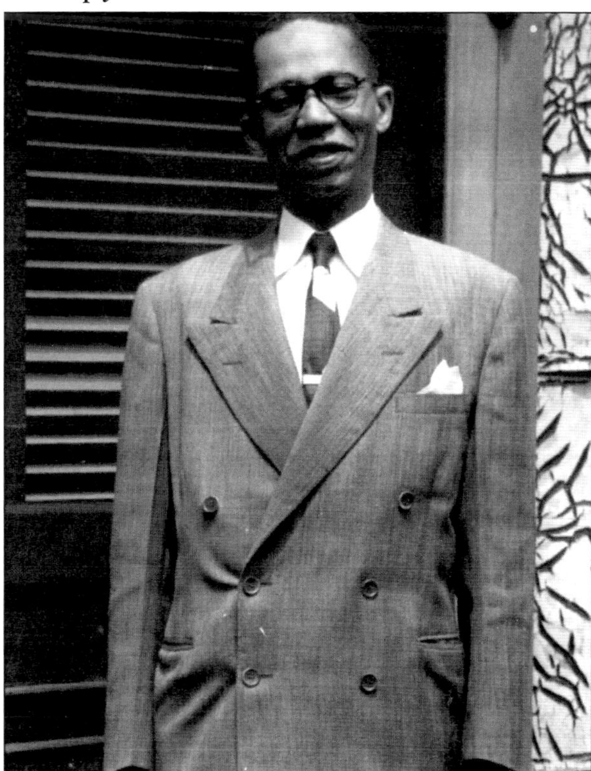

Eugene Goldstein was the Republican liaison for the African American community to city hall, although he was largely a figurehead.

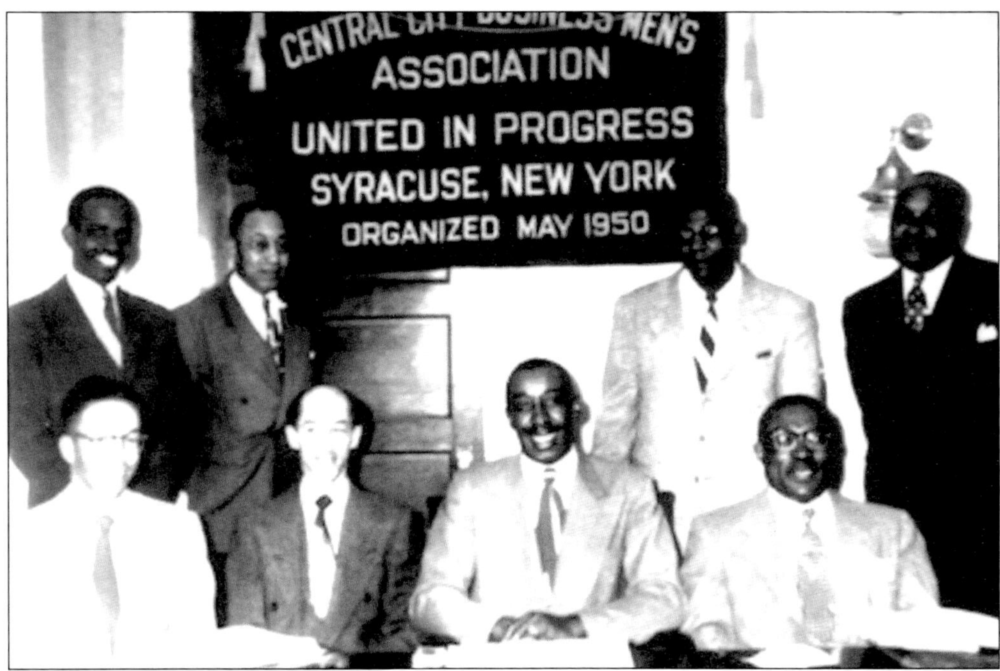


After World War II ended, African American business owners also began to band together. In 1950, Eric Simmons Sr. and a group of other black businessmen created the Central City Business Men's Association as a support network.

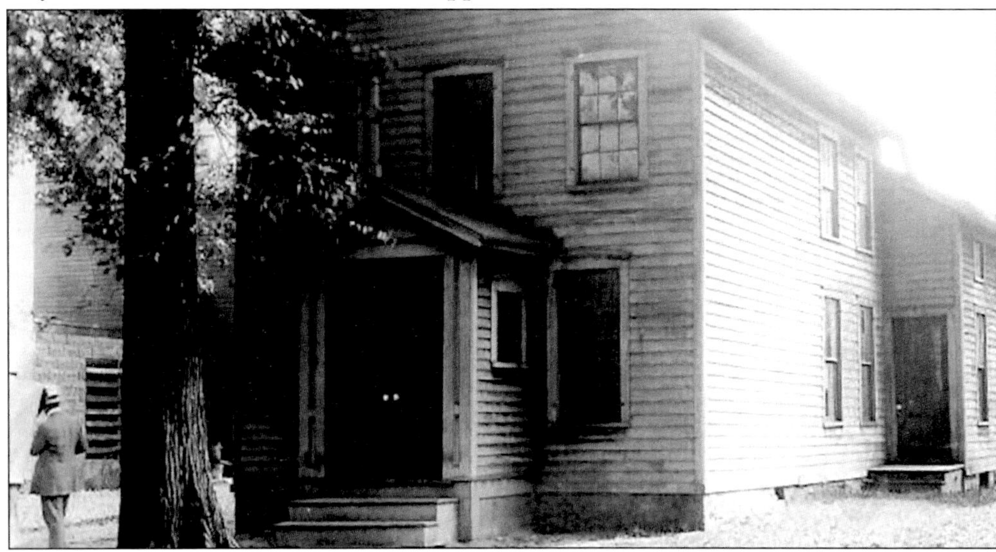

While many remember the Ward with nostalgia, the *Post Standard* painted another picture: "for all the dewy romanticism that is sometimes attached to the old 15th Ward, economic opportunities for African Americans living there were no different from those in the rest of the country." The area had become increasingly rundown. Housing was substandard, and absentee landlords did not correct building violations or keep up their property. In 1961, the City of Syracuse began a massive urban renewal program, razing the 27 blocks of the 15th Ward and displacing its population of owners, renters, and businesspeople. Shown in the photograph is St. Philip's Church, which was razed.

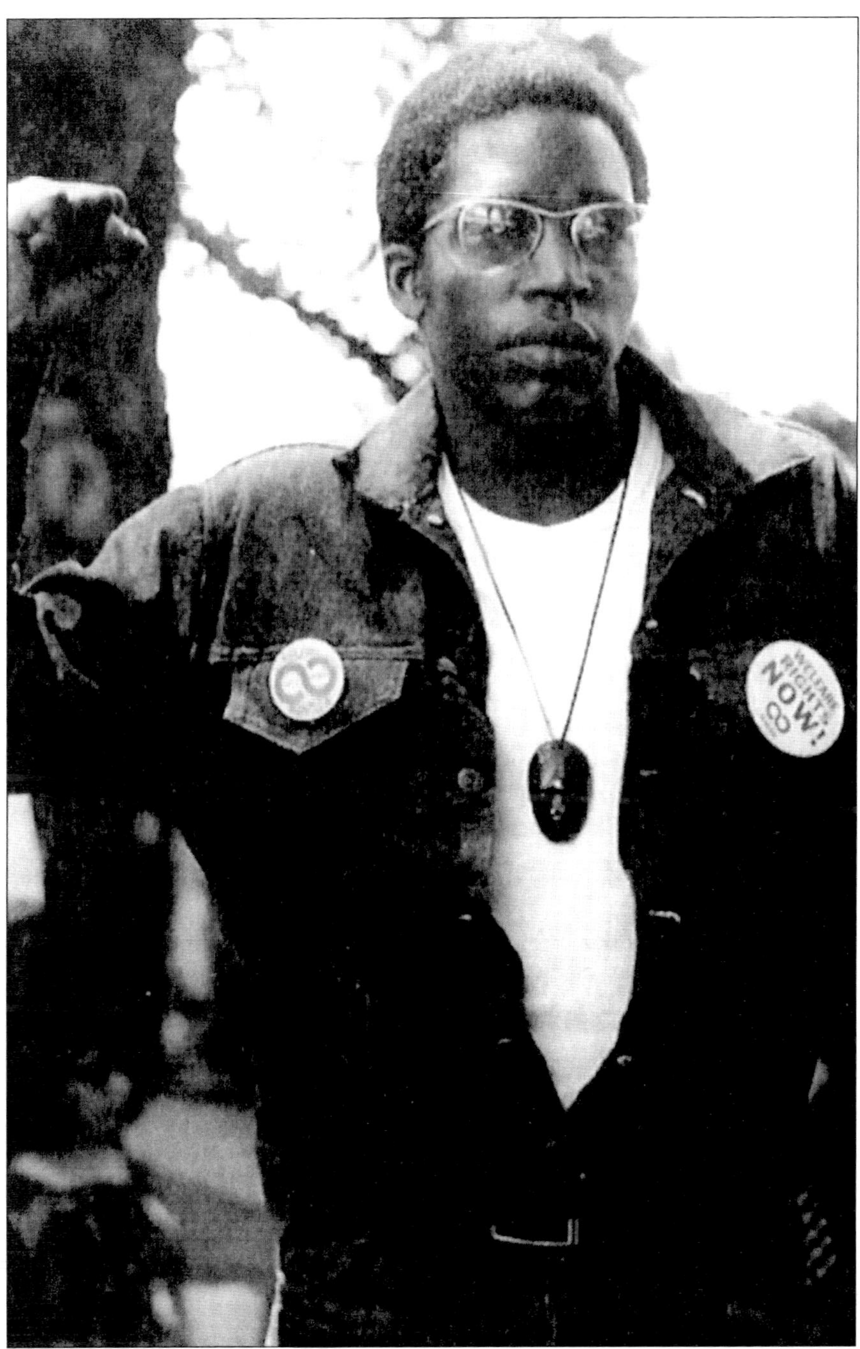


It is revealing of the times that the mayor of Syracuse did not involve the African American community in decision making about urban renewal. He was quoted as saying, "Let's put it this way. You didn't have to consult with anyone to know the 15th Ward was an awful slum. And you didn't need to consult with anyone to know it had to go." Residents of the 15th Ward fought to keep their neighborhood. Hundreds picketed city hall and tried to block wrecking crews as homes and businesses were being demolished. Some chained themselves to construction sites. Protests and picket lines were organized.

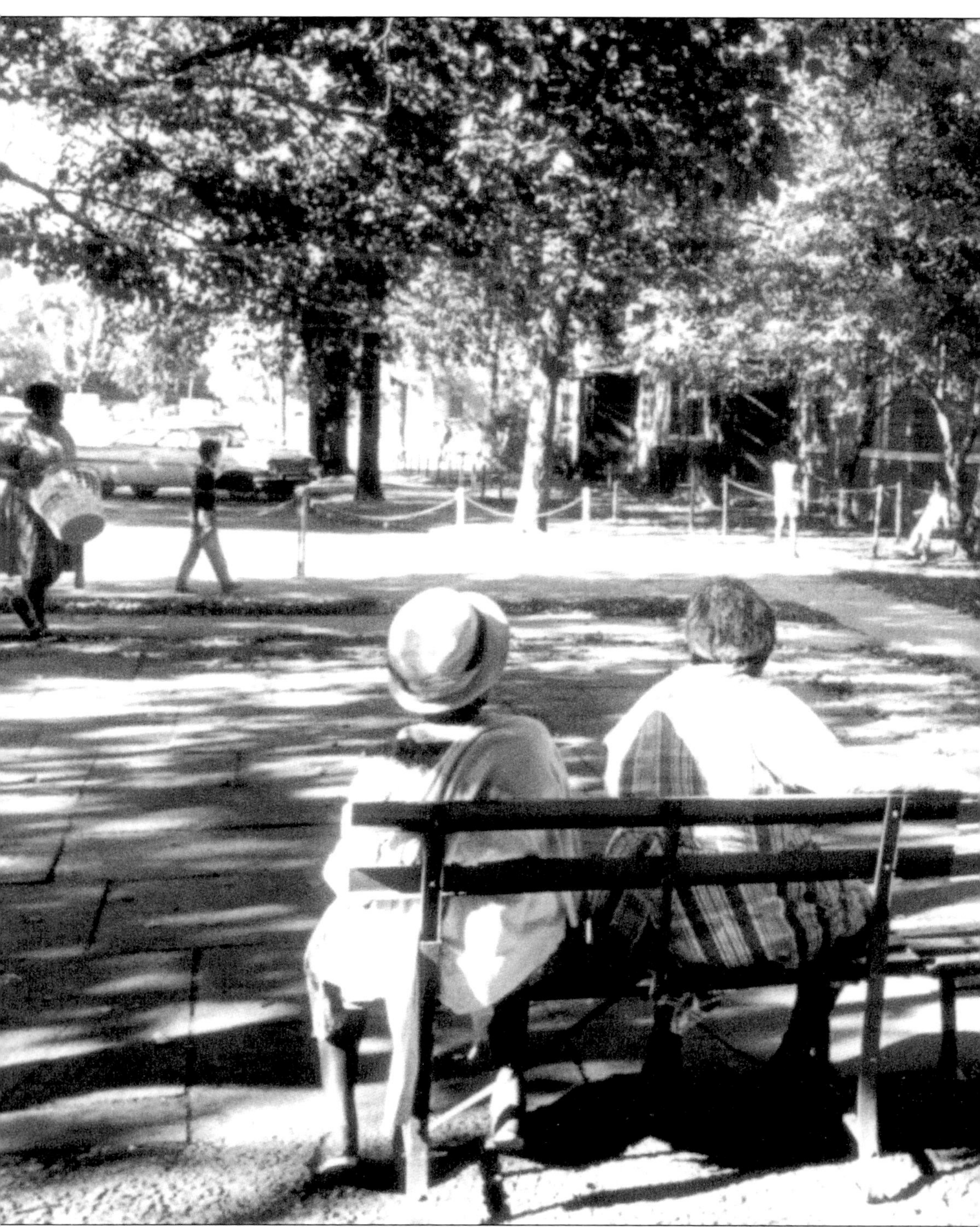

Hopes were high in some quarters, for the new construction and the new buildings were modern. But according to the *Wall Street Journal*, "the relocation job was complicated by basic errors in planning . . . when Syracuse became a laboratory of sorts for housing and renewal authorities." "They were among the best minds in the country," lamented

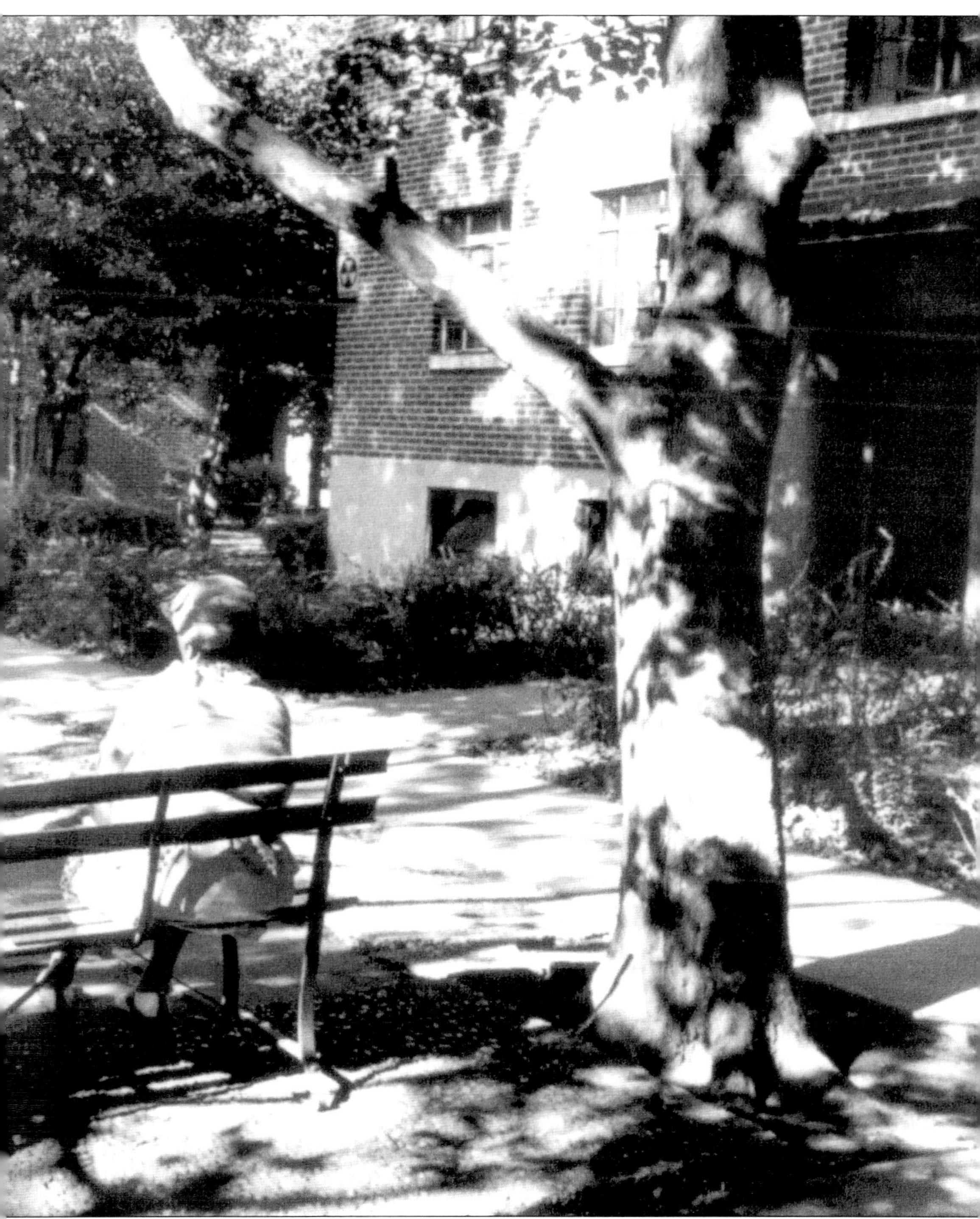

the mayor, "and it's hard to image how anyone could have been more wrong." One of the major flaws in the planning was a completely erroneous assumption that black family size would decrease. As a result, there was not enough housing for displaced families from the Ward.

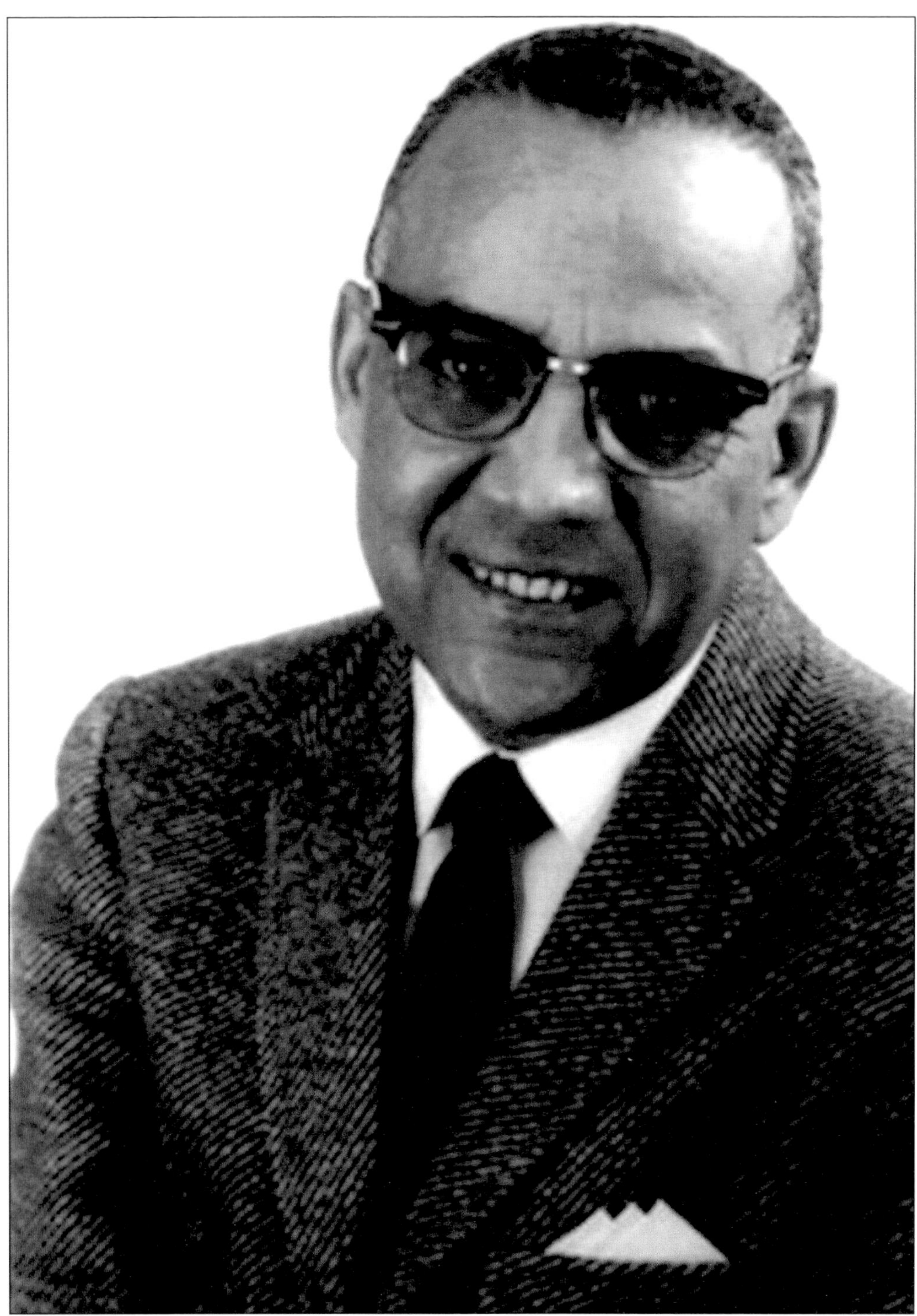

William Chiles, the Syracuse city relocation director charged with finding homes for those displaced by urban renewal, made the following observation: "Urban renewal dispersed the discontented, but it has not eliminated the discontent. Instead of a small, tight ghetto of 27 blocks, we now have a large, loose ghetto of 252 blocks."

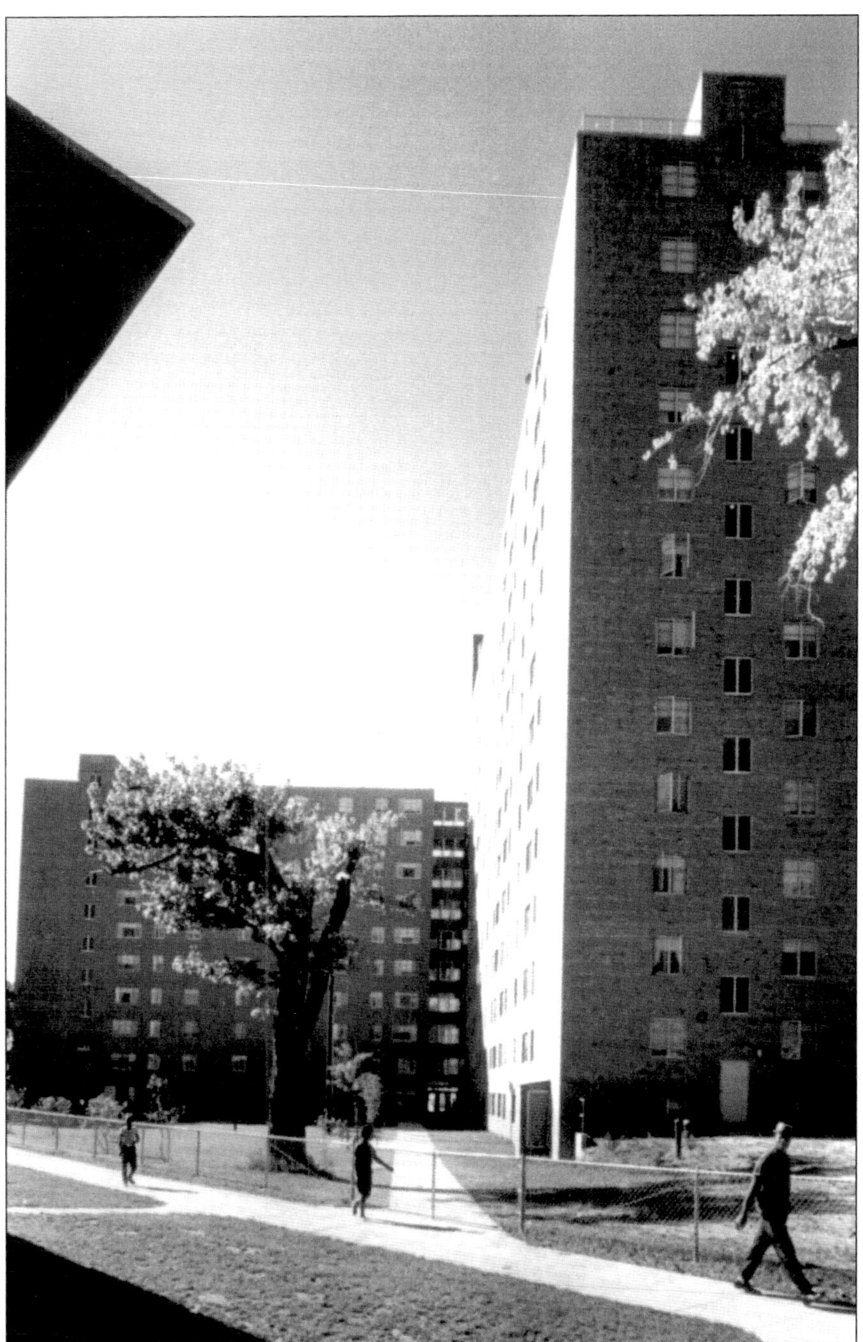

The *Wall Street Journal* published an extensive study entitled "Syracuse and Race: How Economic [and] Other Forces Create the Ghetto" in 1967. It described the results of the urban renewal plan: "27 square blocks of the 15th Ward were razed to the ground, and with them the homes of roughly 75% of the Negro population of the city. Four of the five Negro churches were in the area; so were most Negro-owned stores, bars, restaurants and social centers. The first new structure to rise on the cleared land was a combination jail and police headquarters."

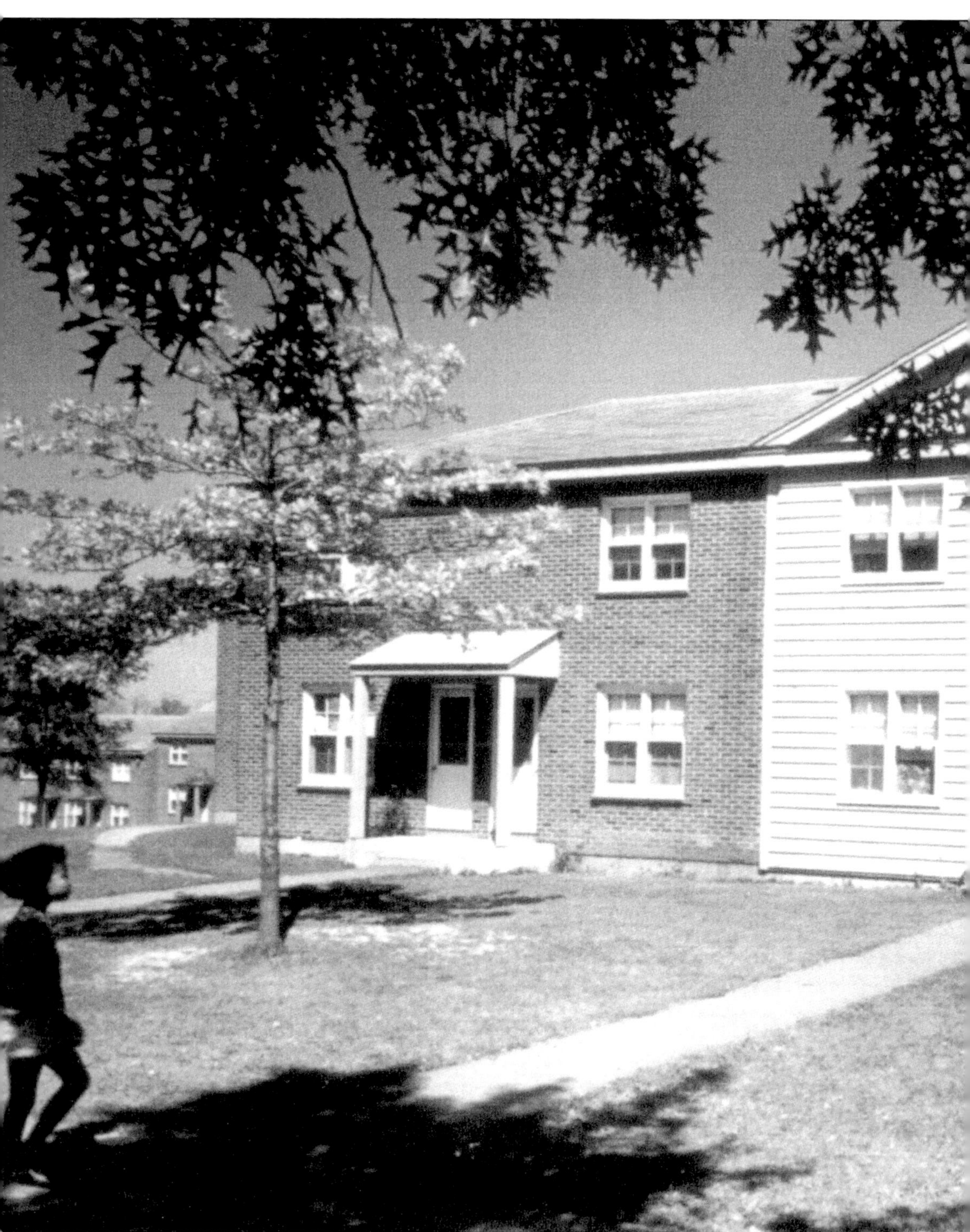

A *Post Standard* article described the long-term effects of the urban renewal program: "Nearly 1,300 residents of the old 15th Ward, once a hub of Syracuse's African American community were displaced. Many of the city's blacks relocated to the South and Southwest

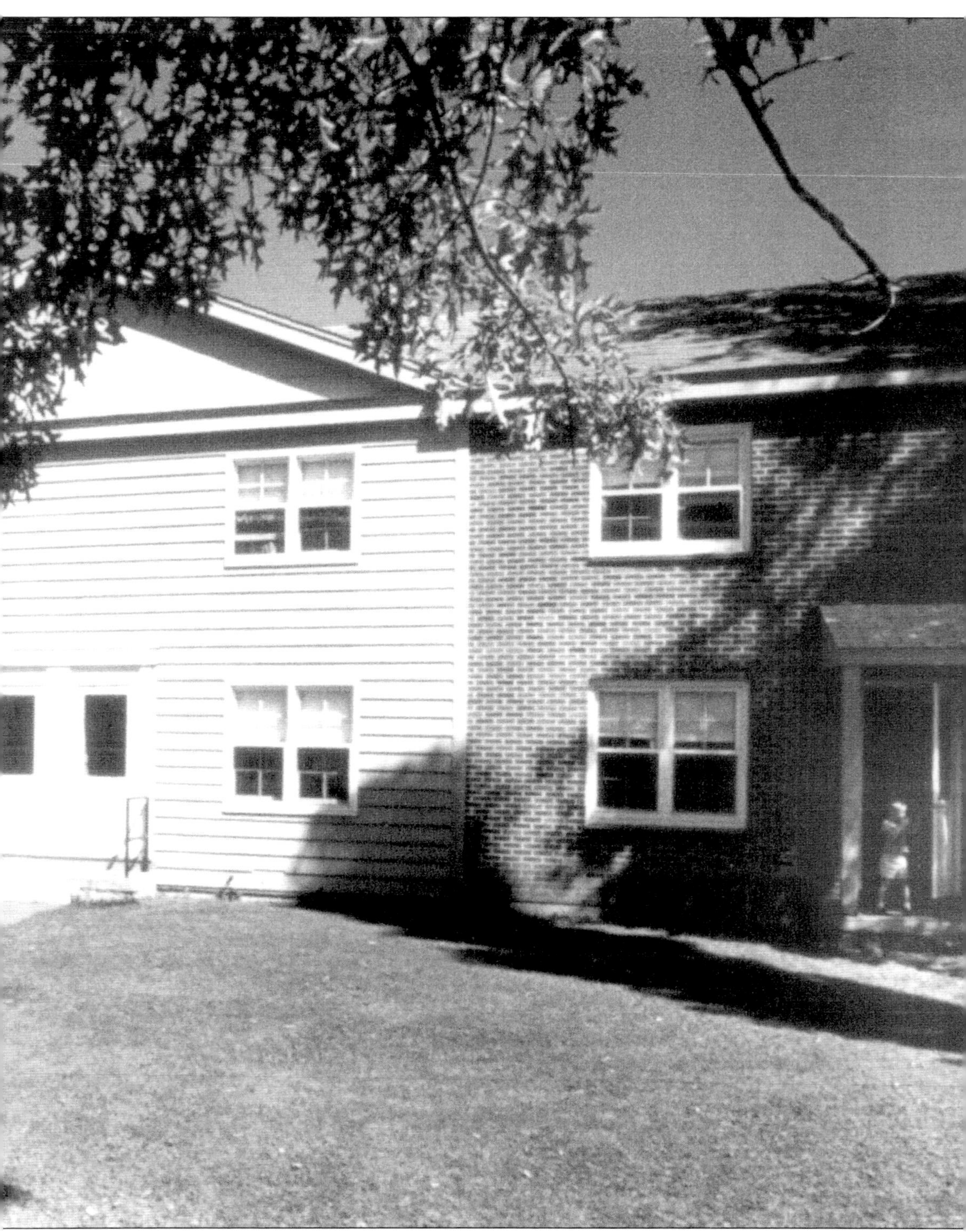

sides and others to the East Side. That, in turn, helped spark white flight to the suburbs. The exodus of longtime residents to the suburbs depleted the city's tax base and created neighborhoods with abandoned and dilapidated buildings."

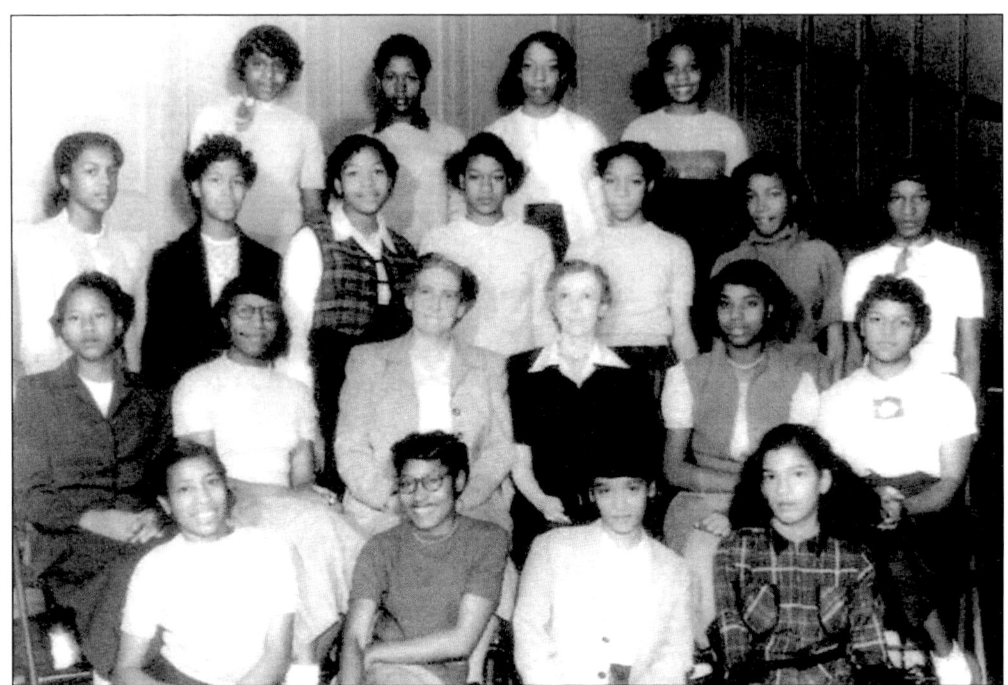

During the 1960s, Syracuse was in the forefront of the struggle to end racial discrimination. In 1961, George Wiley, the second African American on the faculty of Syracuse University, founded the Syracuse chapter of the Congress of Racial Equality (CORE), which worked for equal employment opportunities, housing, education, and political action. This photograph is of Central High School's Euleutherian Society of 1951. An educational society that valued people without regard to race or gender, based on the Greek word *eleutherous,* meaning freedom or equality.

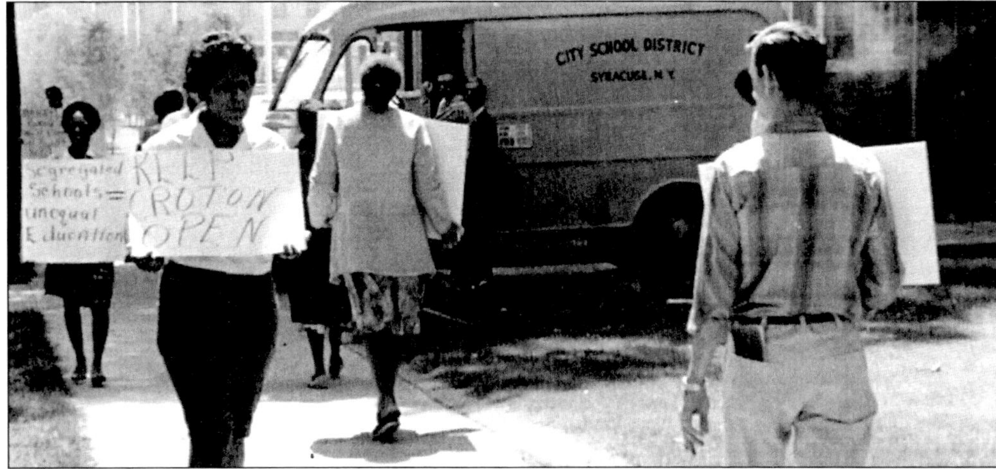


*Human Rights in Syracuse,* published by the Human Rights Commission of Syracuse and Onondaga County, elaborates on the period: "In 1963 CORE began a campaign to involve downtown businesses in the civil rights movement. Since urban renewal helped the center city, CORE felt the merchants should, in turn, assist the dislocated blacks by exerting pressure to end housing discrimination, hiring blacks in public contact jobs, and supporting the creation of a local chapter of Urban League."

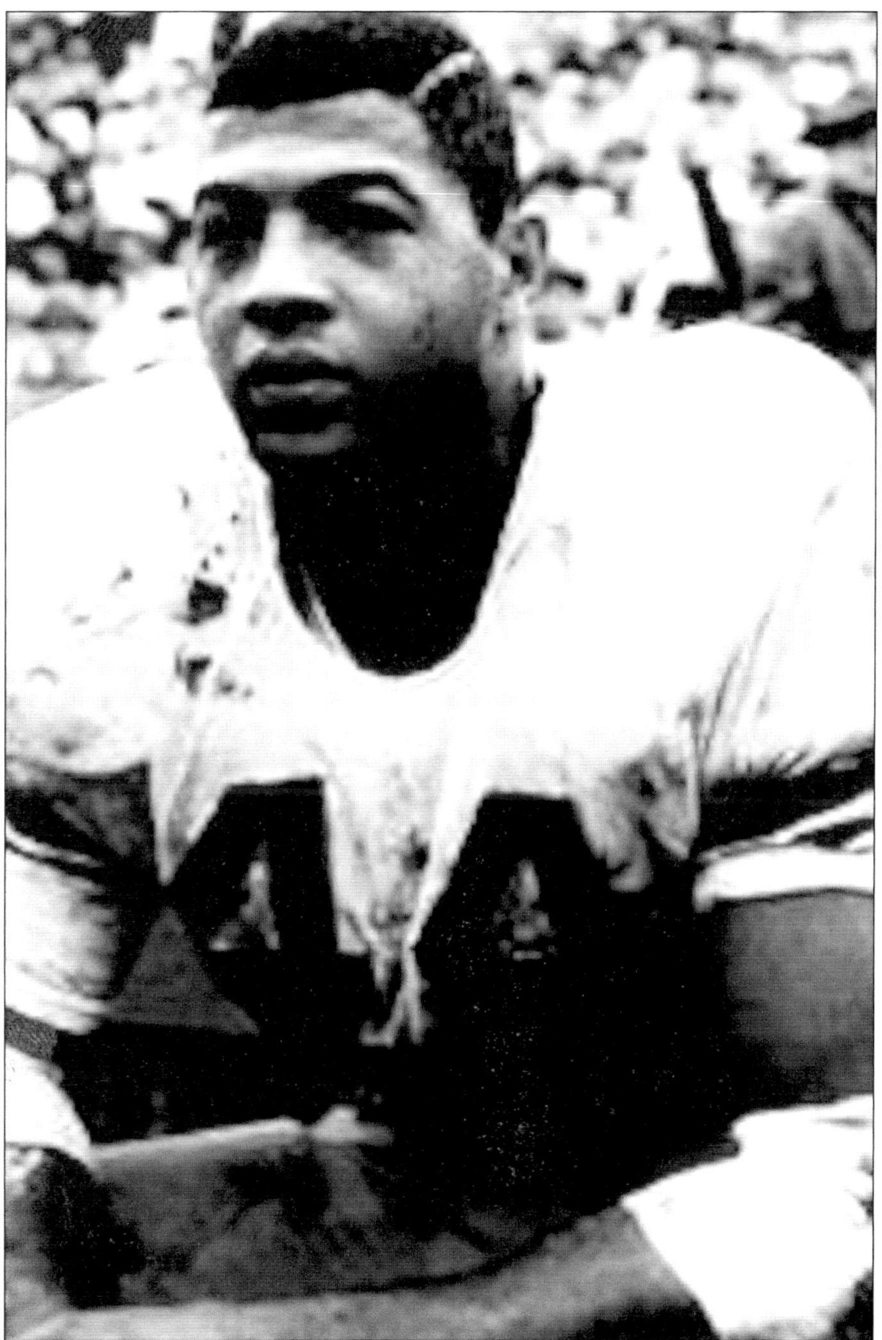

At Syracuse University, the 1960s were also a time of turmoil. At the beginning of the decade, Ernie Davis won the Heisman Trophy, the first Syracuse player and first African American to do so. As the decade progressed, the mood on campus darkened. Accusations of discrimination were leveled at the football program, resulting in a riot at the opening game of the 1969 season. On-campus student protests eventually resulted in the formation of the Afro-American Cultural Center, Afro-American Studies Program, and a Martin Luther King Jr. Memorial Library Collection.

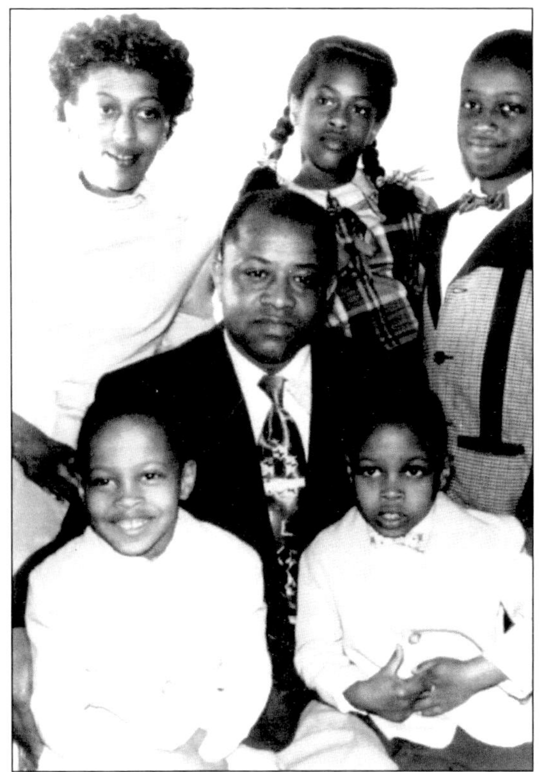

The history of Syracuse's African American community is one of hard work, perseverance, faith, family, and community spirit. Pictured is the family of Sammie and Odessa Adams.

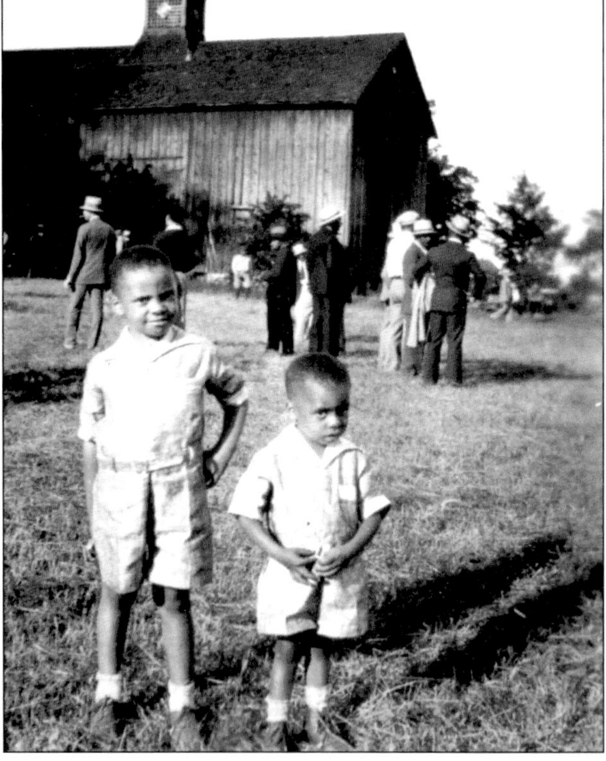

It is a story that needs to be told. The black men and women who have lived in the Salt City since the days of slavery and those who live there now have a rich community heritage of which all Syracusans should be aware. Daniel and Donald Caldwell are children in this photograph.

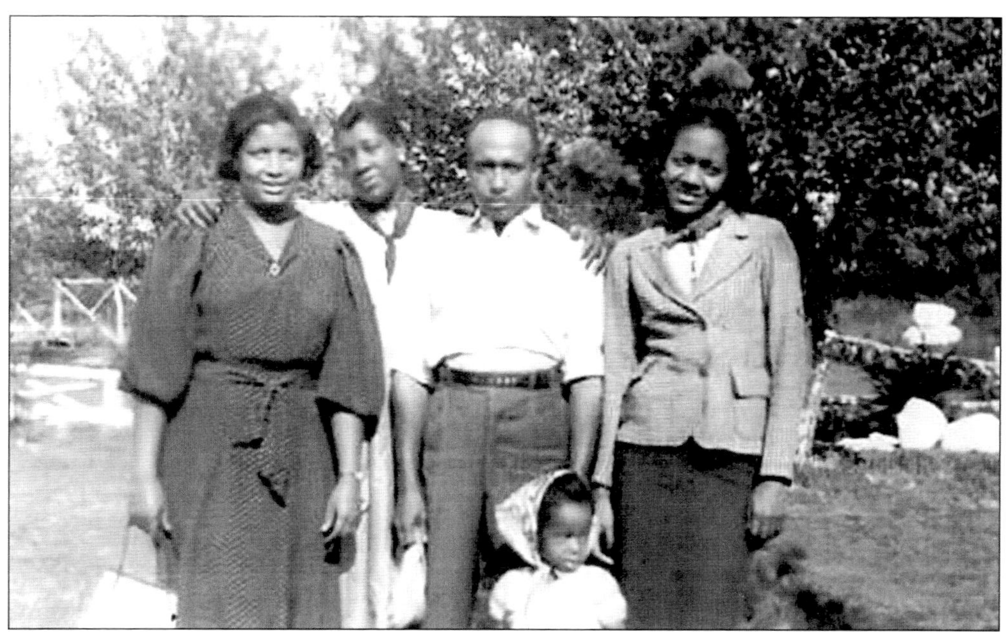

The most recent study of the Syracuse African American community was published in 2000. Reviewing the latter decades of the 20th century, authors George Palumbo and Seymour Sacks noted that at the beginning of the 21st century, about one in five people in the city of Syracuse was African American. Martha and Bertha Benson, Leon Shepard, Louise Benson, and Janice Mitchell are seen in this photograph.

The African American community of the Salt City has seen progress. Many leadership positions in local government (school superintendent, police chief, commissioner of parks, and so on) have been filled by African Americans, and many opportunities in industry, government, business, the media, and education have been opened up. Leenie Henderson, Bryce Henderson, Saddie Hoffman, and Carol Cotton Buchanan are seen in this photograph.

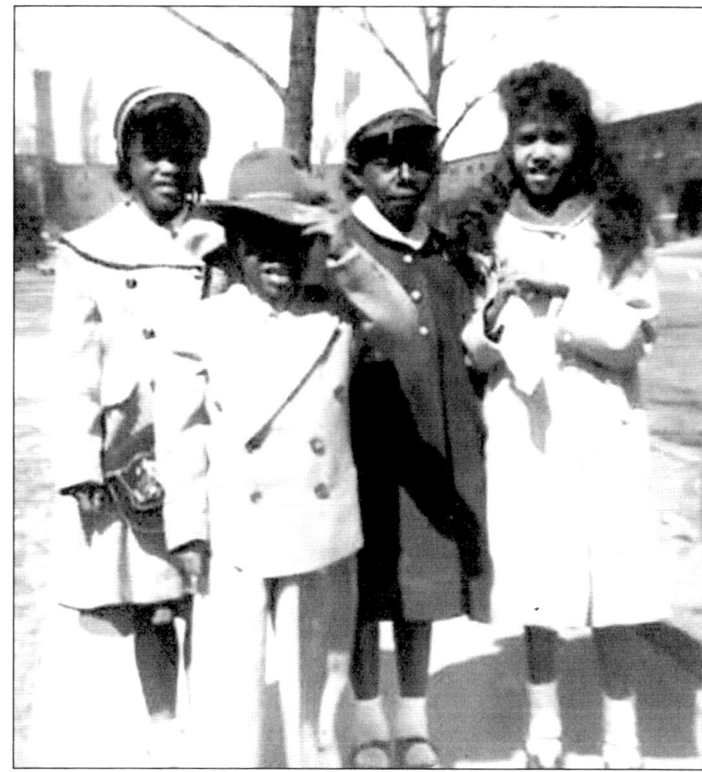

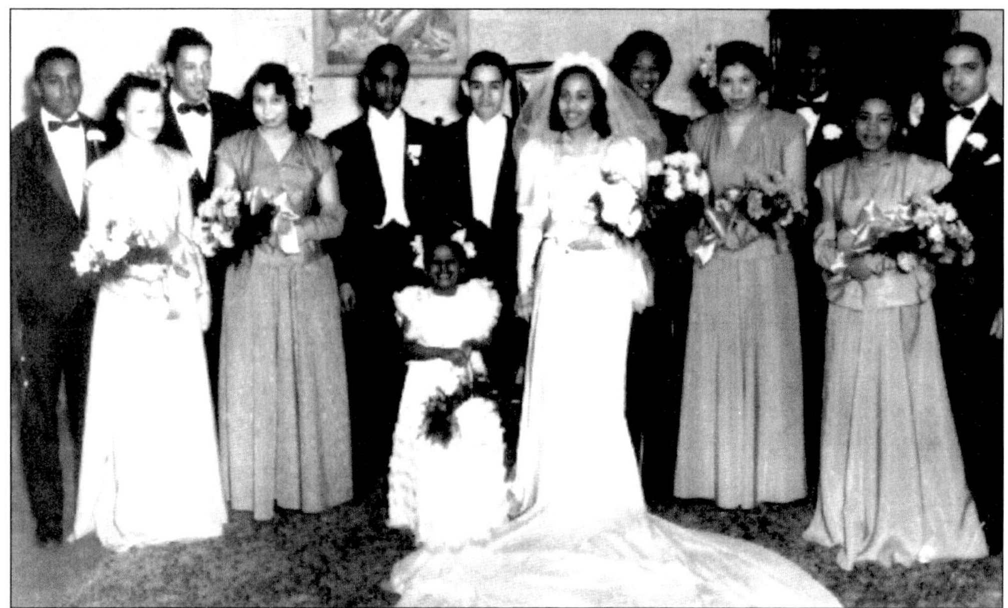

The new study reveals that the average income for married African American couples with children was higher than that of their white counterparts. Shown is a wedding at the Dunbar Center.

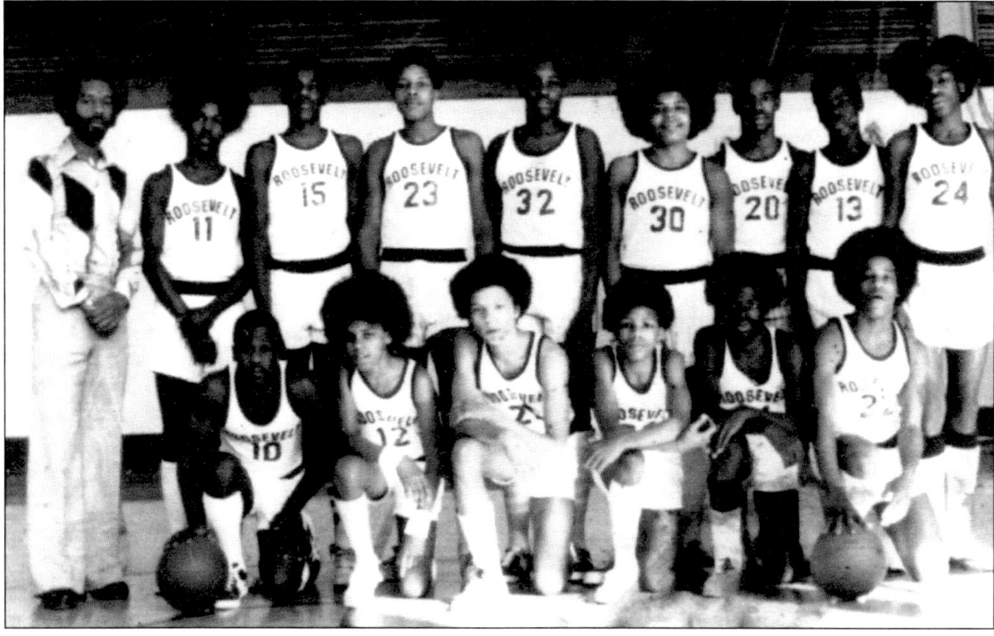

But the study also noted that, overall, the average income for black households was approximately two-thirds that of white households. The number of female-headed households was 2.5 times higher for African American households than for white households, accounting for approximately 85 percent of black family poverty. The trend of the 1980s was that the African American residents of Syracuse were increasingly concentrated in lower-wage clerical and support jobs. The Roosevelt Junior High School championship basketball team is pictured.

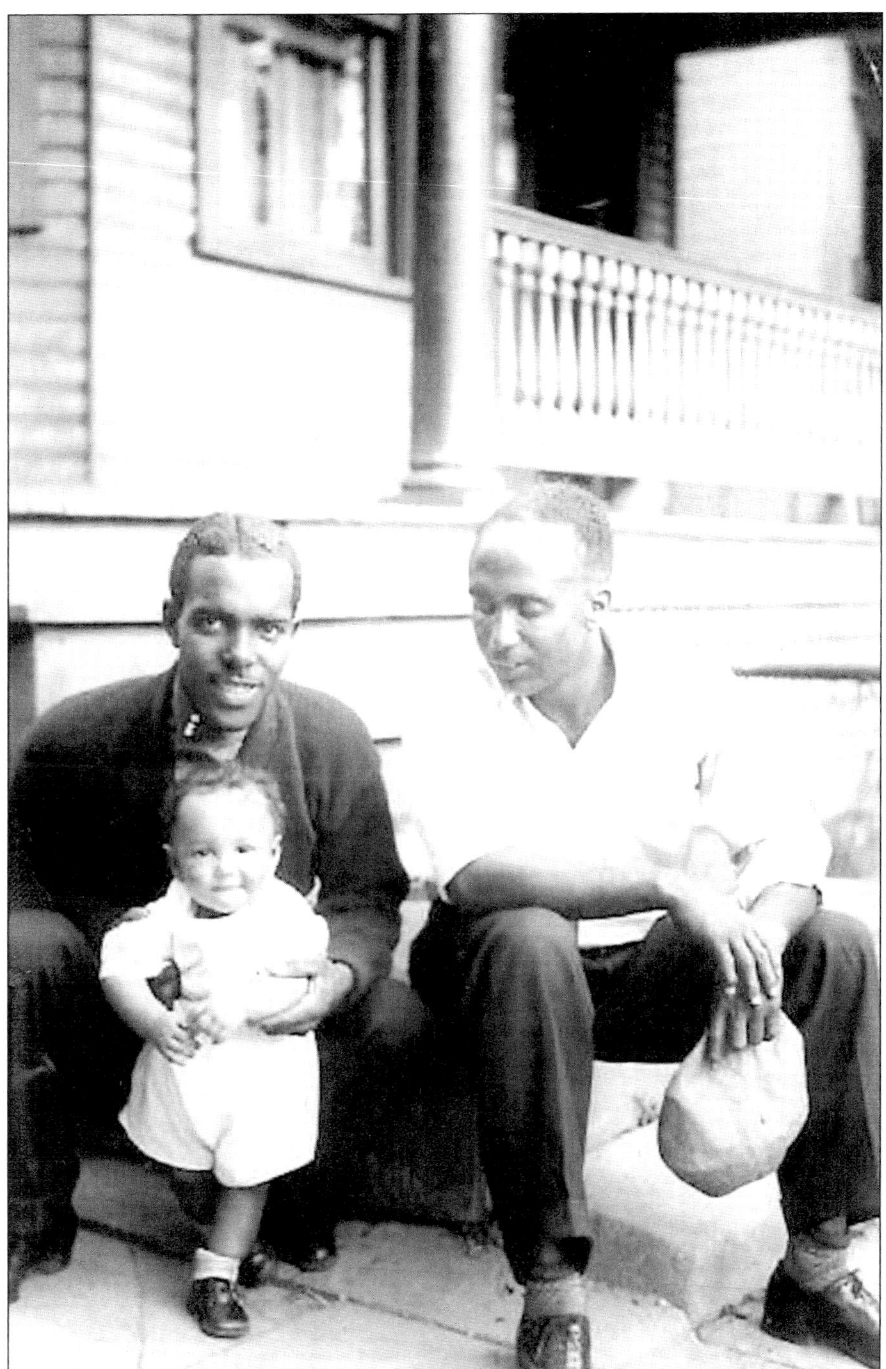

Syracuse is a city in the "rust belt," the Northeast corridor that is losing jobs and population. It needs to develop new economic strengths to prosper in the 21st century. George Palumbo and Seymour Sacks conclude that education is more important than ever to provide African Americans with the skills needed for higher-wage, service-sector jobs. This, they state, "could be the key to the ability of Syracuse to prosper in the next century." John, Herbert, and Leon Shepard appear in this photograph.

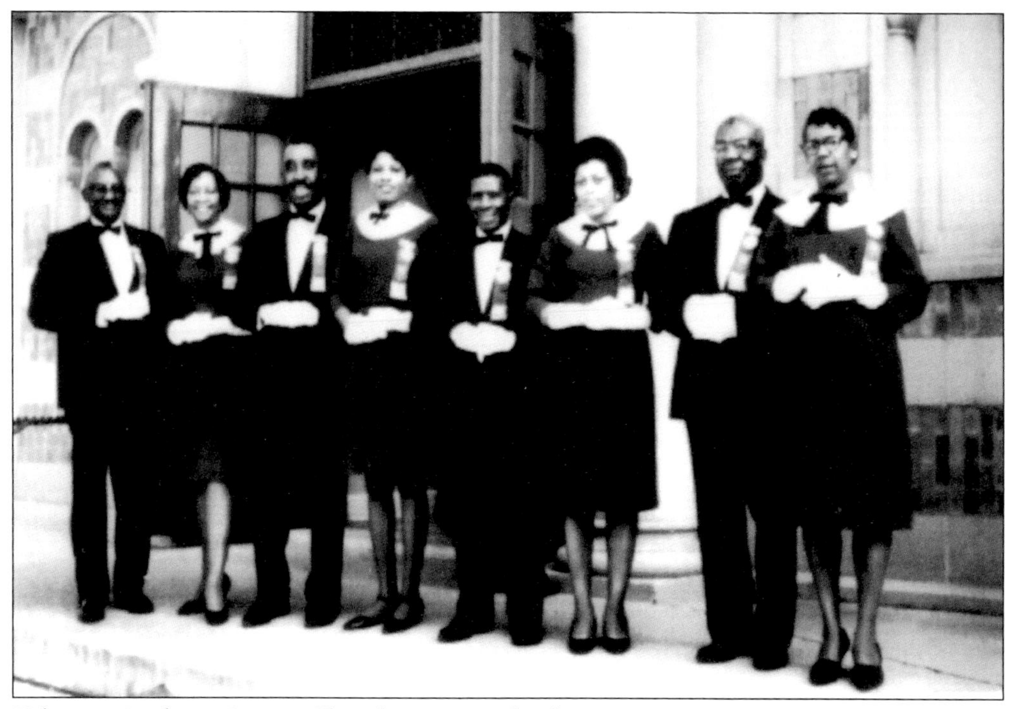

Ushers at Bethany Baptist Church pose on the front steps.

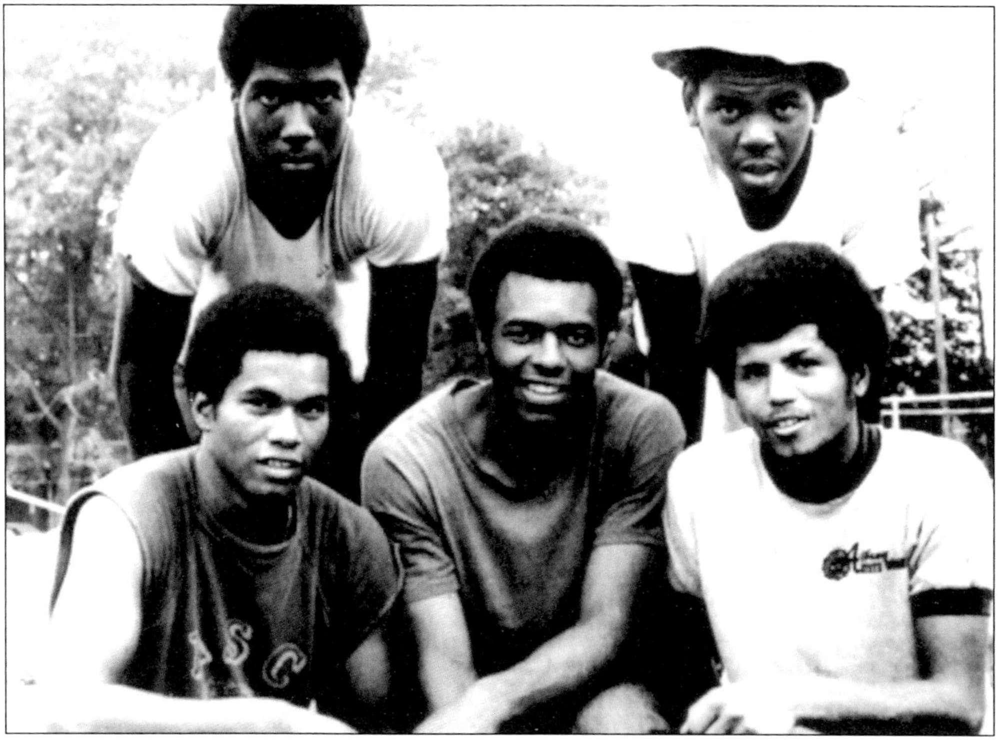

A group of friends gathers for a picture.

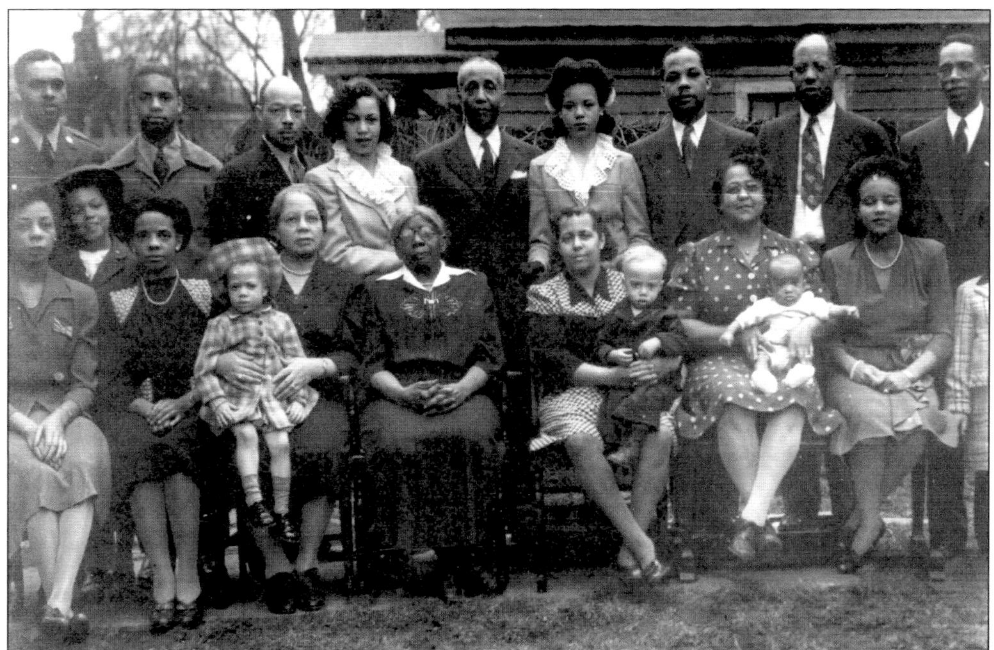

The story of the African American community of Syracuse deserves telling, as Barry Wells, vice president and dean of student affairs at Syracuse University, recently wrote in *Black Issues in Higher Education*, because "the commemoration of the struggles, achievements and milestones of black men and women of the past and present day reminds us of the progress that has been made but equally as important, the distance that our nation has yet to travel." The Hasbrouck-Caldwell family is shown in this photograph.

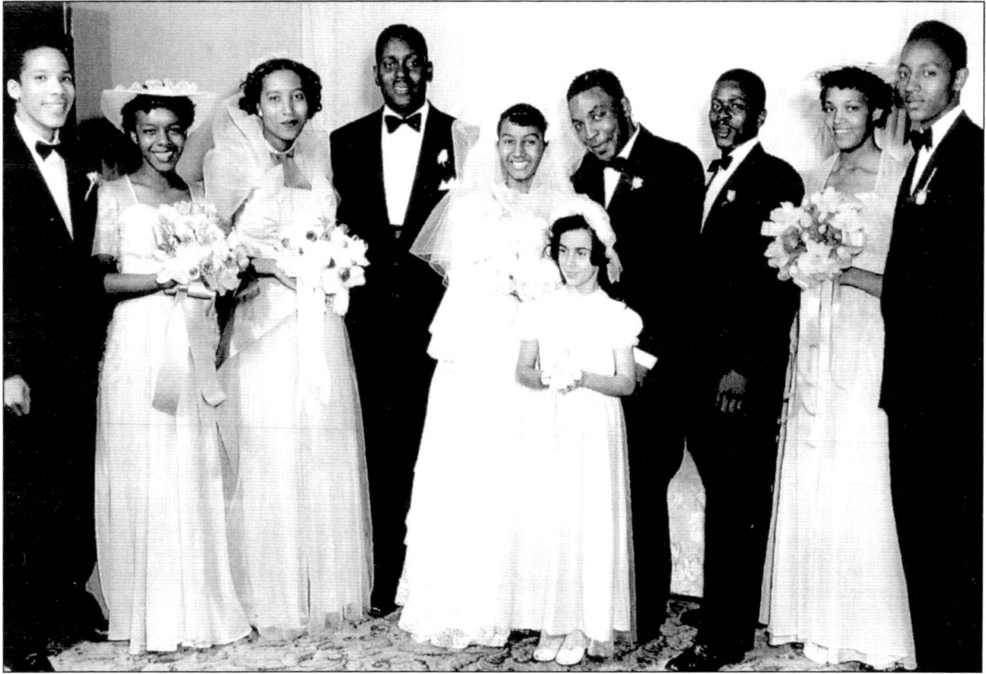

This photograph is of the Branch-Mack nuptials.

# ACKNOWLEDGMENTS

The genesis of this book was an article that appeared in the local Syracuse newspaper in the 1970s about a group of Syracuse African Americans who gathered to reminisce about the early days in the 15th Ward. Not all of their memories were fond. The paper recorded their recollection of segregated theaters and restaurants, as well as their happier memories of a close-knit neighborhood and a vibrant community. Intrigued, I went to a bookstore and located a large, newly published book about Syracuse. Its only reference to an African American was a photograph of Ernie Davis, the Heisman Trophy winner. Thus began a long search for ways to tell the story of a community that deserves far greater recognition.

People need to know their heritage. As Dr. Martin Luther King Jr. said, "We are not makers of history. We are made by history." This book is "a history," clearly not "the history" of the African American community of Syracuse. There are omissions and gaps and undoubtedly errors, for which I apologize. It is my fondest wish that this work serve as a springboard for others to expand it, enlarge upon it, and enrich it with their own histories, stories, and photographs. The 30th celebration in 2005 of the "SyraQue Reunion," an ongoing revisitation of life in the 15th Ward, and the publication of a commemorative album of the reunions, by Marshall and Mary Nelson, are wonderful examples of ways to keep the community's history alive.

This work would not have been possible were it not for the generosity of time, spirit, and resources of many people and institutions, who opened their hearts, archives, and scrapbooks to share. I am honored to have met and worked with these extraordinary individuals, and I extend sincerest appreciation to Marie Cloyd, Mr. and Mrs. Herbert Johnson, Mrs. and Mrs. Ernest Powell, Damon Presley, Dorothy Williams, Donald Caldwell, and Mr. and Mrs. Clarence Dunham, as well as to the Onondaga Historical Association, and the Bezuchamp Library archives, for helping to preserve the past, illumine the present, and light the way to an ever better future.